The Megacorporation In American Society

S. Prakash Sethi and Dow Votaw, *editors*

THE PRENTICE-HALL SERIES
IN ECONOMIC INSTITUTIONS AND SOCIAL SYSTEMS

The Megacorporation In American Society: The Scope Of Corporate Power

Phillip I. Blumberg

Dean
University of Connecticut
School of Law

PRENTICE-HALL, INC., *Englewood Cliffs, New Jersey*

Library of Congress Cataloging in Publication Data

Blumberg, Phillip I
The megacorporation in American society.

(The Prentice-Hall series in economic institutions and social systems)

Includes bibliographies and index.

1. Big business—United States. 2. Institutional investments—United States. I. Title.

HD2791.B58 338.6'44'0973 75-6667

ISBN 0-13-574061-4

ISBN 0-13-574053-3 pbk.

Printed in the United States of America

10 9 8 7 6 5 4 3 2 1

PRENTICE-HALL INTERNATIONAL, INC., *London*
PRENTICE-HALL OF AUSTRALIA, Pty. Ltd., *Sydney*
PRENTICE-HALL OF CANADA, Ltd., *Toronto*
PRENTICE-HALL OF INDIA PRIVATE LIMITED, *New Delhi*
PRENTICE-HALL OF JAPAN, Inc., *Tokyo*
PRENTICE-HALL OF SOUTHEAST ASIA (PTE.) LTD., *Singapore*

TO
JANET

Contents

Preface

The very large public corporations, which I have termed "the megacorporations," are a major center of power in the American society. They dominate the national economy and strongly affect the world economy. They possess important political power and have emerged as one of the fundamental social institutions of our time.

These few hundred corporations, led by an interlocking group of several thousand men and a few women, represent an increasing concentration of the total sales, assets, and net income of American business. This concentration of economic power is matched by an increasing concentration of shareownership in the hands of financial institutions, particularly the trust departments of commercial banks. Largely as a result of the tremendous growth of employee pension and benefit funds and changes in investment philosophy which encouraged the acquisition of equity securities, the financial institutions have accumulated equity holdings of such enormous magnitude that they now possess the power to exercise control over the corporate giants if they are prepared to act in concert. Economic concentration has been compounded by financial concentration.

This dual concentration of economic power—with wide political and social implications—has far-reaching consequences for the nation. To what extent is such a concentration of decision-making in a small unrepresentative group of persons with common backgrounds, values, and experience and an even smaller group of institutions compatible with a free democratic society? Daniel Bell has aptly framed the issue, "Corporate power, clearly, is the predominant power in the society, and the problem is how to limit it."

This volume describes the scope of corporate power in the United States. It is an empirical review of the position of the megacorporations in the American economy and of the emergence of the financial institutions as a source of potential hegemony over the corporate world.

In a companion volume, I will undertake the more difficult objective of describing the restraints or limitations on corporate power and possible institutional reforms by which a democratic society might tame corporate power.

I am glad to acknowledge the assistance of Jerome F. Weihs, Esq., who patiently and tenaciously helped with the research; of Dean Paul M. Siskind of Boston University School of Law, who provided encouragement and support; and of Mrs. Valorie Mulholland of Boston University School of Law, who supervised the typing of draft upon draft of the manuscript.

Phillip I. Blumberg

West Hartford, Connecticut

The Megacorporation In American Society

CHAPTER ONE

The Role of the Megacorporation

This is a study of the very large corporation in American society, the leviathan that gives the American economic order the characteristic feature that distinguishes it from most of the rest of the world. These are enterprises of enormous magnitude with such profound impact on the lives and fortunes of so many human beings, communities, and even nations that they must be regarded as a unique phenomenon. Unless we recognize that these very large corporations, or megacorporations,[1] are different in kind and degree from corporations generally, we cannot understand their implications for democratic society or deal effectively with establishing appropriate political controls over these centers of economic, political, and social power.

A. EMERGENCE OF THE MEGACORPORATION AS A DOMINANT ECONOMIC, SOCIAL, AND POLITICAL INSTITUTION

In addition to its predominant economic role in providing goods, services, and employment, the megacorporation has developed into a social and political organization of profound significance. In fact, it has become a basic social institution and a center of power resembling governmental structures. It has been transformed into a politicized institution in which public concerns and values occupy increasing importance in the corporate decision-making process. A number of observers have been so struck by the political aspects of the megacorporations that they have described them as private governments. Although the term is used in an imprecise manner, its application to the megacorporation indicates the new dimensions involved.

[1] I do not claim any originality for this term. It was suggested by Professor Melvin Eisenberg's use of "megasubsidiaries." I subsequently became aware of Sanford Rose's reference to the "megacorp" in his 1969 *Fortune* article.

The megacorporation has not become any less an economic institution as a result of these developments. However, the pursuit of its economic objectives has become increasingly restricted by the changing climate of opinion concerning socially permissible conduct. If pursuit of profit remains a major objective of the game, the rules of the game have been changed. Public expectations and demands cannot be ignored. The only question is the nature and extent of business' response. This process has been viewed by some as a transformation of the corporation into a social institution to serve social needs, rather than purely economic objectives. It is only realistic, however, to recognize that the economic objectives of the corporation remain paramount and that the social needs reflected in the changing climate of opinion function as restraints that influence the manner in which economic objectives are pursued. Such social factors, while of great importance, are essentially peripheral.

With increasing recognition of the social dimensions of corporate activities, reform groups have used the megacorporation as a forum to bring public issues into view, thereby introducing public opinion into the corporate decision-making process. Social reform groups, particularly church and university groups, have made the megacorporation a useful domestic target at which to direct campaigns against minority and sex discrimination, environmental abuse, military production, colonialism, apartheid, and the Vietnam War. The megacorporation can no longer conduct its operations on a purely economic, *i.e.* value-blind, level, and therefore, political considerations such as these cannot be ignored.

At the same time, the megacorporations and their executives have emerged as social forces of immense significance. Executives of the megacorporations by virtue of their position are widely accepted as leaders of the society, and they provide the leadership of American institutions. Having risen to the top of the ladder within their own enterprises, the executives seek further recognition and fulfillment. They find it on the national level, serving government as members of national commissions, business advisory councils, and White House conferences. They find it on the community level, serving as trustees of museums, orchestras, operas, hospitals, philanthropies, and universities. The interrelationship is mutually satisfying—the institutions are looking for the participation of the powerful and wealthy (or those with access to wealth), and the executives are looking for further recognition and enhanced status as cultural and community leaders.

The large corporation generally—and the megacorporation in particular—has become a social institution which embraces the thousands of human beings whose lives are affected by it and which provides an important focus for the employees' social relationships. In the more complex society, with greater mobility, the loosening of community ties, and urban anonymity, the neighborhood social unit has lost its cohesion and the corporation has assumed some of its role. In Community Chest or United Way fund-raising, for example, individual contributions in the community each year have become less significant and contributions organized around the major employers have become more effective. "I gave at the office," among other things, indicates social allegiance. When strangers meet and want to learn more about each other, "what do you do?" or "for whom do you work?" is one of the earliest questions. The answer categorizes the individual. He is part of the IBM, Xerox, or Exxon family.

With the expansion of group health insurance programs, pension plans, and personal counselling services, the corporation is further strengthening the areas of its participation in the nonbusiness portion of its employees' lives. Finally, more corporations are encouraging personnel to participate in social service programs as a fuller method of mobilizing corporate personnel resources to deal with community problems. Although the volunteers function in their individual capacity, they are recruited and mobilized as part of a corporate program for which the corporation seeks public recognition of a corporate contribution to the community.

In the words of Daniel Bell, "Corporations are institutions for economizing; but they are also ways of life for their members."

B. CHANGING SOCIAL EXPECTATIONS AND DEMANDS

Through a process which I have termed public acceptance, expectation, and demand, the major corporation has been called upon to participate to a greater and greater extent in the solution of social problems. The public first accepts corporate activity in this area, subsequently expects it, and ultimately demands it.

As political objectives of the society crystallize and a consensus emerges, pressures develop for government leadership. When the pressures become more intense, they provide the necessary base which makes it politically feasible for governmental response to occur. Executive or administrative action and legislation follow.

Simultaneously, awareness of the substantial power possessed by business leads to recognition that business participation in the solution of problems which have become the subject of governmental concern is also essential. Thus, as government leads, pressures develop on business to move in the same direction. The history of the struggle to achieve environmental protection, create equal employment opportunities, combat urban blight, and solve the problems of the inner city vividly reflects the interaction between business and government.

In many areas, the apparent inability of government to deal successfully with these problems has led to increased pressures on business. If solution of social problems is to be achieved, it is evident that business must participate. Social thinking proceeds on this assumption, and business is pressed to adapt to the changed climate of opinion.Two illustrations of this process are the programs of the National Alliance of Businessmen to provide 500,000 new jobs for minority group members and the life insurance industry's programs to provide $2,000,000,000 in new urban and ghetto investments.

The expectations of the American public have intensified with the growing social and environmental crises. A 1974 Opinion Research Corporation poll reveals that 70% of the American people believe that business has a moral obligation to help other major institutions to achieve social progress, even at the expense of profitability. At the same time, another Opinion Research Corporation poll reports that overall public attitudes toward business are markedly adverse with only 11% giving "high approval." These polls indicate that public expectations have substantially increased along with increasing dissatisfaction with business performance. These two interrelated factors create almost irresistible pressures that will inevitably be reflected in corporate decision-making. Business must respond to change in order to retain the confidence of society and thereby survive.

C. CHANGING CORPORATE OBJECTIVES AND IDEOLOGY

As a result of public opinion, corporate objectives and ideology have been subjected to intense pressures. Profit-maximization and single-minded dedication to the advancement of shareholder interests no longer satisfactorily explain corporate behavior—if indeed they ever did. George Cabot Lodge points out that American business is an institution in search of an ideology.

Making money for shareholders as the method of achieving the most economic provision of goods and services to society through the operation of the invisible hand of the marketplace no longer receives respect as an adequate statement of business objectives. A rear guard, including such authorities as Professor Milton Friedman, seeks to adhere to the neo-classical standard. Even they, however, recognize that business must compete according to "the rules of the game." As noted above, it is precisely in this area—the rules of the game—that the dramatic change has occurred. Governmental intervention—both existing and potential—as well as public attitudes have forced increasing response from business. Whether regarded as public relations techniques or socially responsible conduct, business behavior in the social or environmental sphere reflects changing corporate objectives. Although such behavior may be picturesquely described as "good citizenship", or "long term profit-maximization," "enlightened self-interest," or as defensive measures to defuse minority hostility or to prevent further government intervention, they all involve an acceptance of the costs involved because of the conclusion that it is required for the long-run welfare of the firm.

The essential point is that the managerial decision in substantial measure is the product of the business environment. It is not wholly an exercise of managerial discretion. In this vein, David Rockefeller justified the cost of the urban and minorities program of The Chase Manhattan Bank by reference to the bank's concern with the urban conditions that might determine the bank's ability to make satisfactory profits five years down the road.

With the organizational structure of almost every major corporation changed to include a community affairs, public affairs, or social responsibility officer, followers of Friedman have recognized the inevitability of corporate response to such social pressures. Thus, Professor Henry G. Manne's criticism essentially relates to what he regards as a more accurate understanding of the nature of such corporate behavior. Business should respond to social pressure only to the extent deemed tactically necessary. It should not assume leadership; it should not endeavor to push out the frontier of business activity in the social or environmental area. Further, the business response should be frankly described as public relations and thereby recognized as economic (*i.e.* profit-generating) behavior rather than being misleadingly proclaimed as "corporate social responsibility."

In this connection, Friedman has pointed out two dangers arising from the rhetoric of social responsibility: (a) public expectations and pressures for business involvement will be further increased as a result of the pronouncements by businessmen; (b) businessmen themselves may lose sight of their "true" function to provide goods and services. The fact of the matter is that the warning comes too late. Public expectations, as we have seen, have dramatically increased. Further, businessmen have not only lost sight of what Friedman may regard as their true function but have increasingly enunciated a different view of the objectives of the corporation.

We find business literature increasingly utilizing the language of managerialism—the view that the corporation has duties to employees, consumers, suppliers, dealers, and the community as well as to shareholders—and that it is the duty of the board to mediate between these competing interests. This statement of the objectives of the corporation, which was expressed as far back as 1919 by William Mackenzie King and repeated in the 1920's by Owen D. Young and Frank Abrams, has become almost traditional in Great Britain. Both the British Institute of Directors and the Confederation of British Industry employ the language of managerialism rather than the traditional legal standard of primary advancement of the interests of shareholders. As will be discussed in greater detail below, these views reflect the changing position of the shareholder in the large public corporation from part owner to investor.

At the same time, the very business leaders who use the language of managerialism find it difficult to discard the primacy of profit as the corporate objective. Yet, it is plain that management cannot give priority to the interests of shareholders and also mediate between the interests of shareholders and the interests of other groups such as employees, consumers, suppliers, dealers, or the community. Business leaders often enunciate contradictory objectives of the corporation reflecting their confusion about the objectives of business in a changing society. These contradictions arise because the familiar goals of the past no longer accurately describe the behavior of the present.

D. ANACHRONISTIC LEGAL FOUNDATIONS

The dilemma described above arises from anachronistic legal and ideological foundations for corporate behavior.

1. The Traditional Legal View.

Let us review the legal foundations of corporate enterprise. Under the traditional legal view, directors must direct the corporation in single-minded dedication to the interests of the shareholders. Thus, in the well known *Ford* case,[2] the Supreme Court of Michigan was faced by Henry Ford's decision in 1916 to reduce dividends which had been averaging over $11,000,000 per year to $1,200,000 in order to reduce prices to customers and to provide more jobs for workers, notwithstanding cash balances of $52.5 million and estimated earnings in excess of $60 million for the year. The Court compelled the payment of a $19 million extra dividend,[3] stating:

> A business corporation is organized and carried on primarily for the benefit of the stockholders . . . it is not within the lawful powers of a board of directors to shape and conduct the affairs of a corporation for the merely incidental benefit of shareholders and for the primary purpose of benefiting others. . . .

Similarly, a more recent English decision in the *Daily News*[4] litigation enunciated the orthodox legal view. Justice Plowman stated:

> The view that directors, in having regard to the question what is in the best interests of their company, are entitled to take into account the interests of the employees, irrespective of any consequential benefit to the company, is one which may be widely held. . . . But no authority to support that proposition as a proposition of law was cited to me; I know of none, and in my judgment such is not the law.

Corporate law forbids so-called corporate waste. Directors may not give away corporate assets without appropriate benefit to the corporation even

[2]*Dodge v. Ford Motor Co.*, 204 Mich. 459, 170 N.W. 668 (1919).

[3]This was one-half of the cash on hand on July 31, 1916, less a $7,000,000 special dividend paid in January 1917. E. Dodd & R.J. Baker, Cases and Materials on Business Associations (Chicago: Foundation Press 1940) at 1198 n.

[4]*Parke v. Daily News, Ltd.*, [1962] 1 Ch. 927, 962-63.

when appoved by a majority of the shareholders. This concept rests on the theory that corporate assets belong to all shareholders and may not be given away over the objection of a single shareholder even if all other shareholders and the directors desire to do so.

"Benefit," as the legal standard for the validity of corporate action, proved manifestly unhelpful in the long series of cases commencing in the latter part of the nineteenth century involving gratuitous corporate expenditures for the advancement of employees and charitable activities. Despite the traditional concept that corporate assets could not be given away, the courts had little difficulty in approving such expenditures notwithstanding their gratuitous form on the ground that they advanced the interests of the corporation. Thus, a succession of employee benefit cases approved gratuitous corporate expenditures—*i.e.* expenditures which the board was under no legal, or even moral, obligation to make—in reliance on the theory that such expenditures benefited the corporation and were, therefore, proper. In the case of employee welfare expenditures—churches or schools in the mill town or benefit funds—the courts found a benefit to the corporation in the increased ease of recruiting and retaining employees.

2. Transformation of Corporate "Benefit" into a Legal Fiction.

With the passage of years, "benefit" was transformed into a legal fiction. In the well-known *Smith* case[5] the New Jersey Supreme Court had little difficulty in finding a corporate "benefit" in a $1,500 contribution by a small New Jersey manufacturing concern to Princeton University. The preservation of the "free enterprise" system and the availability of college-trained persons for managerial positions were found sufficient benefits to the small business in question to uphold the gifts. It is manifest that benefit of this nature relates to the business community as a whole, and only incidentally to this enterprise; to speak of a "benefit" to the corporation in question is to use the term in an entirely different sense from the early decisions and thus to transform it into a legal fiction. In light of the prevailing social climate, the conduct in question served corporate objectives, and as a corollary, shareholder objectives and thus survived judicial scrutiny. This not "benefit," is a more accurate explanation of the *Smith* case. Such an explanation was advanced by an English Court 110 years ago. In a surprisingly modern decision,[6] an English Court upheld a decision by the directors of an English casualty insurance company to honor the claims of 81 Liverpool policyholders whose homes had been destroyed in a celebrated explosion although the policies plainly and unmistakably excluded explosion risks. The Court sensibly concluded that if the insurance company directors thought that honoring the claims would

[5]*A.P. Smith Mfg. Corp.* v. *Barlow*, 13 N.J. 145, 98 A.2d 581, appeal dismissed, 346 U.S. 86 (1953).

[6]*Taunton* v. *Royal Ins. Co.*, 2 H. & M. 135, 71 Eng. Rep. 413 (Ch. 1864).

advance the company's interests in the long run, notwithstanding the immediate out-of-pocket cost, the Court would not interfere. The board could decide for itself whether this was "good business."

Thus, benefit became expanded from direct, short-term benefit to long-term or indirect benefit, from something tangible subject to quantification and involving a causal relationship to something intangible and defying measurement. As a result, the area of corporate directors' discretion became expanded. Courts would not interfere if there was some reasonable basis for concluding that the conduct might somehow prove advantageous to the corporation in the end.

Recognition of social attitudes and the climate of opinion accordingly provides a legal basis for director action. The long-term advancement of shareholder interests is accepted as a satisfactory justification for corporate behavior, if such advancement could conceivably be a reasonable outcome. With so vague a standard, it is apparent that the directors are free to respond to social expectations and demands, notwithstanding a short-term adverse impact on earnings, because of the inability of any shareholder challenging such policies to demonstrate that the conduct would not in the long run prove advantageous to the advancement of corporate interests.

If directors recognize employee, consumer, dealer, supplier, or community demands, their action cannot be challenged, notwithstanding the subordination of short-run shareholder interests, so long as there is some plausible basis for asserting that in the long-run corporate interests (and thereby shareholder interests) will be served, even though demonstration of the long-run advantage may be highly speculative. If management conducts itself according to a standard of what may reasonably be regarded as constituting "good business" in the light of the climate of social opinion, the courts will not interfere. In the process, it is plain that any requirement of the advancement of shareholder interests has ceased to be an effective legal checkrein on corporate behavior.

3. Abandonment of Shareholder Primacy.

Two landmark decisions have gone even further and have abandoned the primacy of shareholder interests.

Herald Co. v. *Seawell* [7] involved a Denver newspaper. The Court of Appeals for the Tenth Circuit upheld the rejection by the directors of a take-over bid by the Newhouse chain and the purchase of shares by the corporation itself in order to assure continued local control of the paper, notwithstanding economic loss to the shareholders.

Previous courts had approved subordination of short-term shareholder interests to the interests of extra-corporate groups because of an assumed

[7] 472 F.2d 1081 (10th Cir. 1972).

long-term advantage to shareholders, however dimly perceived. The Court in the *Herald Company* case upheld directors choosing the public interest in preference to shareholder interests in the absence of any possible basis for contending that shareholders might somehow be better off in the long run. The directors were allowed to act on the basis of what they deemed best for Denver even though it was less advantageous for the shareholders. The Court said:

> In this case we have a corporation engaged chiefly in the publication of a large metropolitan newspaper, whose obligation and duty is something more than the making of corporate profits. Its obligation is three-fold: to the stockholders, to the employees, and to the public.[8]

Similarly, in *Bangor & Aroostook R.R.* v. *Bangor Punta Operations, Inc.*,[9] the Court of Appeals for the First Circuit in 1973 refused to apply an established rule of corporate procedure where a railroad was involved. The court justified its action by reliance upon the overriding public interest in the railroad which it regarded as more important than the ordinary rules of law governing the relations of shareholders to the corporation. Subsequently, this decision was reversed by the Supreme Court by a 5 to 4 vote.

With the *Herald Company* decision and the narrow margin in the *Bangor & Aroostook* case, American courts have begun the process of abandoning the anachronistic legal foundations for corporate behavior which have been exclusively based on the advancement of shareholder interests. Corporations—at least where newspapers and railroads are concerned—involve more profound interests than simply those of shareholders, and the outmoded traditional view of single-minded dedication to shareholder interests is in the process of being jettisoned.

In England the anachronistic nature of the traditional legal standard and its fundamental inconsistency with the generally accepted English view of corporate responsibilities to employees, consumers, suppliers, and the community has been more frankly recognized. Professor L.C.B. Gower pointed this out more than fifteen years ago. Further, in 1973 in reviewing proposed reform of the English Companies Law, the Confederation of British Industry recommended that the provisions of the memorandum of association (the English equivalent of the American certificate of incorporation) be broadened to permit directors to take into account their wider responsibilities in recognition that the corporation exists to serve the interests of employees, consumers, and the community as well as shareholders. The Confederation stated, "Companies must in our view recognize that they have functions, duties and moral obligations that go beyond the immediate pursuit of profit and the requirements of the law."

[8]472 F.2d at 1091 (footnote omitted).

[9]482 F.2d 865 (1st Cir. 1973), *rev'd,*—U.S.—, 41 L.Ed. 2d 418 (1974).

It is plain that the law is moving to reflect changing social opinion. This is true whether or not the law reaches its objectives through the use of convenient fictions to mask the evolution from single-minded advancement of shareholder interests to the recognition of broader social interests or frankly rejects shareholder primacy as no longer reflecting accepted social policy, as was done by the First Circuit and the Tenth Circuit in the *Herald Company* and *Bangor and Aroostook* decisions or as was proposed for the new English Companies Law by the Confederation of British Industry. Anachronistic legal foundations are in the process of restatement so as to avow frankly what the courts have previously recognized in practice, while masking their action with fictions. This is a familiar process in the growth of the law.

4. New Legal Standards.

Shareholder primacy and profit-maximization appear to be on their way to interment as legal standards, at least insofar as the public corporation is concerned. What then is the appropriate legal standard for determination of the fundamental limits of permissible action by a board of directors?

At the threshold, special situations of misconduct should be excluded from discussion. Where board action involves self-dealing, the law essentially insists on fairness and good faith, although in many jurisdictions the elements required to satisfy such standards are less than satisfactory. Where securities transactions are involved, federal statutes establish rules of conduct to safeguard the integrity of the securities markets and to protect public investors.

In the absence of such special features, the law would appear to impose no limitation on the power of the directors to take any corporate action whatsoever so long as there was a reasonable relationship between the action and the business of the corporation in the then prevailing climate of public expectations. As I have elsewhere pointed out, social problems in a very real sense generate their own basis for the legitimacy of corporate response as a legal matter. The social need leads to the development of increased public pressures for corporate involvement, which in turn provide the justification for corporate response. A need to demonstrate single-minded dedication to the advancement of shareholder interests has evaporated.

Where the corporate business involves matters of recognized public concern—newspapers and railroads—we have already seen signs that primacy of shareholder interests may be subordinated to what the courts conclude are more important public interests. Similarly, where corporations voluntarily incur greater costs or reduced income to respond to social needs, without any demonstrable return other than public recognition of the action in question, courts have indicated that shareholders had no legal complaint. Two examples illustrate this: a corporation that needed funds for foreign investment borrowed abroad at higher interest rates than those available at home in cooperation with a government program to improve the nation's balance of payments, and the Chicago Cubs decided not to play night baseball at Wrigley Field because the floodlights would be disturbing to the surrounding community.

As a legal matter the objectives of the corporation have thus transcended the advancement of shareholder interests. Directors are increasingly being permitted to recognize other interests in concluding what is "good business." The changing attitude of the law, at least as far as the large corporation is concerned, recognizes the reality of the changing nature of the relation of the shareholder to the corporation. Shareholders have become investors in corporate equity securities. They are no longer in a position to act as owners in the traditional sense, and the corporation law is gradually ceasing to recognize them as owners in the traditional sense and to accord them the rights of owners.

This perception cannot be pushed too far. The cases indicating change are few. Further, in any event, limited minimum standards will remain.

When an English newspaper corporation was liquidated and the Board proposed to distribute all corporate assets, amounting to about £2 million, to employees as severance pay, the action was successfully challenged in *Parke* v. *Daily News, Ltd.,* which has already been referred to. Although the decision was clearly influenced by the peculiar English doctrine that in the absence of contract or statute, severance pay for employees by a corporation in liquidation is beyond the power of the corporation, there is no reason to suppose that an American court would have decided *Parke* v. *Daily News, Ltd.* differently.

Similarly, if an inner city corporation such as a bank or department store were to make expenditures related to minority employment, minority loans, or urban problems of such magnitude that profits were substantially eliminated, it is not likely that the validity of management action would be upheld. Such a development, of course, is highly unlikely. As a practical matter, business expenditures in the social area have been minimal without any perceptible impact on earnings per share. Only in the environmental field has the dollar response of business reached levels of significant dimensions.[10]

The maintenance of some minimal return on capital would seem to establish an outer legal perimeter on management discretion; in its absence, barring a state of war or other national emergency or catastrophe, it would be difficult to see how the directors could justify the action as "good business."

In the distant future, the law may recognize the corporation as a social

[10]Environmental problems involve a unique area where social and governmental pressures have been profound and where the possibility of *future* governmental action is so lively that it has become a factor that must be considered in making *current* capital expenditures to avoid the possibility of costly corrective work in the future. The nature of corporate response in the environmental area does not foreshadow any similar development in the social sphere.

institution with social objectives transcending economic objectives, but we have not moved so far yet. The business of business is still business, although subject to constraints of a social, moral, and environmental nature. Eventually, the business of business may be changed: social concerns may not simply operate as a restraint but may become the major objective of business, but there is no sign that the courts, legislatures, or society itself are at the present time prepared for such a radical change of business function.

E. RESTRAINTS ON MANAGEMENT CONDUCT OF THE CORPORATION

Moving from the obscure future to the present, what are the restraints imposed on corporate behavior in light of the current ideological objectives of American business?

In the largest corporations, management is largely free of direct shareholder control as a result of the so-called separation of ownership and control, *i.e.* the widespread distribution of shares among millions of individual investors, the pattern of noninterference and almost automatic support of management on the part of institutional investors, management control of the proxy solicitation machinery, and the absence of an organized party system around which institutionalized opposition to management may organize.

Although management functions largely as a self-selected, self-perpetuating group, it is not entirely independent. It operates subject to a series of major restraints, which significantly limit its freedom of action and area of discretion. These restraints are economic, legal, political, and social.

Theoretically, the most formidable economic restraint is the competitive product market where free competition flourishes in all respects. It results in profit-maximization in the neo-classical sense where the businessman responds in essentially an involuntary fashion to the requirements and opportunities of the marketplace, where his actions are not affected by a concern as to the possible reactions of his business rivals, where there is no available area for the exercise of discretion. Except in a very limited area, however, this is recognized as an unrealistic description of the economy.

Economists themselves are divided on the appropriate explanation for business behavior. One thing emerges as relatively clear. Profit-maximization does not appear to explain satisfactorily the way in which business is in fact conducted. Many economists agree that there is a wide area (in addition to the instances of pure monopoly) for the exercise of discretionary judgment by businessmen and that such discretion may be exercised in favor of such objectives as growth, stability, avoidance of risk, or increased managerial returns rather than for maximization of profit. Some economists assert that businessmen appear to satisfice rather than maximize. Profit becomes a minimal restraint rather than the primary objective. Management may seek to achieve a plurality of objectives while maintaining a minimally acceptable level of profits.

Economic constraints also arise from the capital markets and the stock market. Business needs for funds substantially exceed internally generated funds. Management is under pressure to finance through the sale of new securities or reliance on financial institutions. It must operate the enterprise at a level which will command the financial support required. The capital markets impose their discipline on business conduct.

The performance of corporate shares on the stock market is the other major economic restraint. Although minimally acceptable profits are often described as a major restraining factor on management it is not profits as such but earnings per share which are the business objective. Earnings per share play the major, although not exclusive, role in determining the prices at which corporate shares will sell. Higher earnings per share and more importantly a smoothly increasing upward trend line in earnings per share become the key to favorable market recognition of the shares.

Higher market prices for the shares in turn have a series of highly desirable consequences. They reduce the threat of takeover either by proxy contest or tender offer. They achieve public recognition that the corporation and its management are successful, and this has important economic and psychological consequences. They reduce the cost of capital. Higher market prices represent a financial inducement of great significance to management where the pattern of executive compensation follows the usual form and is related to market values through stock option or phantom stock option plans, stock purchase plans, or outright stock ownership. Finally, on the psychological level, the market action of the shares represents a batting average or box score that for many businessmen measures the quality of their performance. It occupies an important role in providing a sense of personal accomplishment and fulfillment and it may also lead to attractive new executive job opportunities.

Legal constraints are provided by state corporation law, increasing federal intervention, and by the private law-making of the New York Stock Exchange. Although state law has become increasingly ineffective, the expanding scope of federal law and the commendable steps taken by the Exchange have provided shareholders (but not other segments of the corporation's public) with substantial, but far from complete, protection against insider manipulation of corporate affairs.

Finally, changing concepts of socially permissible conduct and the realities of potential governmental intervention increasingly shape business decisions. Within the economic and legal restraints sketched above, business retains a wide area of discretionary judgment. Within this discretionary area, consideration of the fundamental political and social attitudes of the time and evaluation of their potential impact on business enterprise involves elements of judgment that are essentially political rather than economic in nature. Business has become a public institution, and business leadership increasingly involves issues of public policy concern. The forces influencing the conduct of business are in many ways increasingly analogous to the conduct of public organizations.

With the changing nature of the conduct of business and relatively novel elements increasingly appearing in the corporate decision-making process, it is plain that the traditional ideological foundations of business are also anachronistic and must be refashioned. American business is indeed an institution in search of an ideology.

BIBLIOGRAPHY

Bell, Daniel, *The Coming of Post Industrial Society: A Venture in Social Forecasting.* New York: Basic Books, Inc., 1973.

Berle, Adolf A., Jr. *Power Without Property.* New York: Harcourt Brace and Co., 1959.

______, *The Twentieth Century Capitalist Revolution.* New York: Harcourt, Brace and Co., 1954.

______, "Economic Power and the Free Society" in *The Corporation Takeover,* ed. Andrew Hacker. New York: Harper and Row, 1964.

Berle, Adolf A., Jr., and Gardiner C. Means, *The Modern Corporation and Private Property.* New York: The Macmillan Co., 1932.

Blumberg, Phillip I., *Corporate Responsibility in a Changing Society.* Boston: Boston University School of Law, 1972.

Cheit, Earl F., ed., *The Business Establishment.* New York: John Wiley & Sons, Inc. 1967.

Committee on Economic Development, *Social Responsibilities of Business Corporations.* New York: 1971.

Friedman, Milton, *Capitalism and Freedom.* Chicago: University of Chicago Press, 1962.

______, "The Social Responsibility of Business Is To Increase Its Profits". *New York Times,* Sept. 13, 1970, §6, p. 32.

Gower, Lawrence, C.B., *The Principles of Modern Companies Law,* 3d ed. London: Stevens, 1969.

Goyder, George, *The Responsible Company.* Oxford: Basil Blackwell & Mott Ltd., 1961.

Hetherington, John A.C., "Fact and Legal Theory: Shareholders, Managers, And Corporate Social Responsibility," 21 *Stanford Law Review* 248 (1969).

Lodge, George Cabot, "Why an Outmoded Ideology Thwarts the New Business Conscience," *Fortune,* Oct. 1970, p. 106.

______, "Top-Priority: Renovating Our Ideology." *Harvard Business Review,* Vol. 48, No. 5 (1970), 43.

Manne, Henry G. "Mergers and the Market for Corporate Control." *Journal of Political Economy,* LXXIII (1965), 110-20.

______, ed., *Economic Policy and the Regulation of Securities.* Washington, D.C.: American Enterprise Institute for Public Policy Research, 1969.

———, "Our Two Corporate Systems: Law and Economics," 53 *Virginia Law Review* 259 (1967).

Mason, Edward S., ed., *The Corporation in Modern Society,* Cambridge: Harvard University Press, 1960.

Nader, Ralph and Mark J. Green, eds., *Corporate Power in America.* New York: Grossman Publishers, 1973.

Note, "Herald Co. v. Sewell: A New Corporate Social Responsibility," 121 *University of Pennsylvania Law Review* 1157 (1973).

Sethi, S. Prakash, ed., *The Unstable Ground: Corporate Social Policy in a Dynamic Society.* Los Angeles, Calif.: Melville Publishing Company, 1974.

Sethi, S. Prakash, *Up Against the Corporate Wall: Modern Corporations and Social Issues of the Seventies.* Englewood Cliffs, N.J.: Prentice-Hall, Inc., 1971.

Sutton, Francis X., Seymour E. Harris, Carl Kaysen, and James Tobin, *The American Business Creed.* Cambridge: Harvard University Press, 1965.

Votaw, Dow and S. Prakash Sethi, *The Corporate Dilemma: Traditional Values versus Contemporary Problems.* Englewood Cliffs, N.J.: Prentice-Hall, Inc., 1973.

CHAPTER TWO

Corporate Size or Aggregate Concentration

Our initial task is to review the dimensions of the major American corporations and their relative position in the American and world economy. This is a study of "bigness" in the economy or aggregate concentration. It should not be confused with market concentration which is reviewed in Chapter 4.

A. THE NEW YORK STOCK EXCHANGE COMPANIES

Examination of the major American corporations should start with the approximately 1,500 companies whose common stock is listed on the New York Stock Exchange (NYSE). These companies—industrial, financial, utility, transportation and trade—dominate the American economy and profoundly influence the world economy.

1. Share of Assets, Sales, Net Income.

In 1971, the NYSE companies represented less than 0.1% of the approximately 1,700,000 American corporations. These relatively few companies had assets of $1,100 billion or more than 40% of total corporate assets, and sales or revenues of $809 billion or about 60% of total corporate revenues. This heavy concentration of assets and sales is exceeded by a remarkable concentration of net income.

In 1971, NYSE companies had total net income after taxes of $42 billion or 88.2% of the total net income of all United States corporations. In 1970, the share of NYSE companies in total net income of all corporations had reached the remarkable level of 94.3%. These top heavy shares represent the culmination of a steady increase from the 63.6% level of 1960 [see Table 2-1]. It is evident that this relatively small number of major American companies receives a dangerously high proportion of total corporate net income.

In this volume filled with statistics, the fact that NYSE companies accounted for 94.3% of total net income after taxes of all United States corporations in 1970 is among the most noteworthy.

2. Number and Distribution of Stockholders.

The number of stockholders in all American corporations has reached notable proportions. The 1970 New York Stock Exchange Census of Shareownership showed that 30.85 million Americans, or one family in four, held stock. Of these, 18.3 million owned shares listed on the New York Stock Exchange.

This widespread participation in corporate ownership has led to such phrase-making as "People's Capitalism" and represents a striking increase from the 6.5 million stockholders of 1952. There are, however, indications that growth has come to an end, at least for the time being. After attaining a record of 32.5 million persons in 1971, the number of shareholders declined in 1972 and 1973 to 30.9 million. Thus, in 2 years, 1.6 million Americans disposed of all stock holdings. The tide of individual stock ownership is apparently ebbing as a result of stock market reverses and the availability of high yields in fixed interest investments.

In early 1973, five corporations (American Telephone & Telegraph, General Motors, Exxon, International Business Machines, and General Electric) had more than 500,000 stockholders each, twenty-one had more

TABLE 2-1

Net Income after Tax
(billions)

Year	*NYSE-Listed Corporations*	*All United States Corporations*	*Percentage*
1973	$ NA	$ 70.2	NA
1972	NA	55.4	NA
1971	42	47.6	88.2%
1970	37	39.3	94.3%
1969	39	44.8	87.1%
1968	37	47.8	77.4%
1967	33	46.6	70.8%
1966	34	49.9	68.1%
1965	32	46.5	68.8%
1964	28	38.4	72.9%
1963	23	33.1	69.5%
1962	21	31.2	67.3%
1961	18	27.2	66.2%
1960	17	26.7	63.6%

Sources: U.S. Department of Commerce, Survey of Current Business, July 1973, Table 6.15; 1973 Statistical Abstract, Table No. 523; New York Stock Exchange Fact Book, 1973.

than 200,000 stockholders each, and fifty listed companies had more than 120,000 stockholders of record each. The fact of fundamental importance is not that American Telephone and Telegraph had 2,992,000 stockholders or General Motors 1,306,000 stockholders in 1973 but that as many as fifty companies had 120,000 or more shareholders of record.

The distribution of stockownership is even more noteworthy when it is recognized that the foregoing substantially understates actual ownership. The available statistics relate to shareholders of record, not to beneficial owners. Thus, the brokerage house with hundreds or thousands of clients holding General Motors or Exxon in their accounts but with the securities registered in the name of the brokerage firm or its nominee is counted as only one stockholder of record. A bank with hundreds or thousands of separate trust or custodian accounts holding General Motors or Exxon will similarly have the securities registered in the name of one or more nominees and similarly constitute only one or several stockholders of record. The actual number of individual beneficial owners is, in fact, unknown and the above data are obvious understatements.

3. Concentration.

The approximately 1,500 NYSE corporations do not comprise a homogenous group. Many are relatively small: the qualifications for listing require only 2,000 round-lot stockholders, after-tax net income of $2.5 million, and aggregate market value of $16 million for the common stock held by the public. Just as the NYSE corporations represent a remarkably high portion of American corporate activity, a limited number of very large corporations represent a substantial portion of the sales, assets, total market value, and net income of all NYSE corporations. A high degree of concentration exists within the 1,500 NYSE companies.

(*a*) *Concentration: Sales.* The fifty largest NYSE corporations (ranked by sales) had sales of $281.3 billion in 1971 or 34.8% of the $809 billion total sales of all NYSE corporations and 20.9% of the $1,347 billion total sales of all American corporations. The ten largest companies accounted for almost half of the sales of these fifty largest:

Companies By Rank	*Total Sales (billions)*	*Percentage of*	
		Largest 50 Companies	*All NYSE Companies*
1-10	$136.0	48.3%	16.8%
11-20	55.0	19.6	6.8
21-30	35.1	12.5	4.3
31-40	29.7	10.6	3.7
41-50	25.5	9.1	3.2
	$281.3	100.0%	34.8%

(*b*) *Concentration: Assets.* Essentially the same high concentration exists in the distribution of corporate assets. The fifty largest NYSE corporations (ranked by assets) had assets of $458.8 billion in 1971, or 40.8% of the $1,125 billion total assets of all NYSE corporations and about 17% of the total assets of all American corporations. The ten largest companies again accounted for almost half of the assets of the fifty largest:

Companies By Rank	*Total Assets (billions)*	*Percentage of*	
		Largest 50 Companies	*All NYSE Companies*
1-10	$211.5	46.1%	18.8%
11-20	95.2	20.7	8.5
21-30	68.0	14.8	6.0
31-40	46.7	10.2	4.2
41-50	37.4	8.2	3.3
Total	$ 458.8	100%	40.8%

(*c*) *Concentration: Net Profits.* Profits also showed a high degree of concentration. The fifty largest NYSE corporations (ranked by sales) had net profits after tax of $16.4 billion in 1971 or 38.9% of the $42 billion total net profits of all NYSE corporations. This represented 34.5% of the $47.6 billion total net profits of all American corporations for the year. The ten largest corporations accounted for almost $10 billion or almost two-thirds of the net profits of the fifty largest.

Companies By Rank	*Total Net Profits (billions)*	*Percentage of*	
		Largest 50 Companies	*All NYSE Companies*
1-10	$ 9.98	61.0%	23.8%
11-20	2.62	16.0	6.2
21-30	1.59	9.7	3.8
31-40	1.15	7.0	2.7
41-50	1.02	6.2	2.4
Total	$ 16.36	100.0%	38.9%

(*d*) *Concentration: Market Value.* As of December 31, 1972, the common stock of the fifty largest NYSE corporations (ranked by market value) accounted for $399 billion, or 47% of the total value of all NYSE common stocks. This represented 34.4% of the total value of all American corporate stock. The $206.3 billion market value of the ten largest corporations alone (ranked by market value) amounted to 24.3% of the $850 billion total value of all 1478 NYSE common stocks then listed.

Companies By Rank	Total Market Value (billions)	Percentage of Largest 50 Companies	Percentage of All NYSE Companies
1-10	$ 206.30	51.7%	24.3%
11-20	75.94	19.0	8.9
21-30	51.37	12.9	6.0
31-40	35.97	9.0	4.2
41-50	28.97	7.3	3.4
Total	$ 398.55	100.0%	47.0%

It is beyond argument that a relatively small number of NYSE corporations—mostly industrial with some financial, utility, and trade corporations—represent a highly concentrated share of the sales, assets, net profits, and total market value of all business firms in the nation.

B. THE CENTRAL ROLE OF THE INDUSTRIAL CORPORATION

Thus far, we have discussed the megacorporations as a single class. In fact, they operate in different industries and in different legal and economic environments. To obtain an adequate framework for comparison, it is necessary to segregate corporations by major industry classifications.

The industrial corporations constitute the core of the economy and are often regarded as characteristic of business as a whole. Thus, the "*Fortune* 500 Largest" is a directory of industrial corporations (manufacturing and mining), with utilities, transportation, merchandising, and financial corporations ranked separately.

While industrial corporations are clearly the single most important component of the economy, they employ only about one-third of all full-time business employees and represent approximately 40% of the overall contribution of business to the national income. Their influence, however, is greater. They account for about one-half of total business sales, about one-half of all capital expenditures, about one-half of corporate profits, and about 98% of nongovernmental expenditures for research and development. The President's Cabinet Committee on Price Stability Study ("Cabinet Committee Study") regarded manufacturing as uniquely important. This sector possesses greater discretionary market power than other areas of business and is highly critical in achieving high employment, growth, and price stability. Notwithstanding the prominence of the industrial corporations, there has been increasing recognition of the major significance of service, trade, and nonprofit organizations. In comparison with the 18,933,000 workers employed in manufacturing in 1972, 15,919,000 were

TABLE 2-2

National Income, 1972
(billions)

		Percentage of Business	*Percentage of Total*
Industrial	$ 312.5	39.4%	33.2%
Transportation	36.0	4.5%	3.8%
Utilities & Communication	38.2	4.8%	4.1%
Wholesale & Retail Trade	139.7	17.6%	14.8%
Services	120.1	15.2%	12.8%
Finance, Insurance and Real Estate	107.9	13.6%	11.5%
Agriculture, Forestry and Fishing	30.4	3.8%	3.2%
Rest of World	7.5	0.9%	0.8%
Total Business	$ 792.3	100.0%	84.1%
Government Total National Income	149.5		15.9%
	$ 941.8		100.0%

Source: U.S. Department of Commerce, Survey of Current Business, July 1973, Table 1.11.

employed in wholesale and retail trade and 14,760,000 in service. Of these, 5,175,000 were employed in medical and other health services and non-profit organizations; an additional 1,281,000 were employed in educational services.

By 1972, services represented $120.1 billion or 12.8% of the total national income and 15.2% of total business income. This compares with $312.5 billion, or 33.2% of total national income and 39.4% of total business income for industrial corporations. Along with services, government itself is responsible for a substantially increased share of national income. National income arising in federal, state, and local government and government enterprises increased to $149.5 billion or 15.9% of total 1972 national income. [see Table 2-2].

C. PROBLEMS INHERENT IN MEASUREMENT OF SIZE

In the measurement of size, corporations are most often ranked in the order of their sales. The amount of assets, the aggregate market value of the stock, the amount of net income after taxes, the number of employees, and the number of shareholders provide additional dimensions, but sales are the most useful index particularly for nonfinancial corporations. The use of assets gives a disproportionate prominence to capital-intensive industries, such as utilities and transportation companies. Moreover, it is the extent of the product resulting from the physical assets, not the stated assets themselves which would appear to constitute the vital element.

In a comparison of companies according to sales, industries with high turnover such as wholesale and retail trade must be segregated since their characteristics are so different. Further, it is evident that in the case of financial institutions, sales are not an appropriate guide. The revenues of banks represent fees for the use of money, not the sale of goods or services. Accordingly, financial institutions are customarily ranked by the size of assets.

As has been frequently noted, statistical comparisons of the "Largest" corporations and of aggregate concentration are subject to a number of distortions. Differences in the degree of consolidation of accounts of subsidiaries and affiliates, exclusion of privately-owned companies, and differences in corporate accounting methods involving alternative methods of reporting inventory, depreciation, and of "pooling" or "purchase" accounting for acquisitions affect the results. Failure to allow for the foreign operations of American concerns and the domestic operations of foreign concerns and inclusion of the nonmanufacturing operations of manufacturing companies and exclusion of the manufacturing operations of non-manufacturing concerns make comparisons of aggregate concentration difficult and not entirely reliable.

Finally, the list of the "Largest" is not stable. From 1966 to 1973, for example, 197 corporations were eliminated from the 500 Largest. If we compare the relative position of the "500 Largest" in 1973 with the "500 Largest" in 1966, we will be comparing different corporations to a significant extent. The alternatives of comparing the corporations in the 1966 group with their performance in 1973 (initial-year group) or the 1973 group with their performance in 1966 (end-year group) are not particularly satisfactory.

Dr. Betty Bock, who has done several studies on the problems inherent in the measurement of aggregate concentration, emphasizes that the validity of findings on aggregate concentration depends on comparable determination of data for the economy and the group of corporations being studied, the methods used to identify the group comprising the largest, and the measures of size used. Use of total assets, sales, or value added by manufacture and selection of the *X* largest in the initial year of the study, in each year of the study, or in the final year of the study can vitally affect the results.

Professor J. Fred Weston also emphasizes the changing composition of the 100 Largest or 200 Largest and suggests that the statistics on aggregate concentration only measure "the fact that the most successful companies are relatively more successful than the average for all manufacturing companies." He points out that to the extent large industrial firms are more diversified in nonindustrial areas or in foreign operations than industrial firms generally, inclusion of their nonmanufacturing and foreign activities in the numerator and denominator of the 200 Largest results in a strong upward bias.

Professor Jules Backman supports these observations. He notes that acquisitions of nonmanufacturing businesses by the 200 Largest industrials of 1968 comprised $14.6 billion of the $50.2 billion total acquisitions between 1948 and 1968 and $7.6 billion of the $15.6 billion of 1968 acquisitions.[1] The Largest industrials are getting bigger but a substantial portion of the growth is in nonindustrial areas. Lumping all acquisitions in a comparison with other industrials is misleading. On the related question of foreign business, Professor Backman notes that between 1950 and 1968, total investment abroad by manufacturing corporations increased 528% from $7.2 to $45.2 billion, while total assets of all manufacturing companies increased only about 250% for the period.

Harold Geneen, chairman of International Telephone & Telegraph Corp., sought to point up the significance of foreign operations in the statistical descriptions of the Largest corporations. He contrasted I.T.T., ranked eleventh Largest, with $4 billion in sales and revenues (about 50% outside of the United States and spread thinly over some thirty-five industries) with Western Electric, ranked twelfth Largest, which does business solely in the United States and all in one industry. He also noted that service and presumably other nonmanufacturing activities of the large corporations were included in the index for measurement of size used to determine the ranking of the Largest.

The question arises whether overstatement in the areas of foreign business and nonmanufacturing business is not offset by other areas of understatement, such as unconsolidated subsidiaries, joint ventures, and commonly-owned companies.

Turnover among the Largest is not a vital factor for our purposes. Since this study is concerned with corporate power as represented by the largest corporations in the economy, the fact that different corporations comprise the "Largest" corporations at different times should not concern us. Aggregate concentration exists although the corporations representing it may change to some extent. Recognition of the likelihood of some change in the ranks of the Largest is important in the evaluation of the significance of the concentration of economic power, but the existence of limited change in the past and the probability of limited change in the future does not impair the present reality of the existence of corporate power. The other elements of imprecision in the data are similarly unimportant provided one recognizes their existence and evaluates the results accordingly.

[1]These totals taken from the Federal Trade Commission Economic Report on Corporate Mergers (1969) do not agree with the later Federal Trade Commission tabulations contained in its Statistical Report, Mergers and Acquisitions, Volume 8 (1973) referred to in Chapter 3 because of definitional changes in the method of computation.

D. THE INDUSTRIAL MEGACORPORATIONS RANKED ACCORDING TO SALES

The most convenient framework for reviewing the industrial corporations is the *Fortune* compilation of the largest American industrial corporations ranked according to sales. It is important to note that the "500 Largest" excludes a number of major privately-owned firms. These include United Parcel with sales in excess of $1 billion, Deering-Milliken, Hallmark Cards, and Hearst Publishing. In addition there are giant privately-owned trading firms such as Cargill and Continental Grain. It is also important to note that *Fortune* classifies a corporation as an industrial if more than 50% of its revenues comes from manufacturing or mining; *all* its operations are then included in the tabulation.[2]

In 1973, the 500 Largest industrials (ranked according to sales) accounted for 65% of the sales, 76% of the employees, and 79% of the profits of all American industrial corporations. In the same year, the 1,000 Largest were responsible for about 72% of the sales, 86% of the employees and 85% of the profits.

Within the ranks of the 1,000 Largest, the core of concentrated industrial power is in the 200 Largest, which represented about three-quarters of the total sales, assets, employees, and net income of the group. Although the classification must necessarily be imprecise, the 200 Largest collectively may be said to constitute the industrial megacorporations which are the subject of this volume:

1972	*Sales (billions)*	*Assets (billions)*	*Employees (millions)*	*Net Income (billions)*
200 Largest Corporations	$ 445.5	$ 392.7	11.258	$ 23.3
800 Next Largest Corporations	171.2	139.2	5.265	6.9
1,000 Largest Corporations	$ 616.7	$ 531.9	16.523	$ 30.2
Percentage Represented by the 200 Largest	72.2%	73.8%	68.6%	77.2%

Source: 1973 Statistical Abstract, Tables Nos. 776,777

The position of the 200 industrial megacorporations has been maintained over the years. Although the degree of concentration in the 100 Largest has

[2]General Telephone & Electronics with sales of $5.1 billion in 1973 was thus ranked as the 17th Largest industrial in 1973 after appearing as the 2d Largest utility in 1972.

reduced somewhat since 1955, the role of the Second 100 Largest has increased. Illustrating the growing importance of the Second 100 Largest as well as inflationary factors, the number of firms with sales in excess of $1 billion climbed to 167 in 1973 from 80 in 1966. As a result, the share of the 200 Largest in the sales of the 500 Largest has remained relatively constant.

	1955	*1960*	*1965*	*1970*	*1971*	*1972*	*1973*
Largest 100	67.1%	65.2%	64.7%	62.3%	62.7%	62.4%	62.6%
Second 100	15.2	15.9	15.8	17.8	17.4	17.5	17.3
Top 200	82.3%	81.1%	80.5%	80.1%	80.1%	79.9%	79.9%

Source: 1973 Statistical Abstract, Table No. 776; Fortune, May 1974

The 500 Largest during the same period have significantly increased their share of the sales, assets, employees, and net income of industrial corporations generally. [see Table 2-3].

TABLE 2-3
The Performance of the 500 Largest Industrials
(Money in billions; employees in millions)

	1955	*1960*	*1965*	*1970*	*1973*
Sales of 500 Largest	161.4	204.7	298.1	463.9	667.1
Total Industrial Sales	278.4	345.7	492.2	708.8	1,017.2
Percentage	58.0%	59.2%	60.6%	65.4%	65.6%
Assets of 500 Largest	122.3	176.2	251.7	432.1	555.5
Total Industrial Assets	190.1	255.9	359.1	578.2	670.1
Percentage	64.2%	68.8%	70.1%	74.7%	82.9%
Employees of 500 Largest	8,605	9,179	11,279	14,608	15,531
Total Industrial Employees	17,514	17,508	18,694	19,972	20,445
Percentage	49.1%	52.6%	60.3%	73.1%	76.0%
Net Income of 500 Largest	11.2	11.6	20.1	21.7	38.7
Total Industrial Net Income	15.1	15.2	27.5	28.6	49.0
Percentage	77%	76%	78%	76%	79%

Sources: 1973 Abstract Tables Nos. 786, 1198; Federal Trade Commission, Quarterly Financial Reports for Manufacturing Corporations; U.S. Department of Labor, Employment and Earnings, July 1974, Fortune, May 1974.

Measurement utilizing the amount of value added by manufacturing may be preferable to use of sales, since it avoids duplication of the product of suppliers in the chain of production from raw material to finished product. Value added is the value of shipments plus receipts for services rendered, less direct costs attributable to other businesses, such as the cost of materials and supplies, fuel and energy, containers, and contract work.

Value-added by manufacture shows a dramatic increase in concentration from 1947 to 1954. Since then, the process of concentration has continued but at a reduced rate. From 1954 to 1970, the share of the 50 Largest firms was relatively constant, but the 100 Largest increased from 30% to 33% and the 200 Largest showed a significantly larger increase from 37% to 43%.

	1947	*1954*	*1958*	*1962*	*1966*	*1970*	*Percentage Increase 1954-1970*
50 Largest	17%	23%	23%	24%	25%	24%	+1%
100 Largest	23%	30%	30%	32%	33%	33%	+3%
200 Largest	30%	37%	38%	40%	42%	43%	+6%

Source: U.S. Department of Commerce, Bureau of the Census, Annual Surveys of Manufactures, 1970, Value of Shipments Concentration Ratios by Industry, Table 1.

The role of the 200 Largest in the economy is steadily increasing, despite the reduced growth rate of the very largest corporations.

Professor John M. Blair points out that while these Census Bureau statistics cannot involve overstatement, there are several sources of understatement. One major area of understatement arises from the fact that the computation of manufacture by value-added is restricted to "manufacturing" concerns, although as we have seen, the 200 Largest "industrials" include "mining" firms (in which petroleum companies are classified). Thus, ten major oil companies included in the 50 Largest industrials are classified under "mining" and are not included in the Census Bureau's 200 Largest "Manufactures" and the value-added data at all. Other possible areas of understatement arise from the exclusion of minority-owned and controlled subsidiaries and joint ventures.

E. THE INDUSTRIAL MEGACORPORATIONS RANKED ACCORDING TO ASSETS

Ranking of industrials according to assets rather than sales does not produce substantial change in the composition of list. About fifty of the 500 Largest lose their places, and the changes in the rank ordering are hardly momentous.

A Federal Trade Commission review of manufacturing corporations shows that the share of total manufacturing assets represented by the very largest manufacturing firms has increased substantially since the end of World War II. From 1947 to 1970, the share of the 100 Largest[3] climbed from 39.3% to 48.5% and the 200 Largest from 47.2% to 60.5% [see Table

[3]Within this select group, the very largest megacorporations are losing some ground. Leo Loevinger points out that the fifty Largest held 54.6% of the assets of the 500 Largest in 1954, against only 52.2% in 1964. By 1973, the share of the fifty Largest had further declined to 48.6%.

2-4]. The share of the 1000 Largest climbed from 61.1% in 1941 to 80.8% in 1968.

The 100 Largest in 1968 held a larger share than the 200 Largest in 1950.

TABLE 2-4

Federal Trade Commission, Economic Report on Corporate Mergers (1969)

Share of manufacturing assets held by the 200 Largest corporations, 1925-41; 1947-68

Year	*Share held by 100 Largest* [1]		*Share held by 200 Largest*	
	Total assets	*Corporate assets*	*Total assets*	*Corporate assets*
1925	34.5	36.1		
1927	34.4	36.0		
1929	38.2	39.7	45.8	47.7
1931	42.2	43.9	49.4	51.4
1933	42.5	44.2	49.5	51.4
1935	40.8	42.3	47.7	49.6
1937	42.1	43.7	49.1	50.9
1939	41.9	43.5	48.7	50.5
1941 [2]	38.2	39.6	45.1	46.7
1947	37.5	39.3	45.0	47.2
1948	38.6	40.3	46.3	48.3
1949	39.5	41.1	47.1	49.0
1950	38.4	39.8	46.1	47.7
1951	38.1	39.4	46.1	47.7
1952	39.3	40.6	47.7	49.2
1953	40.3	41.7	48.7	50.3
1954	41.9	43.3	50.4	52.1
1955	43.0	44.3	51.6	53.1
1956	43.9	45.0	52.8	54.1
1957	45.2	46.3	54.3	55.6
1958	46.0	47.1	55.2	56.6
1959	45.4	46.3	54.8	56.0
1960	45.5	46.4	55.2	56.3
1961	45.8	46.6	55.4	56.3
1962	45.5	46.2	55.1	56.0
1963	45.7	46.5	55.5	56.3
1964	45.8	46.5	55.8	56.6
1965	45.9	46.5	55.9	56.7
1966	45.8	46.4	56.1	56.7
1967	47.6	48.1	58.7	59.3
1968	48.8	49.3	60.4	60.9
Percentage Point Increase				
1925-1968	14.3	13.2	—	—
1947-1968	11.3	10.0	15.4	13.7
Percent Increase in Share				
1925-1968	41.4	36.6	—	—
1947-1968	30.1	25.4	34.2	29.0

[1] Ranked according to asset size in each year.

[2] Data are not available for the years between 1941 and 1947 because some large corporations did not publish balance sheets for reasons of wartime security.

Source: Bureau of Economics, Federal Trade Commission, Appendix C.

Just over 200 corporations in 1968 held the same share as the 1000 Largest as of 1941 [see Table 2-5].

TABLE 2-5
Federal Trade Commission, Economic Report on Corporate Mergers (1969)

Number of Companies in 1941, 1964 and 1968 Holding Identical Shares of All Corporate Manufacturing Assets

Share of assets (percent)	Number of companies holding share in:		
	1941	1964	1968
38%	100	59	53
46	200	97	86
50	300	125	104
53	400	150	124
55	500	175	141
57	600	197	156
58	700	218	170
59	800	236	182
60	900	255	195
61	1,000	272	207

Source: Bureau of Economics, Federal Trade Commission, Appendix A.

The absolute size as well as the relative share of the manufacturing megacorporations have continued to increase with inflation obviously contributing to this development. From 1960 to 1973, the number of manufacturing corporations with assets of over $1 billion increased from 28 to 138 and the number of corporations with assets of over $250 million increased from 142 to 391. [see Table 2-6].

TABLE 2-6
Number of Corporations with $250 Million and $1 Billion of Assets or More

	1960	1970	1971	1972	1973
Number of Corporations with $250 Million of Assets or More	142	320	333	348	391
Number of Corporations with $1 Billion of Assets or More	28	102	111	115	138

Source: 1973 Statistical Abstract, Table No. 787, 1972 Statistical Abstract, Table No. 771.

From 1960 to 1972, the manufacturing megacorporations with over $1 billion of assets increased their relative position at a substantial rate. Their

TABLE 2-7
Share of Manufacturing Assets and Net Profits Held By Corporations with Assets of $1 Billion or More

Assets (Billions)	*1960*	*1970*	*1971*	*1972*
All Manufacturing Corporations	$ 251,314	$ 554,046	$ 584,253	$ 623,823
Corporations with Assets of $1 Billion or more	69,011	267,733	296,610	321,158
Percentage	27.5%	58.3%	50.8%	51.5%
Net Profit (Millions)				
All Manufacturing Corporations	$ 4,220	$ 6,894	$ 6,995	$ 7,934
Corporations with Assets of $1 Billion or more	1,598	3,645	4,309	4,420
Percentage	37.9%	52.9%	61.6%	55.7%

Source: 1973 Statistical Abstract, Table No. 781.

share of total assets of all manufacturing corporations almost doubled from 27.5% to 51.5% and their share of net profits rose from 37.9% to 55.7% [see Table 2-7]. Concentration represented by manufacturing corporations with over $250 million of assets also increased substantially but not at the same remarkable rate. From 1960 to 1972, these corporations increased their share of total assets from 50.8% to 69.9% and their share of net profits from 58.5% to 72.5% [see Table 2-8].

TABLE 2-8
Share of Manufacturing Assets and Net Profits Held By Corporations with Assets of $250 Million or More

Assets	*1960*	*1970*	*1971*	*1972*
All Manufacturing Corporations	$ 251,314	$ 554,046	$ 584,253	$ 623,823
Corporations with Assets of $250,000,000 or more	127,627	374,439	404,765	435,973
Percentage	50.8%	67.6%	69.3%	69.9%
Net Profit (Millions)				
All Manufacturing Corporations	4,220	6,894	6,995	7,934
Corporations with Assets of $250,000,000 or more	2.468	5.082	5,569	5,749
Percentage	58.5%	73.7%	79.6%	72.5%

Source: 1973 Statistical Abstract, Table No. 781, 1972 Statistical Abstract, Table No. 771.

TABLE 2-9

Studies by the Staff of the Cabinet Committee on Price Stability, Study Paper No. 2 (1969)

Concentration of Assets and Profits in American Manufacturing Corporations, 1st Quarter of 1968

Asset size (millions)	*Corporations*	*Total assets*		*Total net profits*	
		Millions	*Percent*	*Millions*	*Percent*
$ 1,000 and over	78	$ 194,580	43	$ 3,665	49
$ 250 to $ 1,000	194	92,842	21	1,478	20
$ 100 to $ 260	257	39,404	9	594	8
$ 50 to $ 100	284	20,817	5	275	4
$ 25 to $ 50	507	18,259	4	283	4
$ 10 to $ 25	1,117	17,905	4	286	3
Under $ 10	*185,000	65,011	14	893	12
Total	187,407	448,898	100	7,429	100

*Estimate

Source: Federal Trade Commission and Securities and Exchange Commission.

By the first quarter of 1968, the 2,437 manufacturing companies with assets of $10 million or more held 86% of the assets and earned 88% of the profits of the estimated total of 187,000 manufacturing companies in the country [see Table 2-9].

In the case of the manufacturing corporations, it is plain that the largest firms (ranked by asset size) represent a concentration of assets and net profits which has been constantly increasing and which will likely increase still further.

Professor Weston seeks to explain high aggregate concentration in terms of the very heavy capital investment required in six capital-intensive industries (petroleum refining, motor vehicles and equipment, primary iron and steel, basic chemicals, nonferrous metals, and aircraft and parts.) He points out that in 1968 these six industries accounted for fifty-three of the 100 largest manufacturing firms and for $205.1 billion or 42.2% of total assets of $485.9 billion. This percentage of total assets has remained constant since 1954.

F. RECAPITULATION OF THE INDUSTRIAL MEGACORPORATIONS

The tremendous scale of operation of the megacorporations is illustrated by the position of the 100 Largest industrial corporations in 1972, ranked separately according to sales, assets, net income, and employees:

Ranked According to Sales

Total Sales of 100 Largest	$ 347.8 billion
Total Industrial Sales	850.6 billion
Percentage of Total Sales	40.9%
Sales of Group Median	$ 2.1 billion
Sales of Smallest	1.4 billion

Ranked According to Assets	
Total Assets of 100 Largest	$ 310.8 billion
Total Industrial Assets	663.4 billion
Percentage of Total Assets	46.8%
Assets of Group Median	$ 2.0 billion
Assets of Smallest	1.2 billion
Ranked According to Net Income	
Total Net Income of 100 Largest	$ 18.8 billion
Total Industrial Net Income	36.5 billion
Percentage of Total Net Income	51.5%
Net Income of Group Median	$ 111.7 million
Net Income of Smallest	60.8 million
Ranked According to Employees	
Total Employees of 100 Largest	8.5 million
Total Industrial Employees	19.7 million
Percentage of Total Employees	43.2%
Employees of Group Median	58.6 thousand
Employees of Smallest	36.6 thousand

Sources: 1973 Statistical Abstract, Table 777; Survey of Current Business, July 1973, Tables 6.4, 6.15, 6.19; NYSE 1973 Fact Book. Economic Report of the President, 1974, Table C-75.

In Table 2-10, the ranking of the largest corporations is recapitulated according to a variety of indicators to indicate the relative position of each company.

We are thus dealing with institutions of size and strength resembling states. Their net income exceeds the gross national product of many countries (although the comparison loses some strength when analyzed on a value-added basis). Let us compare the relative level of the economies of the smaller European countries:

Country	*Gross 1971 National Product (Billions)*
Austria	$ 17.84
Denmark	18.24
Finland	11.50
Greece	10.77
Ireland	4.97
Norway	13.57
Portugal	7.43
Turkey	13.03
Total	$ 97.35

Source: World Almanac (1974), pp. 619-20.

The $97.35 billion aggregate gross national product of these eight nations is less than the total $136 billion sales of the ten largest NYSE corporations (ranked by sales).

TABLE 2-10

Rank of the 50 Largest Industrial Corporations of 1973 (According to Sales)

	1973				*1972*		*Fiscal 1973*
	Sales	*Assets*	*Net Income*	*Employees*	*Share holders*	*Market Value*	*Defense Production*
General Motors	1	2	2	1	1	3	22
Exxon	2	1	1	12	2	4	23
Ford	3	4	5	2	6	19	24
Chrysler	4	14	26	6	19	—	30
General Electric	5	11	11	4	4	5	2
Texaco	6	3	4	33	9	7	65
Mobil Oil	7	7	6	37	14	13	54
International Business Machines	8	5	3	5	3	1	18
ITT	9	8	12	3	33	20	21
Gulf	10	9	8	59	8	21	85
Standard Oil of California	11	10	7	98	11	16	34
Western Electric	12	19	18	7	—	—	11*
U.S. Steel	13	13	17	10	7	—	71
Westinghouse	14	20	44	9	29	28	13
Standard Oil (Indiana)	15	12	13	81	23	18	68
Dupont	16	18	10	16	15	11	60
General Telephone	17	6	14	8	6	37	47
Shell	18	16	16	127	—	32	100
Goodyear	19	25	37	11	—	—	39
RCA	20	29	38	13	10	43	20
Proctor & Gamble	30	35	19	80	—	9	—
LTV	23	66	176	44	—	—	17
International Harvester	22	34	62	20	37	—	9
Eastman Kodak	25	21	9	15	13	2	38
Continental Oil	21	26	29	96	—	—	—
Atlantic Richfield	26	17	24	170	36	33	90
Tenneco	29	15	32	28	12	—	25
Union Carbide	28	22	22	19	18	—	—
Swift (Esmark)	27	126	179	119	—	—	—
Kraftco	31	99	73	71	—	—	—
Bethlehem Steel	24	23	35	17	16	—	—
Greyhound	32	104	115	55	30	—	—
McDonald Douglas	39	41	59	32	—	—	7
Firestone Tire & Rubber	37	36	42	18	—	—	—
Caterpillar Tractor	34	47	27	35	—	36	—
Litton	47	51	199				
Phillips Petroleum	40	27	31	117	34	—	—
Occidental Petroleum	36	32	108	129	20	—	—
Lockheed Aircraft	44	63	342	42	—	—	1
General Foods	46	74	65	75	—	—	—
Xerox	41	30	20	24	37	8	—
Dow Chemical	38	24	23	67	—	31	—
Beatrice Foods	43	127	85	51	—	—	—
Boeing	33	79	171	41	—	—	3
Rockwell International	35	54	57	22	—	—	10
W.R. Grace	42	55	98	34	—	—	—
Monsanto	45	40	30	54	—	—	—
Borden	48	90	120	82	—	—	—
Union Oil of California	49	31	39	253	—	—	—
Minnesota Mining & Manufacturing	50	45	21	31	—	10	—

Western Electric would rank #11, if ranked separately of its parent, American Telephone which ranks #6 largely because of Western Electric's contracts.

G. NONINDUSTRIAL MEGACORPORATIONS

The position of the largest industrial corporations may now be compared with the largest corporations in other areas of the economy. The *Fortune* 1973 directory provides a useful summary of the 300 nonindustrial giants representing the fifty Largest corporations in each of six nonindustrial areas:

	Assets (Billions)	*Revenues (Billions)*	*Employees (Millions)*	*Net Income (Billions)*
50 Largest Commercial Banks	$ 459.0	(A)	.4	$ 2.4
50 Largest Life Insurance Companies	204.8	$ 42.8	.4	1.1
50 Largest Diversified Finance Companies	123.8	33.1	.4	2.2
50 Largest Retailing Companies (B)	44.3	100.5	2.7	2.1
50 Largest Transportation Companies (B)	48.2	30.6	.9	.9
50 Largest Utilities	181.2	55.8	1.3	7.2
Total	$ 1061.3	$ 262.8	6.1	$ 15.9

Source: Fortune, July 1974, at 122-133)
(A) Not relevant for comparative purposes.
(B) Ranked by revenues; others ranked by assets.

These 300 nonindustrials compare with the 200 Largest industrial megacorporations as follows:

	Assets	*Revenues*	*Employees*	*Net Income*
300 Nonindustrials	$ 1061.3	$ 262.8	6.1	$ 15.9
200 Largest Industrials	459.9	532.9	12.3	33.7

Although the aggregate assets of the 200 Largest industrials are only about 40% of those of the 300 nonindustrials, their revenues,[4] employees, and their net income were all more than twice as large. This helps explain why the industrials are looked upon as the most important component of business.

H. THE MULTI-NATIONAL DIMENSION

The foreign content of the sales, production, assets, earnings and employment of the major American manufacturing corporations (ranked according

[4]Revenues of the 50 Largest commercial banks have not been included in the revenues of the 300 nonindustrials.

to sales) was shown to be enormous by a United Nations study of multinational corporations as of 1971, Multi-national Corporations in World Development (1973) ("Multi-national Corporations Study") [see Table 2-11]. Although part of this is represented by exports, much of it reflects American-owned or partly-owned operations abroad. Thus, from 1962 to 1971, United States direct investment abroad increased from $37.1 billion to an estimated $94 billion.

In 1969, United States corporations had a total of 9,691 affiliates abroad, most of which were wholly-owned and almost all of the balance majority-owned; in 1967, only about 7% of affiliates in developed economies and about 11% in developing economies were less than 50%-owned. As many as 291 United States corporations had affiliates in ten or more foreign countries.

American investment played a major role in the economies of most of the highly developed countries of the world. Thus, in 1970 United States plant and equipment expenditures in foreign manufacturing ranged from 5.8% in France to 20.9% in the United Kingdom and 32.2% in Canada.

Country	*1966*	*1970*
Canada	42.7%	32.2%
United Kingdom	16.3%	20.9%
Belgium-Luxembourg	17.0%	14.1%
West Germany	9.2%	12.3%
France	4.3%	5.8%

Source: Multinational Corporations Study, p. 170.

Thus, it is apparent that the economic development of even such a highly developed country as the United Kingdom was influenced significantly by decisions made in the United States affecting 20.9% of total capital formation in manufacturing. The impact is even more important in those particular industries where United States investment is pronounced. For example, in 1970 United States expenditures for plant and equipment in the machinery industry represented 23.3% of total for the industry in France and 29.0% in the United Kingdom.

The United Nations study of multi-national corporations not only showed the importance of foreign operations of the major American corporations but it demonstrated the predominance of American corporations in the world economy. Of the 650 largest industrial corporations in the world, 358 were American. Of the 211 corporations with sales of $1 billion or more, 127 were American. Of the 16 with sales of $5 billion or more, 12 were American. It is clear that the American megacorporations cast a world-wide shadow.

TABLE 2-11

United Nations, Multinational Corporations in World Development (1973)
Foreign Content of Operations and Assets of Manufacturing Corporations of Market Economies with Sales of Over $1 Billion, 1971

Rank[a]	*Company*	*Nationality*	*Total sales (millions of dollars)*	*Foreign content as percentage of*					*Number of subsidiary countries*[c]
				Sales[b]	*Production*	*Assets*	*Earnings*	*Employment*	
1	General Motors	USA	28,264	19[j]	...	15[g]	19[j]	27[e]	21
2	Standard Oil (N.J.).......	USA	18,701	50[j]	81[e]	52[h]	52[j]	...	25
3	Ford Motors	USA	16,433	26[j]	36[h]	40[h]	24[j]	48[e]	30
5	General Electric	USA	9,429	16[j]	...	15[h]	20[j]	...	32
6	International Business Machines	USA	8,274	39[j]	...	27[h]	50[j]	36[e]	80
7	Mobil Oil	USA	8,243	45[j]	...	46[h]	51[j]	51[h]	62
8	Chrysler	USA	7,999	24[j]	22[e]	31[h]	...	24[e]	26
9	Texaco	USA	7,529	40[j]	65[e]	...	25[e]	..	30
11	International Telephone and Telegraph Corp. ...	USA	7,346	42[j]	60[h]	61[h]	35[j]	72[h]	40
12	Western Electric..........	USA	6,045	...	...	...	...	...	...
13	Gulf Oil.................	USA	5,940	45[j]	75[e]	38[h]	21[j]	...	61
16	Standard Oil of Calif......	USA	5,143	45[j]	46[j]	9[h]	43[h]	29[h]	26
18	United States Steel........	USA	4,928	54[j]	...	48[e]	62[e]	70[e]	...
19	Westinghouse Electric.....	USA	4,630	...	...	...	...	...	...
21	Standard Oil (Ind.)	USA	4,054	...	...	16[e]	...	...	24
22	Shell Oil (subsidiary of Royal Dutch/Shell) ...	USA	3,892	...	...	...	...	...	...
23	E.I. du Pont de Nemours ..	USA	3,848	18[j]	12[h]	12[g]	...	...	20
26	RCA	USA	3,711	...	...	...	...	...	18
28	Goodyear Tire and Rubber	USA	3,602	30[g]	...	22[g]	30[g]	...	22
32	Ling-Temco-Vought	USA	3,359	..	...	...	...	...	...
37	Procter and Gamble	USA	3,178	25[j]	...	16[h]	25[j]	...	24
38	Atlantic Richfield	USA	3,135	...	...	...	...	...	12
41	Continental Oil	USA	3,051	...	...	20[d]	...	...	27
42	Boeing..................	USA	3,040	...	...	...	...	...	...
43	Union Carbide	USA	3,038	29[j]	25[h]	26[h]	22[e]	43[h]	34
44	International Harvester	USA	3,016	25[j]	19[h]	26[h]	10[g]	32[e]	20
45	Swift	USA	2,996	16[j]	...	...	...	..	...
46	Eastman Kodak	USA	2,976	33[k]	20[h]	27[k]	19[j]	40[k]	25
47	Bethlehem Steel	USA	2,964	2[e]	...	...	...	...	...
48	Kraftco	USA	2,960	..	...	...	...	...	16
51	Lockheed Aircraft	USA	2,852	3[d]	...	...	...	...	10
52	Tenneco	USA	2,841	...	...	...	...	...	14
			2,836	14[j]	...	...	...	12[j]	33
58	Greyhound	USA	2,616	...	...	...	...	...	...
60	Firestone Tire and Rubber	USA	2,484	...	...	...	26[e]	24[d]	33

Source: Centre for Development Planning, Projections and Policies of the Department of Economic and Social Affairs of the United Nations Secretariat, based on table 1; *Belgium's 500 largest companies* (Brussels, 1969); *Entreprise,* No. 878, 6-12 July, 1972; Rolf Jungnickel, "Wie multinational sind die deutschen Unternehmen?" in *Wirtschafts dienst,* No. 4, 1972; Wilhelm Grotkopp and Ernst Schmacke, *Die Grossen 500* (Dusseldorf, 1971); Commerzbank, *Auslandsfertigung* (Frankfurt, 1971); Bank of Tokyo, The President Directory 1973 (Tokyo, 1972); *Financial Times,* 30 March 1973; *Vision,* 15 December 1971; *Sveriges 500 Största Företag* (Stockholm, 1970); Max Iklé, *Die Schweiz als internationaler Bankund Finanzplatz* (Zurich, 1970); Schweizer Bankgesellschaft, *Die grössten Unternehmen der Schweiz* (1971); *Financial Times,* 15 May 1973; J.M. Stopford, "The foreign investments of United Kingdom firms", London Graduate School of Business Studies, 1973, (mimeo); *Multinational Corporations,* Hearings before the Sub Committee on International Trade of the Committee on Finance, United States Senate, 93rd Congress, First Session, February/March 1973; Nicholas K. Bruck and Francis A. Lees, "Foreign content of United States corporate activities", *Financial Analyst Journal,* September-October 1966; *Forbes,* 15 May 1973; *Chemical and Engineering News,* 20 December 1971; *Moody's Industrial Manual,* 1973; Sidney E. Rolfe, *The International Corporation* (Paris, 1969); Charles Levinson, *Capital, Inflation and the Multinationals* (London, 1971); *Yearbook of International Organizations,* 12th ed., 1968-69, and 13th ed., 1970-71; Institut für Marxistische Studien and Forschung, *Internationale Konzerne and Arbeiterklasse* (Frankfurt, 1971); Heinz Aszkenazy, *Les grandes sociétés européennes* (Brussels, 1971); *Mirovaja ekonomika i mezdunarodnyje otnosenija,* No. 9, 1970.

[a]Corporations are ranked in descending order of sales.

[b]Total sales to third parties (non-affiliate firms) outside the home country.

[c]Countries in which the parent corporation has at least one affiliate, except in the case of Japan, where the number of foreign affiliates is reported.

[d]1964. [g]1967. [j]1970.

[e]1965. [h]1968. [k]1971.

[f]1966. [i]1969. [l]1972.

Number of Corporations
with Sales of

Country	*Over $10 Billion*	*$5 to $10 Billion*	*$1 to 4.999 Billion*	*$300 Million to $999 Million*	*Total*
United States	3	9	115	231	358
Rest of The World	1	3	80	208	292
Total	4	12	195	439	650
Total Sales (Millions)	$76,131	$77,807	$382,297	$233,772	$773,007

Source: Multi-national Corporations Study, p. 127.

The foreign operations of American corporations present questions of power and social control for the countries involved that differ markedly from such issues in the United States. The size, level of economic development, and dependence on foreign capital, as well as the political and social structure of the various foreign countries present different questions. The ability of the host country governments to impose their own objectives and restraints on the multi-nationals operating within their borders ranges widely, and the degree of freedom of the multi-national to function free of governmental intervention is correspondingly affected. The significance of the size and power of the megacorporations as reflected within the United States is manifestly not an accurate indication of the significance of their size, power, and influence in the countries involved in their overseas operations. Further, governmental policies abroad, particularly in the area of race relations, may be in conflict with social attitudes at home. A country-by-country analysis is required.

It must be recognized that to the extent that governmental intervention in the United States does not affect foreign operations and the host countries do not impose effective controls of their own, the multi-nationals can function with significantly greater freedom than is apparent from a review of their domestic operations. The importance of this absence of overall political constraints is emphasized by the substantial proportion of American corporate operations represented by foreign affiliates. Further, foreign operations may provide the occasion for the multi-national to pursue policies that are contrary to American legal constraints or moral climate.

Reflecting these factors, the foreign operations of American multinational corporations have provoked controversies at home that have contributed to the politicization of the American corporation. Compliance with the legal constraints or prevailing social attitudes of the host countries does not shield the multi-national corporation from controversy at home. "Value-blind" conduct of the over-seas business in compliance with local law or custom does not constitute a satisfactory answer to social critics. Thus,

American corporate employment practices and even the very conduct of business in South Africa, Angola, Rhodesia, mining ventures in Puerto Rico, and oil exploration in South West Africa (Namibia) have all produced vigorous public controversy in the United States. Approval of the host country has either been irrelevant or contributed to the very matters complained of. The multi-national is the subject of pressure from social reform groups that seek to modify policies that are not discouraged by the United States government and may be expressly approved by the host country. Its policies have an inescapable political dimension, for which governmental approval does not necessarily provide a protective umbrella. This important aspect of foreign operations underscores the political significance of the megacorporations.

The scale of the operations of the megacorporations as reflected in the data on aggregate concentration in the United States and their operations abroad demonstrate the central role of the megacorporations in the American and international economy.

BIBLIOGRAPHY

Blair, John M. *Economic Concentration.* New York: Harcourt Brace Jovanovich, Inc., 1972.

Bock, Betty, *Statistical Games and the "200 Largest" Industrials: 1954 and 1968.* New York: The Conference Board, Studies in Business Economics No. 115, 1970.

Cabinet Committee on Price Stability, Staff of, *Industrial Structure and Competition Policy.* Study Paper #2, Washington, D.C.: Government Printing Office, 1969.

Eisenberg, Melvin, "Access to the Corporate Proxy Machinery," 83 *Harvard Law Review* 1489 (1970).

______, "The Legal Roles of Shareholders and Management in Modern Corporate Decision-making." 57 *California Law Review* 1 (1969).

______, "Megasubsidiaries: The Effect of Corporate Structure on Corporate Control," 84 *Harvard Law Review* 1577 (May, 1971).

Federal Trade Commission, *Economic Report on Corporate Mergers.* Washington, D.C.: Government Printing Office, 1969.

New York Stock Exchange, *1970 Census on Shareownership.* New York: 1971.

______, 1973 Fact Book. New York, 1973.

Senate Committee on Finance, *Report on Implication of Multinational Firms for World Trade and Investment and for U.S. Trade and Labor.* 93rd Cong., 1st sess., Feb. 1973. Washington, D.C.: Government Printing Office, 1973.

Symposium, "Conglomerate Mergers and Acquisitions: Opinion & Analysis" 44 *St. John's Law Review,* Special Edition, Spring 1970.

United Nations, *Multinational Corporations in World Development.* New York: 1973.

Weston, J. Fred and Stanley I. Ornstein, eds., *The Impact of Large Firms on the United States Economy.* Lexington, Mass: D.C. Heath & Co., 1973.

CHAPTER THREE

The Significance of Size or Aggregate Concentration

We have examined the dominant position of the megacorporations in the American economy with their dramatically high percentages of total industrial assets, total industrial sales, and net income. What is the significance of this concentration of economic power in a relatively small number of corporations?

If size contributes to the impairment of competition, it obviously represents a consequence of grave significance for an economic order that professes to be governed by market forces and "free enterprise." According to neo-classical economic theory, the evils of monopoly will tend to appear in the form of higher prices, lower production, above-normal profits, wealth transferred from consumers to the producer (and perhaps to labor), inefficient allocations of resources, and underemployment. These are matters for the antitrust laws which are discussed in Chapter 4 in connection with market concentration. In this chapter, we will review the significance of bigness, in and of itself, without regard to market concentration.

A. GENERAL IMPLICATIONS OF SIZE

The emergence of the megacorporation is a development of great social, economic, and political importance. It concentrates the focal points of American economic decision-making as well as major political and social influence in a relatively small group of corporate power centers. This concentration is exacerbated by the significant overlapping of the boards of directors with the ultimate responsibility for the conduct of corporate affairs as a result of the widespread existence of multiple or interlocking directorships among the relatively small group who comprise the leadership of the megacorporations.

In an incisive analysis of the dimensions of corporate power,[1] Professor

[1]Edwin M.Epstein, *Dimensions of Corporate Power,* California Management Review, Winter 1973, vol. XVI, no. 2, p. 9, Summer 1974, vol. XVI, no. 4, p. 32.

Edwin M. Epstein, has emphasized the importance of distinguishing between the power of corporations generally, the power of a particular group of corporations acting in concert, and the power of a single corporation or plant. He observes that the corporate system is not monolithic and that deeply rooted conflicts of interest exist among corporations, concluding that it is an oversimplification to review the problem in terms of the corporations vis-a-vis the rest of society.

Size means profound economic power in the society, whether or not it may represent market power. Through the vast scale of the megacorporation's operations, its impact on its tens of thousands of employees and the many communities in which its plants operate, and its visibility on the national scene, the megacorporation can and does exert influence over the economy, the nation, the community, and the labor force. In determining levels of new capital investment, wage policies, employment opportunities, and pollution control, the megacorporation has great impact on those whose lives and businesses are affected by it. Its decisions may set a pattern for an industry or even the nation. Further, by reason of the mammoth size and prominence of the megacorporations, the senior business management generally occupy positions of leadership where their attitudes and values serve as models for corporation executives generally.

On the social level, size can make for significantly greater impact on the persons and communities affected by corporation behavior. In the sphere of plant closings or relocations, lay-offs, and employee recruitment, the impact of corporate decision-making becomes more profound as the size of the corporate operation increases. The closing of the large plant obviously affects a larger number of employees and has greater impact on the surrounding community than the closing of a smaller plant. The consequences of the decisions made by a large multi-plant firm will be more grave than those of the firm with a single or only a few plants.

At the same time, the very visibility of the megacorporation renders it more likely to be the subject of public reaction and thus will tend to restrict its ability to act. The decision of the large corporation becomes a *cause celebre* while the more obscure action of the smaller firm is less likely to become the center of social storm. In brief, there is a critical mass required to trigger aroused public attention, which may not be involved in the acts of smaller business.[2] Professor Peter Drucker suggests that this element may constitute the realistic limit on the growth of firms. In Drucker's view, the optimal firm should not be so large in relation to its environment that its freedom of action is impaired.

[2]In this connection, M. Rathbone, president of Standard Oil of New Jersey (Exxon), the second largest industrial, observed, ". . . the large organization may actually have a narrower range for its decision-making than the small, closely held corporation which is not so much in the public eye and hence not so exposed to criticism." (quoted in Paul A. Baran and Paul M. Sweezy, *Monopoly Capitalism* (New York: Monthly Review Press 1966), p. 22n. Copyright © 1966 by Paul Sweezy. Reprinted by permission of Monthly Review Press.

Does the very large corporation have greater control over the lives of its employees? Is it more authoritarian? Does it insist on greater conformity or suppress individuality to a greater extent? In the case of blue collar employees, this is far from clear. To the extent that the major manufacturing firms are apt to be more highly unionized, there may be greater protection for employees of the megacorporation against authoritarian intrusion into their personal sense of dignity and privacy. White collar employees, however, may present a different picture, particularly as one moves into managerial levels. The pressures for conformity as a condition to success are increased. Frequent changes of assignment within the corporation are a normal pattern in the giant multi-plant and multi-national concern, requiring repeated changes of location. Such transfers are an undesirable side effect of corporate life, tending to destroy identification with communities and to impair family life. However, in terms of numbers, it would appear that only a relatively small fraction of corporate personnel is exposed to these adverse influences.

There are other currents which could change the social impact of the megacorporation. Changing attitudes and values of younger persons will inevitably be reflected at management levels as junior executives assume more responsible positions. Affirmative action programs required by governmental pressures will introduce increasing numbers of previously under-represented minorities with different social and cultural values into the corporate structure. The changing society will be reflected in the corporate world.

Political power remains. This is the area in which—market control aside—corporate size creates the most serious problems. The megacorporation that is politically active has a potentially dangerous degree of influence over both the executive and the legislative branch of government at all governmental levels: federal, state, and local. Political campaign contributions by corporate executives (if not the corporation), well-financed lobbying activities, service of company executives on the 1,250 advisory councils of the federal government, corporate personnel shuttling back and forth between senior positions in the government and industry (sometimes supported by corporate subsidies), and other forms of corporate political interaction provide big business with an ability to influence and, on occasion, control the determination of governmental policy.

Large corporations have the political influence to achieve governmental assistance to protect their interests. The oil industry provides an outstanding example. In the years before the energy crisis, corporate political influence produced such advantageous governmental action as high depletion allowances related to income not assets, import restrictions, pro-rationing devices, and state quotas under the Interstate Oil Compact. This can be viewed as the establishment and maintenance by the government of a degree of monopoly power for the benefit of the industry.

The public exposure of the involvement of International Telephone and Telegraph in the high councils of the Nixon administration is another example of the reality and significance of corporate political power. Other illustrations include the symbiotic interaction between weapons and other military producers, on one hand, and the Department of Defense on the other, and the extensive influence of transportation, communication, utility, and other companies over the policies of the regulatory agencies presumably regulating their activities.

At the same time we should recognize that political involvement has its costs, particularly in highly regulated industries where even the largest firms may be vulnerable to political pressures. The illegal 1972 campaign contributions of American Airlines illustrates this aspect of the problem.

On the state level, domination of state governments by powerful corporate influences—industrial companies in the East, railroads and mining concerns in the West—are well known chapters of American political history.

Professor Edwin M. Epstein has concluded that while large business corporations are the "single most important nongovernmental determinants" of public policy, "no definitive, empirically verifiable assessment of this power is currently feasible."

Such political power is clearly an area of justifiable concern; it flows from size. Yet, we should recognize that even if the number of business units were significantly increased through some program of corporate breakup or divestiture, the problem of the collective power of larger business would remain. In place of the individual action of particular companies or a small number of major companies in a particular industry, the organized effort of a larger group of producers would be required. The highly successful political record over the years of the industry associations of fragmented industries such as agriculture or milk demonstrates how effective such organized political effort can be, notwithstanding the smaller size of the constituent firms.

Nevertheless, the fragmentation and dispersal of power is an important assurance for the preservation of democratic government. The local firm sensitive to local influences and opinion is apt to be more responsive than the local unit of a large multi-plant enterprise. It makes a difference whether decisions are made at home by principals who must live with and justify their actions to their neighbors or whether decisions are made 1,000 miles away. When the local firm is acquired by the national firm, an unquestionable loss of accountability results. Further, the degree of identification of individual and firm interests with the interests of the local community will tend to be greater in the case of the local firm controlled by principals with community roots than with the transient manager assigned by absentee management to assume responsibility for the plant for a limited period before moving on to the next location.

With firms of lesser size, the problem of the maintenance of adequate social and political controls and the establishment of the primacy of political decision-making by democratic institutions becomes manifestly easier. This, then, is a question of the relation between size and liberty. In contrast, such questions as the relation between size, efficiency, prices, and innovation—as important as they may be—become much less significant.

In reviewing the implications of the power of large corporations, Professor Grant McConnell, a political scientist, presented a number of fundamental questions:

- Do these large corporations . . . have such a massive influence on the quality of American life that they form the social and political climate in a multiple of ways?
- Do the leaders of these corporations constitute an elite, or part of an elite, which make the important decisions on which the character of life . . . in America depends?
- Do these large corporations exercise great power directly over the acts of government?
- Are these large corporations so completely self-governing and self-perpetuating that they must be regarded as a revolutionary species of social and political organization?[3]

McConnell concluded that the corporation was a political institution because it exercised appreciable influence over public policy and because its partisans treat it as a self-governing society. He observed that where the corporation develops power to make choices without the limitations once imposed by the market, it is exercising governmental power and thus is, to some degree, public in nature. The lack of definite and unchallenged criteria for corporate managers to observe in their exercise of power and the lack of legitimacy of the corporation create serious problems. McConnell views corporations as private governments because of the power over the larger society they have the autonomy to exercise.

Professor Robert Dahl similarly insists that every "large corporation should be thought of as a political system, that is, an entity whose leaders exercise great power, influence, and control over other human beings."

In contrast, Professor Earl Latham's analysis of the large corporations as systems of private government focuses on its internal elements, in which he notes characteristics common to all bodies politic: an authoritative allocation of principal functions, a symbolic system for ratification of collective decisions, an operating system of command, a system of rewards and punishments, and institutions for the enforcement of common rules.

Latham's analysis is helpful in reviewing the nature of the impact of the corporation with respect to the role and position of its employees. On the other hand, his examination of the internal functioning of the large corporation provides little assistance in appraising its relationship to the society as a

[3]Grant McConnell, *Private Power and American Democracy* (New York: Vintage Books, Random House, 1970), pp. 248-49. Copyright © 1966 by Alfred A. Knopf, Inc.

whole and in devising a framework for constraining the external exercise of corporate power.

The critical questions are presented by the specific ways in which size contributes to corporate power over governmental policy, social well-being, and individual freedom. Notwithstanding loose analogies to the large corporations as "private governments," the external problems flowing from the exercise of corporate political influence over governmental policy provide a much clearer demonstration of the interrelation between corporate size and corporate power than the internal problems arising from alleged corporate authoritarian policies toward employees.

We turn now to the economic corollaries of size: its relationship to profits, merger activity, innovation, charitable contributions, social performance, and defense production.

B. SIZE AND PROFITABILITY

The initial problem in attempting to ascertain the existence of any correlation between size and profitability is the possible distortion created by market power. Larger size may be accompanied by an element of monopoly power. Increased profitability may then be the product of market control rather than size.

A recent study by Professor John M. Blair concluded that in only a minority of industries did size contribute to increased efficiency, *i.e.* increased profitability. In an examination of thirty industries, he found that increasing size was accompanied by increasing profitability in only six industries (and in three of these, higher profits were related at least in part to monopoly power), and by decreasing profitability in eight industries. No discernible correlation appeared in the remaining sixteen industries. This illustrates the no-win dilemma of the megacorporation. High profitability is often attributed to monopoly power, and low profitability is seized upon as an indication of inefficiency.

In addition to the possibility of the development of market power, increased size permits economies of scale in production, administration, marketing, and research and thereby can contribute to increased efficiency. Size reduces production costs. Larger plants are more efficient plants but only up to a point; diminishing returns set in. Thus, the very existence of multi-plant operations indicates the limitations on economies of scale of production. If the economies of production were more substantial, they would create pressures for fewer and larger plants rather than lead to multi-plant operation.

Professor Weston, however, notes that in the six capital-intensive industries responsible for 42.2% of total manufacturing assets, the value added by manufacture per plant in 1969 was $8.4 million or more than ten times the $0.8 million average for all industry groups. He suggests that this indicates that increasing size may lead to increased efficiency. On the other hand, there is no reason to suppose that the major firms in these very industries do not operate on a multi-plant basis.

Size permits administrative economies through centralized administration, including accounting, engineering, financial, and legal services. Savings occur through more effective division of labor and reduced supervision expense. On the other hand, as the separation between the administrative level and the corporate activities being served widens, the administrative machinery inevitably becomes less sensitive, less responsive, and further insulated from operating realities.

Size may facilitate financing. The large, better-known borrower finds easier access to capital. Its credit rating tends to be higher. It is able to issue securities on a scale large enough to interest major investors. Hence in the 1974 credit crunch, we saw proposals that interest rates for small concerns be lowered by governmental action while higher rates continued for larger corporations.

Size eases procurement. It may assure sources of supply in times of shortage and lower prices for increased quantities generally.

Finally, size may achieve greater political recognition of the corporation's requirements and objectives. For example, on the federal level, we may inquire whether if less prominent companies had been involved, the Congress would have changed the tax laws to defer taxable consequences to duPont shareholders on the distribution of the General Motors shares held by duPont in the celebrated 1962 divestiture required by an antitrust action. On the state level, one may ask whether the state of New York would have bailed out Consolidated Edison in the wake of the 1974 crisis caused by the passing of the utility dividend if the largest utility in the state were not involved.

That efficiencies arising from size have their limits, most but not all economists agree. Size produces managerial problems, particularly where growth occurs as a result of mergers and acquisitions. In addition to impairment of effective managerial control, increased size may also lead to inflexibility. The critical mass for acceptable projects increases, and otherwise desirable projects may be weeded out simply because they are regarded as too small for the enlarged firm.

Managerial limitations have been advanced as the ultimate barrier to economies of scale; Professor Kenneth Boulding suggests that the increasing remoteness of the decision-maker from the realities of the problem inevitably leads to diminishing returns. Professor Oliver Williamson, however, notes that there is less than unanimity on the question of whether the problems of assuring accurate information to the top of the hierarchy are responsible for diminishing returns of scale.

As Professor Peter Drucker sees it, the basic problem is not one of manageability except in the limited case of giant service institutions. As already noted, he regards size as disadvantageous only when the company becomes so big in relation to its environment that its size impairs its freedom of action. Only then is optimum size below maximum size. General Motors, concerned that its market share may exceed 50% of the automobile industry, may conclude that it is politically unwise for it to expand into smaller cars; the dominant employer in an area may conclude that a plant closing would have so severe an impact on the community and lead to so strong a public reaction that it is not free to relocate. Size has then become a handicap.

Professor John K. Galbraith also rejects the view that the economics of the firm yields an optimum size that limits growth. Galbraith asserts that technology has transformed modern industrial organization making very large corporate size inevitable because of economies of scale in production, research, and innovation. As he sees it, the power of the giant firm to control its environment—costs, technological processes, prices, the responses of consumers and the government—makes continued growth desirable. Thus, he sees the "most basic tendency of modern economic society" as the propensity "for constituent firms to become vast and to keep on growing". He ignores the possibility emphasized by Drucker that the size of the firm in relation to its environment has built-in limitations.

Professor Willard Mueller, however, contends that Galbraith's view is not supported by the evidence. He asserts that there is little disagreement that productive efficiency does not dictate high concentration, except in a small and declining share of manufacturing industries, and that there is no persuasive evidence that vast size and market power are essential to successful innovation and planning.

The *Fortune* Studies of the 500 Largest companies and of the Second 500 indicate that the very largest companies generally speaking tend to have greater resistance to adverse economic developments and greater stability of operations. The earnings of the Second 500 have been more volatile than those of the 500 Largest. In the 1970 recession, the earnings of the Second 500 declined by 27.3%, or more than double the 12.2% decline for the 500 Largest. In the 1971 and 1972 recovery, the earnings of the Second 500 increased at almost double the rate of the earnings of the 500 Largest.

Change in Profits Over Preceding Year

	500 Largest	*Second 500*
1973	39.0%*	27.5%
1972	18.9	36.1
1971	8.1	15.9
1970	−12.1	−27.3

*If twenty-four major oil companies included in the 500 Largest are excluded from the computation, the increase in 1973 profits over 1972 profits is reduced to 32.8%.

Although for years the 500 Largest enjoyed higher returns on stockholders' equity and higher profit margins than the Second 500, this is no longer the case. In the ten years ending in 1973, the median growth in earnings per share for the Second 500 amounted to 10.91% in comparison to 9.73% for the 500 Largest.

At the same time, it is plain that the larger the firm, the less likely it is to experience a decline in sales or to incur losses. In the four years from 1970 to 1973, there was an aggregate of 279 instances of corporations in the 500 Largest with reduced sales against 370 corporations in the Second 500 Largest with reduced sales. Similarly, in the same period, 97 members of the 500 Largest reported losses in comparison with 207 loss corporations in the Second 500.

Although the data shows the greater stability of the 500 Largest, it also shows that the very largest corporations are not immune from economic decline. In 1970, for example, 130 of the 500 Largest operated at a loss, and 284, or more than one half, reported decreased net income. Even in the boom year of 1973, seventy-five of the 500 Largest experienced a down turn in net income. Losses and depressed earnings became common in the 1974 recession.

As a result of the foregoing factors and of merger activity, membership in the 500 Largest is not permanent. There is significant turnover, with a total of 203 corporations disappearing from the group in the period from 1966 to 1973, with mergers or acquisitions responsible for the elimination of eighty-six corporations.[4] During the 1967-69 period when merger activity was at its peak, mergers and acquisitions accounted for sixty-one out of a total of ninety-five eliminations (or about 64%). From 1970 to 1973, however, mergers and acquisitions accounted for only eleven of eighty-six (or 12.8%).

Collins and Preston's study of the changes within the 100 Largest over six decades from 1909 to 1958 concluded that turnover and mobility were declining. This, however, was prior to the intensified merger activity of the 1960's which has contributed to increased turnover.

In the twenty years from 1954 to 1973, there was considerable attrition among the ranks of the 1954 Largest corporations:

Class	*Number of 1954 Class Not Included in 1973*	*Percentage Eliminated*
50 Largest	19	38%
100 Largest	38	38%
200 Largest	68	34%
500 Largest	214	43%

[4]Some of these subsequently returned to the group. In 1973, five of the twenty new companies joining the 500 Largest had been included in the list in a previous year. It should also be noted that from 1966 to 1973, eight companies were eliminated because they were no longer classified as industrials.

Technological changes, changing consumer preferences, management weaknesses, and acquisitions all contributed to their elimination.

Where the "disappearance" of one of the Largest is the result of corporate combination between companies already in the group, the economic function of the "disappearing" entity has been continued by the acquiring corporation. The conduct of its business has simply been added to the operations of the acquiring corporation. In brief, with the addition of the new companies to fill the places vacated as a result of n business combinations, the 100 Largest have in effect become the "100 + n Largest," conducting the same operations previously conducted by the 100 + n firms.

The significance of the "disappearance" is the elimination of the acquired company as an independent entity, with a resulting increase in aggregate concentration.

What do the economists generally say? In reviewing the major empirical findings in the economic literature on the relationship between what he described as the three-way interdependence of profitability, growth, and size of the firm, John L. Eatwell (Marris and Wood, *The Corporate Economy,* Appendix A) observed how little is still known about the dynamic behavior of firms. While expressing skepticism about across-the-board studies because of the variables affecting different industries, he concluded that the profitable growing corporation may expect to encounter, on the whole, increased certainty of profit which could in turn reinforce the expansion process. This conclusion is consistent with our review of the performance of the 1000 Largest.

C. SIZE AND MERGER ACTIVITY

According to the Federal Trade Commission Economic Report on Corporate Mergers (1969) "FTC Merger Report", the ebullient merger movement, which climaxed in 1967 to 1969, contributed to a substantial growth in aggregate concentration. Commencing in 1970, acquisitions substantially declined.

1. Merger Activity.

From 1948 to 1972, there were 1,746 "large acquisitions" (*i.e.* acquisitions involving \$10 million or more) of manufacturing and mining concerns involving \$76.982 billion of assets [see Table 3-1].

The merger movement reached a crescendo in the late 1960's. In 1948, there had been only four "large" acquisitions involving assets of \$63.2 million. In the nineteen years from 1948 to 1966, there were 784 large acquisitions involving \$28.0 billion. In the next three years, 1967 to 1969, the merger movement reached unprecedented levels with 447 "large" acquisitions involving \$31.8 billion, or more than had been involved in the previous

TABLE 3-1

Federal Trade Commission, Statistical Report, Mergers and Acquisitions, Volume 8, Table 17 (1973)

Large Acquisitions in Manufacturing and Mining By Firms Ranked Among the 200 Largest Manufacturing Firms in 1971, By Year, 1948-1972

	Total large acquisitions[1]		*Large acquisitions by 200 largest firms*[2]		*Percentage of total large acqusitions by 200 largest firms*	
Year	*Number*	*Assets (Millions)*	*Number*	*Assets (Millions)*	*Number*	*Assets*
1948	4	$ 63.2	4	$ 63.2	100.0	100.0
1949	6	89.0	4	45.3	66.7	50.9
1950	5	186.3	1	20.0	20.0	10.7
1951	9	201.5	4	114.4	44.4	56.8
1952	16	373.8	6	174.7	37.5	46.7
1953	23	779.1	12	397.4	52.2	51.0
1954	37	1,444.5	15	930.2	40.5	64.4
1955	67	2,168.9	32	1,199.5	47.8	55.3
1956	53	1,882.0	28	1,260.8	52.8	67.0
1957	47	1,202.3	20	703.7	42.6	58.5
1958	42	1,070.6	20	721.1	47.6	67.4
1959	49	1,432.0	20	806.2	40.8	56.3
1960	51	1,535.1	23	871.1	45.1	56.7
1961	46	2,003.0	22	1,499.7	47.8	74.9
1962	65	2,241.9	25	1,052.5	38.5	46.9
1963	54	2,535.8	33	1,867.3	61.1	73.6
1964	73	2,302.9	31	1,055.7	42.5	45.8
1965	62	3,232.3	24	1,845.4	38.7	57.1
1966	75	3,310.7	29	1,953.6	38.7	59.0
1967	138	8,258.5	59	5,751.7	42.8	69.6
1968	173	12,554.2	83	8,225.7	48.0	65.5
1969	136	10,966.2	49	5,963.8	36.0	54.4
1970	90	5,876.0	29	2,670.0	32.2	45.4
1971	58	2,443.4	17	960.6	29.3	39.3
1972[3]	56	1,748.8	17	646.8	30.4	37.0
Total	1,435	69,902.0	607	40,800.4	42.3	58.4

[1]Acquired firms with assets of $10 million or more.

[2]Ranked by 1971 total assets.

[3]Figures for 1972 are preliminary.

Note: Not included in above tabulation are companies for which data were not publicly available. There were 311 such companies with assets of $7,080.1 million for period 1948-72, of which 109 companies with assets of $2,653.6 million were acquisitions by the 200 largest firms.

Source: Bureau of Economics, Federal Trade Commission.

nineteen years. From 1948 to 1958, no companies with assets of $250 million or more were acquired. From 1959 to 1966, only six companies with assets of $250 million or more were acquired. In the three years from 1967 to 1969, twenty-four more companies with assets of $250 million or more involving total assets of $13.0 billion were acquired. In 1968 and 1969, five megacorporations with assets in excess of $1 billion were acquired: Jones & Laughlin

TABLE 3-2

Federal Trade Commission, Economic Report on Corporate Mergers (1969), Appendix Table 1-10, p. A-10 and Statistical Report, Mergers and Acquisitions, Volume 8, Table 20 (1973)

Acquisitions of Companies with Assets of $250 Million or More, By Year of Acquisition, 1948-72[1]

Year	*Acquiring company*	*Acquired company*	*Assets $ [millions]*
1959	General Tel. & Electron.	Sylvania Electric	$ 264.9
1963	F M C	American Viscose	334.8
1965	Union Oil Co. of Calif.	Pure Oil	766.1
1966	Continental Oil	Consolidation Coal	446.1
1966	Atlantic Refining	Richfield Oil	449.7
1966	Phillips Petroleum	Tidewater Oil (Western manufacturing & marketing properties)	305.0[2]
1967	U. S. Plywood	Champion Papers	335.3
1967	McDonnell	Douglas Aircraft	564.7
1967	Tenneco	Kern County Land	253.9
1967	Signal Oil & Gas	Mack Trucks	303.0
1967	North American Aviation	Rockwell Standard	391.2
1967	Studebaker	Worthington	296.6
1968	Montgomery Ward	Container Corp. of America	397.4
1968	Colt Industries	Crucible Steel	303.9
1968	Singer	General Precision Equipment	322.7
1968	Occidental Petroleum	Hooker Chemical	366.5
1968	Ling-Temco-Vought	Jones & Laughlin Steel	1,092.8
1968	Loew's Theatres	P. Lorillard	375.3
1968	Kennecott Copper	Peabody Coal	315.6
1968	Northwest Industries	Philadelphia & Reading	318.6
1968	International Telephone & Telegraph	Rayonier	296.3
1968	Glen Alden	Schenley Industries	570.7
1968	Sun Oil	Sunray DX Oil	749.0
1968	American Standard	Westinghouse Air Brake	302.7
1969	General Host	Armour	560.5
1969	Rapid-American	Glen Alden	1,252.5
1969	Martin Marietta	Harvey Aluminum	277.7
1969	Amerada Petroleum	Hess Oil & Chemical	491.5
1969	Atlantic Richfield	Sinclair Oil	1,851.3
1969	Lykes	Youngstown Sheet & Tube	1,026.7
1970	Greyhound	Armour (from General Host)	607.2
1970	Standard Oil of Ohio	British Petroleum Holding	657.3
1970	Honeywell	General Electric (Computer Components)	547.7
1970	Nestle Alimentana	Libby, McNeil & Libby	267.0
1970	Warner Lambert	Parke Davis	399.2
1971	National Steel	Granite City Steel	312.7

[1]No acquisitions of firms with assets of $250 million or more took place in the period 1948 through 1958.

[2]Consideration paid.

Source: Bureau of Economics, Federal Trade Commission.

Steel, Commercial Credit, Sinclair Oil, Glen Alden, and Youngstown Sheet and Tube [see Table 3-2]. The merger frenzy included smaller companies as well. In 1968 alone nearly 10% of all independent manufacturing corporations with assets of $10 million or more were acquired.

After 1969, the merger movement tapered off. In 1972 there were only fifty-six "large" acquisitions involving $1.7 billion of assets. This was the smallest number of large mergers since 1963 and involved the smallest amount of acquired assets since 1960.

2. Acquisitions by the Megacorporations.

The impact of merger activity on aggregate concentration was particularly severe: "large" firms were being acquired and the acquisitions were being made by the very large corporations. From 1948 to 1972, the 200 Largest accounted for 607 "large" acquisitions or 42.3% of the total number and for $40.8 billion of assets, or 58.4% of total assets acquired. The share of the 200 Largest reached its height in 1967 where they were responsible for 69.6% of all acquired assets.

3. Impact on Aggregate Concentration.

As a result of aggressive acquisition activity from 1948 to 1968, the acquired assets of the 200 Largest industrials (as of 1968) amounted to 94% of their 1948 assets and 17% of their 1968 assets [see Table 3-3].

From 1947 to 1968, most of the substantial increase in the share of total assets of all industrial corporations represented by the 200 Largest (as of 1968) was due to mergers. If it had not been for mergers, the Federal Trade Commission estimated that the share of the 200 Largest would have increased from 42.4% in 1947 to 45.3% in 1968 instead of to 60.9%.

Year	*Share of Assets*	*Merger Contribution*	*Share of Assets without Merger Contribution*
1947	42.4%	—	42.4%
1960	54.1%	5.6%	48.5%
1968	60.9%	15.6%	45.3%

Similarly, the share of the 100 Largest would have increased from 38.2% in 1947 to 40.7% in 1968 instead of to 49.3%. It should be noted, however, that these estimates rest on assumptions by the Commission Staff as to the presumed growth of the acquired businesses *after* acquisition.

The effect of widespread acquisitions on the elimination of major firms from the economy was obvious. Mergers and acquisitions were responsible for the elimination of 135 companies from the 500 Largest in the twelve years

TABLE 3-3

Federal Trade Commission, Economic Report on Corporate Mergers (1969) Table 3-8. p. 3-25

Total Acquisition Growth of the 200 Largest Manufacturing Corporations of 1968 as a Percent of Their Total Growth, 1948-1968

Size of acquiring corporation[1]	Assets of group[2] (Millions)		Asset growth[2] 1948-1968 (Millions)	Acquisitions January 1, 1949-December 31, 1968		Acquired assets as percent of: Assets		Asset growth
	1948	1968		Number	Value of acquired assets (Millions)	1948	1968	1948-68
5 largest	$ 10,101	$ 55,935	$ 45,834	65	$ 1,293	12.8	2.3	2.8
6 - 10	6,472	30,932	24,460	42	675	10.4	2.2	2.8
11 - 20	7,463	35,205	27,742	151	4,483	60.1	12.7	16.2
21 - 50	10,447	59,713	49,266	512	11,976	114.6	20.1	24.3
51 - 100	8,979	57,218	48,239	1,181	13,334	148.5	23.3	27.6
101 - 150	6,071	33,591	27,520	1,019	13,478	222.0	40.1	49.0
151 - 200	3,630	23,013	19,383	894	4,765	131.3	20.7	24.6
Total	53,164*	295,607	242,443*	3,864	50,003*	94.1	16.9	20.6

[1] Companies ranked by total assets in 1968.

[2] Total assets at year end.

[3] These figures include all acquisitions (including partial acquisitions) made by the acquiring company during the period 1949-1968, and are not limited to acquisitions of mining and manufacturing companies. In instances where asset data were unavailable, asset estimates or consideration paid has been used. Asset information (including asset estimates or consideration) was available for 2,683 of these acquisitions.

*Detail does not add to total due to rounding.

Source: Bureau of Economics, Federal Trade Commission.

from 1962 to 1973. This was particularly notable during the three-year period from 1967 to 1969 when mergers and acquisitions accounted for sixty-one companies disappearing from the list.

The very pattern of merger activity contributes to increased concern about an increase of centralized private decision-making arising from intensified aggregate concentration that may be incompatible with a free society. Along with the development of the conglomerate merger, a fusion of traditionally separate industries and sectors of the economy has been occurring. Manufacturing concerns have been acquiring nonmanufacturing firms. In like fashion, holding companies, most often based on such nonindustrial concerns as the major banks and railroads, have been obtaining influence over the manufacturing sector through acquisition of major industrial concerns. In 1968, forty-three major industrial corporations with combined assets of $6.15 billion were controlled by nonmanufacturing companies. By 1972 it was clear that mergers between manufacturing and nonmanufacturing concerns were becoming more common. Over 20% of all industrial acquisitions were being made by nonmanufacturing companies.

According to the FTC Merger Report, the level of aggregate concentration is understated. Many of the 200 Largest do not consolidate all their subsidiaries, others have common owners, and a number participate in joint ventures that are only partially included. In the first quarter of 1969, joint ventures involving one or more of the 200 Largest included twenty-two major corporations with aggregate assets of $2.436 billion. Seventeen others with combined assets of $5.439 billion were controlled by companies included in the 200 Largest. From 1960 to 1968, 164 of the 200 Largest (as of 1968) formed 705 joint ventures creating a total of 1,153 joint venture company ties, of which 256 were represented by other companies in the 200 Largest.

Dr. Betty Bock's study of the 200 Largest in 1954 and 1968 led to somewhat different conclusions as to the significance of mergers for the growth of these firms. Her study reported that "large" acquisitions amounted to only 13% of the growth of the 200 Largest (as of 1968) from 1954 to 1968. Dr. Bock observed, however, that "large" acquisitions played an important part in the growth of the fifty-nine corporations included in the 200 Largest (as of 1968) which had not been in the 1954 group. These fifty-nine corporations increased their combined assets by approximately 839% over the period, with about 25% of the increase (or about 210% of the 839%) contributed by "large" acquisitions.

This conclusion is doubly significant. Unlike the FTC Merger Report, Dr. Bock considered only the size of the acquired company on acquisition and disregarded any increase in the magnitude of the acquired operations after acquisition. In other words, all internal growth of the firm was attributed to its assets as of the start of the study and none to the acquisitions over the fifteen-year period in question. This results in an obvious understatement of considerable magnitude. Further, Dr. Bock disregarded all "small" acquisitions although these amounted to $12.9 billion or about 25% of all acquired assets from 1954 to 1968.

These matters do not affect Dr. Bock's conclusion that a major contribution of mergers or acquisitions to the growth of the large corporations was to enable corporations outside of the 200 Largest to grow large enough to be included. Thus, mergers or acquisitions including conglomerate acquisitions have enabled aggressive newcomers to upset more complacent managements and achieve greater economic power. To the extent that such developments mean change, fresh leadership, and access of new groups to corporate power, they have some constructive aspects whatever their other limitations.

D. MERGERS AND PROFITABILITY

According to Professor Oliver Williamson, there are virtually no vigorous supporters among academics with respect to the efficiencies arising as a result of conglomerate mergers, except in the area of finance. In finance, he points out that the very disparate nature of the business operations of the conglomerate firm will present unique opportunities for the reinvestment of internally generated funds in areas of greatest profitability and that the internal allocations of the conglomerate may serve as a more efficient miniature capital market. Williamson also suggests, as does Professor Bruce R. Scott, that the comparative performance of the various divisions within the conglomerate firm may provide an effective measure of managerial performance and thereby act as a discipline contributing to increased efficiency.

Testimony before the Hearings on Economic Concentration of the Subcommittee on Antitrust and Monopoly of the Senate Judiciary Committee ("Economic Concentration Hearings") by Professors Reid, Eslick, Kelly, Fogarty and Arnould all concluded that there was no relation between merger activity and efficiency as reflected by profitability.

A study by Professor Samuel Richardson Reid of the growth and profit performance of 478 of the 500 Largest industrials indicated that as merger intensity increased, the relative increase in profitability of firms declined. Reid concluded that management interest in growth of the firm was in conflict with profit maximization.

Similarly, a study by Donald F. Eslick found that there was a strong tendency for diversified firms to be less profitable in comparison with others of the same size. Since merger activity, as distinct from internal growth, tends to involve greater diversification, this study is consistent with Reid's findings that merger activity does not lead to increased profitability. In referring to the Reid and Eslick studies, Dr. John M. Blair observed that in the largest firms, it is the single industry firm which makes no acquisitions that displays superior earnings compared with firms that are either diversified or active in acquisitions.

E. SIZE AND INNOVATION

Professor Joseph A. Schumpeter and his disciples including Galbraith have emphasized the relation between the giant firm and technological development. This has led to assertions that larger firms are more innovative because of their greater ability to expend funds for research and development, to provide capital and operating funds for the new operations, and to tolerate the risks involved. The correlation rests both on size and concentration. Size contributes to greater financial power, broader horizons, and greater diversification. Concentration (and implicitly market power) permits greater research as a result of greater profits or the substitution of quality competition. Thus, a familiar example is the fact that duPont expended $27 million in the development of nylon from 1928 to 1940 before the sale of the first pound from commercial production.

Studies of the relation of size and innovation made by Professors Jewkes, Schmookler, Scherer, Mansfield, Hamberg, Weiss, Worley and others, however, do not confirm the proposition that, as a general rule, larger firms are more innovative.

Professor Dean Worcester's review of the literature thus concludes that the analyses of economists who have sought to associate the quantity of research effort and results with the size of the firm do not disclose any unambiguous relationship between firm size and research or between monopoly and increased research. Worcester found that research intensity varied from industry to industry and that economies of scale of research were not important. He observed that many large firms (over 10% of firms with 5,000 employees or more) did little or no research and that some of the very smallest firms had the highest percentage of research and development personnel. He concluded that the evidence was against any general relationship between firm size and the efficiency of research and development expenditures.

Jewkes, Sawers and Stillerman found that large corporations accounted for only twelve of sixty-one major inventions over a period of fifty-five years. Turner and Williamson also concluded that larger firms, if anything, play a minor role in major inventions.

Professor Schmookler concluded that while big firms are much more likely to be performing research and development than smaller, the small firms engaged in research and development did relatively as much as larger firms and in some industries did more. (Government-financed research and development were excluded in the comparison.)

Professor F.M. Scherer's study of the number of patents awarded and also of the employment of research and development personnel in relation to firm size (ranked by sales) indicated that large scale is not essential for vigorous research and the smaller firms may be doing more in proportion to their sales. Mansfield also found no consistent relationship between firm size and research and development as a percentage of sales. His review of the petroleum refining, coal, and steel industries over a period of forty years indicated that the optimal size for maximizing innovations was smaller than the largest firms in each industry. J.S. Worley found that in every industry the *average* small firm tended to have a larger share of personnel allocated to research than *some* of the largest firms in the industry.

Finally, Professor James M. Utterback has observed that smaller firms place a greater value on the technologies involved and have less complex decision-making processes which may lead to earlier adoption of innovations.

General Electric and United States Steel are giant companies that are frequently held out as examples of noninnovative concerns. Theodore K. Quinn's discussion of General Electric, of which he had been a vice-president, asserts that it was responsible for no original product invention in the domestic appliance field with one possible exception, over many years. Professor Daniel Hamberg has noted that not one of the thirteen major innovations in the steel industry introduced between 1940 and 1955 was the result of efforts of American companies. The basic oxygen process is an example. This major advance was developed by an Austrian concern. McLouth Steel, a small producer, was the first American firm to adopt the process in 1954. Jones & Laughlin did not adopt the process until 1957 and the two largest steel producers, United States Steel and Bethlehem Steel, did not introduce it until 1964. This delay is said to have meant lost profits for the steel industry of $216 million after taxes by 1960.

Professor Richard Caves points out that established firms are frequently backward about radically new innovations. The aircraft engine companies would not work on the new jet engines, for instance. Bell Telephone and General Electric, well established in communications, were not interested in radio. Innovations which promise great advances may thus require the establishment of a new firm.

F. SIZE AND DEFENSE PRODUCTION

A number of megacorporations do a huge amount of defense business which in turn is directly responsible for their tremendous size. These companies which are strongly identified with military production may be regarded as the defense industry. In addition, there are a number of megacorporations which are included among the major defense producers because their products (petroleum, automobiles, trucks, and tires, for example) are as indispensable for military, as for civilian, activity. In these corporations, however, the proportion of defense business to total sales is relatively small. Except in the case of large aircraft and some electronics manufacturers, defense contracts constitute an unimportant portion of the total business of the major industrial corporations.

The outstanding fact about the defense business is the high degree of concentration. The largest five defense producers (ranked according to the net value of prime contracts) received 20.1%, the largest ten producers, 31.8%, the largest twenty-five producers, 48.8%, and the largest 100 producers, 68.6% of all prime contracts.

The top ten defense producers with $10.03 billion or 31.8% of the $31.6 billion prime contracts awarded in fiscal 1973 were all either aircraft manufacturers or electronics firms. Except in the case of General Electric and American Telephone (included because of the substantial contracts awarded to its subsidiary, Western Electric), military sales represented a significant percentage of total sales:

Corporation	*Defense Contracts (FY 1973) Millions*	*National Rank According to Sales, 1973*	*Percentage of Average Annual* Sales, 1972 and 1973*
Lockheed Aircraft	$ 1,659	# 44	63.4%
General Electric	1,416	5	12.9%
Boeing	1,229	33	43.1%
McDonnell Douglas	1,143	39	39.9%
Grumman	909	156	100.0%
American Telephone**	775	1 (utilities)	3.5%
Textron	747	83	42.3%
United Aircraft	741	59	34.4%
General Dynamics	707	96	44.4%
Rockwell International	704	35	25.4%
	$ 10,030		

*Since defense contracts are reported on the basis of the fiscal year ended June 30 while most corporations report on the basis of the calendar year, 1972 and 1973 corporate sales have been averaged to provide a basis for comparison with defense contracts for the fiscal year ended June 30, 1973.

**Western Electric accounted for $564 million (or 72.7%) of this total.

As we review the twenty-five largest industrials, we find that their aggregate defense contracts, even when sufficiently large to include them among the 100 largest defense contractors, represent a negligible amount of total sales, except in the case of five electronics firms [see Table 3-4]. Twenty of the twenty-five largest had defense business of 3.10% of total sales or less. Electronics firms comprised the remaining five firms led by General Electric with defense business of 12.9% of sales.

The relative unimportance of defense contracts to the megacorporations is particularly true in the petroleum industry where the military business of Exxon (twenty-third largest defense contractor), Texaco (sixty-fifth largest), Mobil (fifty-fourth largest), Standard Oil of California (thirty-fourth largest) range from 0.71% to 1.95% of sales. Similarly, in the automobile and related industries, the military business of General Motors (twenty-second largest defense producer) is 0.76% of sales, Ford (twenty-sixth largest), 0.99% of sales, Chrysler (thirtieth largest) 1.41% of sales, and Goodyear (twenty-ninth largest) 2.63% of sales.

TABLE 3-4
Largest 25 Industrials (Ranked by Sales, 1972)
and Defense Contracts, FY 1973

1972 Rank (By Sales)	*Corporation*	*Defense Contracts FY 1973 (millions)*	*Average Annual Sales 1972 & 1973 (millions)*	*Percentage*
1	General Motors	$ 249.1	$ 33,116.8	0.76%
2	Exxon	237.6	23,017.0	1.03
3	Ford	213.9	21,604.8	0.99
4	General Electric	1,416.2	10,907.4	12.9
5	Chrysler	152.3	10,766.7	1.41
6	International Business Machines	301.8	10,262.9	2.94
7	Mobil Oil	98.1	10,278.2	0.95
8	Texaco	71.8	10,049.9	0.71
9	ITT	249.2	9,369.9	2.66
10	Western Electric	563.5	6,794.2	8.29
11	Gulf	45.4	7,330.0	0.62
12	Standard Oil of Calif.	132.4	6,795.7	1.95
13	U.S. Steel	64.1	6,176.8	1.04
14	Westinghouse	504.7	5,394.5	9.36
15	Standard Oil (Indiana)	67.5	6,795.7	0.99
16	DuPont	77.3	4,820.8	1.63
17	Shell	35.9	4,479.9	0.80
18	Goodyear	114.8	4,373.4	2.63
19	RCA	253.8	4,042.5	6.28
20	Proctor & Gamble	—	—	—
21	LTV	347.1	3,845.6	9.02
22	International Harvester	41.3	3,842.9	1.07
23	Eastman Kodak	116.5	3,756.6	3.10
24	Continental Oil	—	—	—
25	Atlantic Richfield	41.7	3,651.7	1.14

Source: Department of Defense, 100 Companies Receiving the Largest Dollar Volume of Prime Contract Awards, Fiscal Year 1973; Fortune, May 1974, Fortune, May 1973.

There is little correlation between the largest corporations and the largest defense producers. Only one of the ten Largest industrial corporations[5] is included in the ten largest defense producers.

Largest Industrial Corporations	*Number Included in the Largest 10 Defense Producers*	*Largest 25*	*Largest 50*
Largest 10	1	5	7
Largest 25	1	9	15
Largest 50	5	15	21

[5]If the defense business of American Telephone (the Largest utility) and its subsidiary Western Electric (the tenth Largest industrial) are pooled, their combined business would place them in the top ten defense producers. If not combined, Western Electric was the tenth largest defense producer.

It is evident that defense business does not represent the major operations of the leaders in the economy. Nor do the companies with businesses primarily directed towards defense production include a broad spectrum of American industry.

G. SIZE AND SOCIAL CONSEQUENCES

In the area of corporate social responsibility, a number of the major corporations have been cited as outstanding. However, the question arises whether improved social performance reflects the more ample resources of the giant firms, the greater discretionary area available to management, or whether the managerial sensitivity reflected in the social performance has also been responsible for the growth of the firm. Further, the giant firms which are highly visible to the public eye have had responsibility thrust upon them. Unlike smaller firms, they operate in the glare of public exposure as well as under governmental and other public pressures for leadership in urban and environmental areas. Finally, for each of those giant corporations which has been commended for its performance in the social and environmental sphere, there are other giants which have been strongly criticized. In fact, larger firms may have poorer records in the support of philanthropic institutions and in minority employment. Thus, Professor William Shepherd has concluded that smaller firms, which are more subject to competitive pressures, are less discriminatory in their employment policies.

Merger activity of the megacorporations has produced important shifts in the geographic pattern of control. From 1949 to 1968, the 200 Largest (as of 1968) acquired 3,908 companies with assets of $50.2 billion. Of these, New York corporations gained a *net* transfer of control of 986 companies involving $13.228 billion of assets previously headquartered in other states. As a result, from 1929 to 1968, the percentage of the companies among the 200 Largest with headquarters in New York increased from 31.0% to 41.0% and the assets controlled increased from 36.5% to 45.8%.

As the Federal Trade Commission and the Subcommittee on Antitrust of the House Judiciary Committee have pointed out, this shift of decision-making power from local communities to great metropolitan centers has important political and social implications. An acquisition creates a drain on the top managerial talent of the acquired companies who relocate as a result of the acquisitions, as well as reduced reliance on local financial, legal, accounting, advertising and other service industries in the community in which the acquired firm was based. It also diminishes identification with the local community, reduces executive participation in community affairs, and even perhaps reduces contributions to the United Fund. Further, an acquisition inevitably results in the subordination of local management to absentee management less familiar with local problems and lacking a local point of view.

C. Wright Mills compared three cities characterized by local businesses with three others in which the dominant businesses were absentee-owned. The local business cities ranked higher on public facilities, social services, and civic participation. Mills concluded that there is more incentive for community-based owners to participate and improve their communities while larger firms tend to hire, promote, and move managers with little attention to participation in local civic affairs.[6]

Corporate support of charitable, educational, and philanthropic institutions was one of the earliest manifestations of so-called corporate social responsibility. It provides a useful index of corporate commitment to the solution of social problems.

The Council for Financial Aid to Education, Inc. estimates that corporate charitable contributions increased from $352 million, or 0.59% of pre-tax net income in 1950 to $1.055 billion or 1.24% of pre-tax net income in 1969. For the next four years, the ratio of contributions to pre-tax net income continued to decline. Preliminary estimates for 1973 show contributions of $940 million or an estimated 0.75% of pre-tax net income [Table 3-5]. This level is in marked contrast to the 5% maximum which is deductible under the Internal Revenue Code.

Corporate charitable contributions are not only low but are highly vulnerable to economic conditions. The level of contributions is apparently re-

[6]The Mills study is noted in Leonard Broom and Philip Selznick, eds., *Sociology* (Evanston, Ill.: Row, Peterson, 1955), pp. 623-26.

TABLE 3-5

Corporate Contributions and Total
Corporate Pre-Tax Net Income

Year	*Corporate Pre-Tax Net Income (Billions)*	*Corporate Contributions (Millions)*	*Percentage*
1950	$ 42.6	$ 252	0.59%
1960	49.7	482	0.97
1961	50.3	512	1.02
1962	55.4	595	1.07
1963	59.4	657	1.11
1964	66.8	729	1.09
1965	77.8	785	1.01
1966	84.2	805	0.96
1967	79.8	830	1.04
1968	87.6	1005	1.15
1969	84.9	1055	1.24
1970	74.0	797	1.08
1971	85.1	840*	0.99
1972	98.0	840*	0.86
1973	126.7*	950*	0.75

*Estimate of American Association of Fund Raising Counsel.
Source: Council for Financial Aid to Education, Inc., 1972 *Corporate Support of Higher Education.*

garded as discretionary, and reductions occur when earnings decline. Contributions may, in this sense, be regarded as a corporate social dividend, which is cut when earnings decline and which is only slowly restored as earnings recover.

The 1972 Survey of the Council involving 475 corporations (of which 246 were manufacturing corporations) revealed that the percentage of contributions to pre-tax income declined directly with size, whether measured by net income or sales. The larger the income of the corporation, the less the rate of contribution. In comparison with a 1972 average of 0.86% of pre-tax net income for all corporations the fifty corporations in the Survey with net income of between $100 and $500 million gave only 0.66% and the thirteen giant corporations with pre-tax net income of $500 million or more gave only 0.49% of pre-tax net income. In contrast twenty-six corporations with less than $5 million net income contributed an average of 1.44% of their pre-tax net income [Table 3-6].

TABLE 3-6

Corporate Contributions and Corporate Pre-Tax Net Income of Various Sizes of Corporations, 1972

Corporate Pre-Tax Net Income	*Number of Companies in the Sample*	*Percentage of Contributions to Pre-Tax Net Income*
Less than $5 million	26	1.44%
$5 million to $10 million	26	1.09
$10 million to $25 million	53	1.30
$25 million to $50 million	39	0.98
$50 million to $100 million	32	0.76
$100 million to $500 million	50	0.66
$500 million and over	13	0.49
Total		0.62%

Source: Council for Financial Aid to Education, Inc., 1972 *Corporate Support of Higher Education.*

The 1973 performance of some of the nation's leading megacorporations in this area were very poor indeed:

Corporation	*Charitable Contributions (Millions)*	*Pre-Tax Net Income (Millions)*	*Contributions as Percentage of Pre-Tax Net Income*
General Motors	$ 16.6	$ 4,513.1	0.37%
E. I. DuPont de Nemours	5.5	1,043.5	0.51%
International Business Machines	17.7	2,946.5	0.60%
The Chase Manhattan Bank	1.6	240.7	0.66%
Xerox	6.6	735.8	0.91%

Corporate charitable contributions are of great importance to the well-being of the nation. They provide essential support to the full spectrum of private charitable agencies dealing with social problems of every description as well as indispensable support for private higher education. They constitute the basis for maintaining a private alternative to increasing government domination of education and the numerous social agencies dealing with community needs throughout the country. Although some economists, particularly Milton Friedman, have criticized corporate contributions as usurping the shareholder's freedom to determine for himself the charitable or educational activities to be supported with "his" money, even these critics recognize that the deductibility of corporate contributions in the computation of federal corporate tax enables the corporation to make double the contribution that the shareholder could make if an equal amount (less 48% corporate tax) were distributed to the shareholder as a dividend and contributed directly by him.

There is some shareholder opposition to corporate contributions. Thus, as we have seen, shareholder proposals to restrict corporate charitable contributions to activities directly related to the corporations' operations have received almost 10% of the votes cast at recent annual shareholder meetings of such corporations as American Telephone and Bethlehem Steel. Further, some utility commissions still refuse to recognize utility charitable contributions as an allowable expense in rate-making proceedings, although the general movement of administrative and judicial attitudes is unmistakably moving in that direction.

Corporate charitable contributions are a permanent element of the corporate scene and may be expected to remain so, at least as long as the tax laws are unchanged. An increase in the level of corporate annual giving could have great potential significance. Each 1% of pre-tax corporate net income represented by additional contributions would provide philanthropic support that would be the equivalent of the creation of five new Ford Foundations. A number of corporations, such as Dayton-Hudson and Cummins Engine, have prospered with a policy of corporate contributions amounting to the full 5% of pre-tax net income deductible under the Internal Revenue Code. If this salutary policy were widely followed, it could have great effect on the development of nongovernmental efforts in the educational, social service, and charitable areas. An allocation of funds of such a magnitude could produce a remarkable improvement in the American scene. Further, it would be the product of "private" efforts, encouraged by governmental tax policy. The business spokesmen who so strongly favor greater nongovernmental decision-making might well reflect on the immense potential which is implicit in a substantially increased level of corporate contributions.

BIBLIOGRAPHY

Adams, Walter and Joel B. Dirlam, "Big Steel, Invention, and Innovation" Quarterly Journal of Economics, LXXX, No. 2 (1966), 167.

Baran, Paul A., and Paul M. Sweezy, *Monopoly Capitalism.* New York: Monthly Review Press, 1966.

Blair, John M., *Economic Concentration,* op. cit.

Bock, Betty, *Statistical Games and the "200 Largest" Industrials: 1954 and 1968. op.* cit.

Caves, Richard, *American Industry: Structure, Conduct, Performance* (3d ed.) Englewood Cliffs, N.J.: Prentice-Hall, Inc., 1969.

Council on Financial Aid to Education, Inc., *Corporation Support for Higher Education.* New York: 1972.

Dahl, Robert, "Governing the Giant Corporation" in Ralph Nader and Mark J. Green, eds., *Corporate Power in America,* op. cit.

Drucker, Peter F., *Management: Tasks, Responsibilities, Practices.* New York: Harper & Row, 1974.

Eatwell, John L., "Growth, Profitability and Size: The Empirical Evidence" in Robin Marris and Adrian Wood, eds., *The Corporate Economy,* Appendix A. New York: Macmillan, 1971.

Epstein, Edwin M., "Dimensions of Corporate Power", *California Management Review,* XVI, No. 2 (1973), 9, XVI, No. 4 (1974), 32.

Federal Trade Commission, *Economic Report on Corporate Mergers,* op. cit.

Friedman, Milton, *Capitalism and Freedom,* op. cit.

______, "The Social Responsibility of Business Is To Increase Its Profits", op. cit.

Galbraith, John K., *Economics and the Public Purpose.* Boston: Houghton Mifflin Company, 1973.

______, *The New Industrial State* (2d rev. ed.). Houghton Mifflin Company, 1971.

Hall, Marshall, and Leonard Weiss, "Firm Size and Profitability" *Review of Economics and Statistics,* XLIX, No. 3 (1967), 319.

Hearings on Controls or Competition, Subcommittee on Antitrust and Monopoly, Senate Committee on the Judiciary, 92d Cong., 2d sess., January 18-21, 1972 (Symposium on the Economic, Social and Political Effects of Economic Concentration) Washington, D.C.: Government Printing Office, 1972.

Hearings on Economic Concentration, Subcommittee on Antitrust and Monopoly, Senate Committee on the Judiciary, 89th Cong., 1st sess., 1965. Part 3. *Concentration, Invention, and Innovation.* Washington, D.C.: Government Printing Office, 1965.

Jewkes, John, David Sawers, and Richard Stillerman, *The Sources of Innovation* (2d ed.) New York: Macmillan, 1969.

Latham, Earl, "The Body Politic of the Corporation" in *The Corporation in Modern Society,* ed. E.S. Mason, op. cit.

______, "The Commonwealth of the Corporation", 55 *Northwestern Law Review* 25 (1960).

McConnell, Grant, *Private Power and American Democracy.* New York: Vintage Books, Random House, 1970.

McGee, John S. *In Defense of Industrial Concentration.* New York: Praeger Publishers, 1971.

Mansfield, Edward, "Size of Firm, Market Structure, and Innovation", *Journal of Political Economy,* LXXI, No. 6 (1963), 556.

______, "Industrial Research and Development Expenditures: Determinants, Prospects, and Relation to Size of Firm and Inventive Output", *Journal of Political Economy,* LXXII, No. 4 (1964), 319.

Mills, C. Wright, "Small Business and Civic Welfare" in Leonard Broom and Philip Selznick, eds., *Sociology,* Evanston, Ill.: Row, Peterson, 1955.

Mueller, Willard F., A Primer on Monopoly and Competition, New York: Random House, 1970.

Quinn, Theodore K., *Giant Business: Threat to Democracy.* New York: Exposition Press, 1953.

Scherer, F.M., "Firm Size, Market Structure, Opportunity, and the Output of Patented Invention", American Economic Review, LV (1965), 1097.

Schmookler, Jacob, in *The Corporation in Modern Society,* ed. Edward S. Mason. Cambridge, Mass.: Harvard University Press, 1960.

______, "Bigness, Fewness and Research", *Journal of Political Economy,* LXVII, No. 6 (1959), 628.

Scott, Bruce R., "The Industrial State: Old Myths and New Realities", *Harvard Business Review,* Vol. 51, No. 2 (1973), 133.

Senate Subcommittee on Monopoly, Senate Select Committee on Small Business, *Role of the Giant Corporations,* 1st sess., Part 2. Washington, D.C.: Government Printing Office, 1971.

Symposium, "Conglomerate Mergers and Acquisitions: Opinion and Analysis", op. cit.

Utterback, James M., "Innovation in Industry and the Diffusion of Technology", *Science,* February 15, 1974, p. 620.

Weston, J. Fred and Stanley I. Ornstein, eds., *The Impact of Large Firms on the United States Economy,* op. cit.

Williamson, Oliver E., "Corporate Control and the Theory of the Firm", *Economic Policy and the Regulation of Securities.,* Washington, D.C.: American Enterprise Institute for Public Policy Research, 1968.

______, *Corporate Control and Business Behavior,* Englewood Cliffs, N.J.: Prentice-Hall, Inc., 1970.

Worcester, Dean, *Monopoly, Big Business and Welfare in the United States.* (1967).

CHAPTER FOUR

Market or Industry Concentration

Aggregate (or overall) concentration deals with the economy as a whole and reflects the dominant position of the megacorporations as a group. It has economic, political, and social significance. It has been studied principally by economists who have been interested almost exclusively in its economic aspects. The political and social dimensions tend to receive minor consideration although they would appear to be more important.

Market (or industry) concentration is an economic phenomenon. It refers to the share of the leading producers in the total sales of the market or industry. The critical concern is whether high concentration gives the leading producers power over the market by facilitating collusive or interdependent conduct and thereby adversely affects competitive forces. Accordingly, the concept plays a crucial role in antitrust policy.

At the outset, we should recognize that market concentration ratios are not trustworthy. The definition of the "market" boundary involves severe distortions as a result of the diversification of business activity. Further difficulties arise from the exclusion of imports and the inclusion of exports in the determination of the ratios, the impact of product substitution, the irrelevancy of national data when the market in question is regional or local, and the existence of product specialization within industries. Thus, market concentration ratios may not be reliable and may overstate or understate actual concentration. Aside from the question of accuracy, market concentration ratios are only one of the factors of industrial structure affecting the extent of competition. Ease of entry to the market, the number of major firms in the market, the extent of competition. Ease of entry to the market, the number of major firms in the market, the extent of product differentiation, and the relative stability or lack of stability of the market also play an important role and should be considered along with market concentration ratios.

A. THE EXTENT OF MARKET CONCENTRATION

Subject to possible areas of understatement and overstatement from the factors discussed above, the available data show serious areas of high or moderate concentration:

4-Firm Concentration	*1966 Industries* Number	Percent	*1970 Industries* Number	Percent
75% and over	33	9%	34	8%
50% – 74%	90	24%	86	21%
25% – 49%	154	40%	171	42%
Under 25%	105	27%	119	29%
Total	382	100%	410	100%

4-Firm Concentration	*1966 Value of Shipments* Total (billions)	Percent	*1970 Value of Shipments* Total (billions)	Percent
75% and over	$ 66	14%	$ 56	10%
50% – 74%	89	19%	104	18%
25% – 49%	189	40%	239	41%
Under 25%	124	27%	181	31%
Total	$ 468	100%	$ 580	100%

Sources: Cabinet Committee Study, p. 57; U.S. Department of Commerce, Bureau of the Census, Annual Surveys of Manufactures, 1970, Value of Shipments Concentration Ratios By Industry.

The Cabinet Committee Study reported that in 1966, there were thirty-nine four-digit industries with shipments in excess of $500 million in which 4-firm concentration ratios exceeded 60%. These thirty-nine most highly concentrated major industries, including autos, steel, computers, aircraft, tires and tubes, photographic equipment, aluminum rolling, cigarettes, cans, soaps, and detergents, accounted for shipments of $76.3 billion or 16.6% of the $459.1 billion total manufacturing shipments in 1966. In 1970, these thirty-nine industries accounted for shipments of $104 billion or 16.4% of the $634 billion total. [See Table 4-1]. Five industries of this group of thirty-nine highly concentrated industries—autos, steel, computers, aircraft, and tires and tubes—were responsible for more than one-half of the shipments of this group. With this strong concentration in a small cluster of industries, the significance of concentration in the economy as a whole is somewhat reduced.

TABLE 4-1
Industries in Which 4-Firm Concentration Ratio Exceeded 60% and Shipments Exceeded $500,000,000 in 1966 and Comparison with 1970

		1966		*1970*		*1966-70*
SIC Code	*Industry*	*Value of Shipments (millions)*	*4-Firm Concentration Ratio*	*Value of Shipments (Millions)*	*4-Firm Concentration Ratio*	*Change In Ratio*
3717	Motor Vehicles	$ 15,449	79%	$ 27,751	91%	+12%
33121	Coke Ovens and Blast Furnaces	1,298	68)			
33122	Steel Ingots and Semi-finished Shapes	2,030	70)	9,328	47	NA
33124	Hot Rolled Bars, Shapes	3,608	63)			
33126	Steel Pipes and Tubes	1,137	61)			
3571	Computing and Related Machines	4,833	63)	2,817(A) 888(B)	57) 83)	NA
3721	Aircraft	4,675	67	10,996	65	−2
3011	Tires and Inner Tubes	3,716	71	4,587	72	+1
3861	Photographic Equipment	3,285	67	4,373	75	+8
3352	Aluminum Rolling	3,100	65	3,454	57	−8
2111	Cigarettes	2,860	81	3,503	84	+3
3411	Metal Cans	2,631	71	3,913	72	+1
2841	Soap and Other Detergents	2,395	72	2,989	70	−2
2824	Organic Fibers	1,992	85	2,822	73	−12
3632	Household Refrigerators	1,675	72	2,022	82	+10
2032	Canned Specialties	1,457	68	1,634	66	−2
3661	Telephone Apparatus	1,432	94	2,247	94	—
2141	Tobacco Stemming	1,387	69	1,288	66	−3
3694	Engine Electrical Equipment	1,342	72	1,570	66	−6
2052	Biscuit Crackers	1,327	59	1,546	59	—
2647	Sanitary Paper Products	1,186	64	1,659	63	−1
3612	Transformers	1,052	66	1,393	59	−7
2087	Flavorings	974	63	1,319	61	−2
3633	Household Laundry Equipment	947	79	1,081	83	+4
3229	Pressed and Blown Glass	926	72	1,052	67	−5
2823	Cellulose Man-Made Fibers	924	85	685	NA	NA
3511	Steam Engines and Turbines	867	87	1,791	77	−10
3672	Cathode Ray Tubes	812	89	519	88	−1
2812	Alkalies and Chlorines	783	63	660	71	+8
2046	Corn Milling	755	67	831	64	−3
2043	Cereal Preparations	743	87	953	90	+3
3741	Locomotives	701	98	NA	NA	NA
3211	Flat Glass	638	96	669	92	−4
3691	Storage Batteries	616	60	783	56	−4
2816	Inorganic Pigments	582	64	635	56	−8
2063	Beet Sugar	579	68	727	65	−3
2813	Industrial Gases	549	72	665	75	+3
3572	Typewriters	534	79	635	NA	NA
3313	Electrometallurgical	509	74	516	77	+3
	Total	$ 76,307		$ 104,301		
	Total for all manufacturing	459,071		634,322		
	Percent	16:6%		16.4%		

(A) SIC #3573; Computing Machines
(B) SIC #3574: Calculating and Accounting Machines
Source: U.S. Department of Commerce, Bureau of the Census, Annual Surveys of Manufactures, 1966 a 1970, Value of Shipments Concentration Ratios By Industry, Cabinet Committee Study, Appendix Tabl p. 93.

Professor John M. Blair[1] describes industries as "concentrated" when the four largest firms account for 50% or more of the output, as "moderately concentrated" when they account for 25% to 49%, and as "unconcentrated" when they account for less than 25%. On this basis, he classified one-third of manufacturing output in 1963 as "concentrated" industries; in this group, the average share of the largest four producers was 66%. Another one-third was represented by "moderately concentrated" industries.

Professors Carl Kaysen and Donald F. Turner reached substantially similar results in a 1954 study. To avoid the distortion created by blurred industry boundaries, they isolated 191 industries with reasonably well-defined industry boundaries. They then analyzed these industries in terms of their extent of concentration and their participation in national or regional markets. They found sixty-four highly concentrated industries (8-firm, 50% concentration; 20-firm, 75% concentration) with 23.5% of total value of shipments, fifty-six moderately concentrated industries (8-firm, 33⅓% concentration; 20-firm under 75% concentration) with 35.6% of total value of shipments and 71 unconcentrated industries with 41.1% of total shipments.

B. THE TREND IN MARKET CONCENTRATION

Most authorities agree that the general level of market concentration since World War II has been relatively stable.

The Cabinet Committee Study reported that average 4-firm concentration ratios in 213 industries had increased only from 41.2% in 1947 to 41.9% in 1966.[2] Concentration in producer goods industries had declined from 45.1% to 43.4% and in consumer goods industries had increased from 34.8% to 39.6%. The only significant change was in highly differentiated consumer goods in which concentration increased sharply from 48.2% in 1947 to 59.0% in 1963 and then slightly further to 60.2% in 1966. [see Table 4-2]. Eight-firm concentration ratios showed a somewhat greater increase.

A Cabinet Committee Study of 213 comparable industries found that the number of industries with a 4-firm concentration ratio of 75% or more declined from thirty in 1947 to twenty-two in 1966, in contrast to industries with 4-firm concentration ratios between 50% and 74% where there was an increase from forty-one to fifty-one [see Table 4-3].

Notwithstanding relative stability with respect to overall market concentration, significant movement in different industries occurred between 1947 and 1966. In the period from 1947 to 1966, 4-firm concentration ratios increased in eighty-eight industries and declined in 78.[3] In forty-seven indus-

[1]John M. Blair, *Economic Concentration* (New York, N.Y.: Harcourt Brace Jovanovich, Inc., 1972).

[2]As pointed out by Leo Loevinger, long-term comparisons of concentration ratios for about one-half of the more than 400 industry categories are not possible because of changes in classifications.

[3]3 percentage points or more.

TABLE 4-2

Cabinet Committee Study, Table 3, p. 58

Average four and eight firm concentration ratios by type of industry 1947-66

	213 Industries	Producer goods	Consumer goods, degree of differentiation			
			All	*Low*	*Mod.*	*High*
			Average four-firm concentration			
1966 (adjusted)*..	41.9	43.4	39.6	25.9	40.5	60.2
1966 (unadjusted)	41.8	43.4	39.3	25.2	40.5	60.2
1963............	41.4	43.3	38.2	23.8	39.6	59.0
1958............	40.2	43.1	35.5	22.0	37.3	54.7
1954............	40.6	43.8	35.4	22.9	36.4	53.6
1947............	41.2	45.1	34.8	25.0	36.	48.2
Change, 1947-66 .	0.7	−1.7	4.8	0.9	4.5	12.0
			Average eight-firm concentration			
1966 (adjusted)*..	55.2	57.4	51.7	36.5	53.3	73.1
1966 (unadjusted)	55.1	57.4	51.3	35.4	53.3	73.1
1963............	54.4	57.2	50.0	38.6	52.2	72.2
1958............	53.0	56.8	47.0	30.9	49.7	68.5
1954............	53.3	57.4	46.6	32.1	48.5	66.4
1947............	53.3	57.7	46.2	34.8	48.1	60.9
Change, 1947-66 .	1.9	−0.3	5.5	1.7	5.2	12.2

*The adjusted data shown for the year 1966 are estimates which adjust for the fact that 1966 4-firm concentration ratios were not reported by Census for 24 industries and 8-firm concentration ratios were not available for 35 industries. The unadjusted average for 1965 included 1963 data for industries for which 1966 data were not available.

Sources: Annual Survey of Manufactures: 1966, Value-of-Shipment Concentration Ratios by Industry, U.S. Bureau of the Census; and Industry Classification and Concentration, Federal Trade Commission, March 1967.

tries, there was little or no change. Consumer goods industries showed a marked increase as a result of increased product differentiation resulting from increased advertising expenditures, particularly television advertising. At the same time, concentration in consumer goods industries involving undifferentiated products increased only moderately, and concentration in producer goods with generally undifferentiated products declined.

Changes in 4-Firm Concentration, 1947-1966

Type of Industry	*Total*	*Increased**	*Number of Firms Where 4-Firm Concentration Little Change**	*Decreased**
Producer Goods	132	41	31	60
Consumer Goods	81	47	16	18
Total	213	88	47	78

Source: Cabinet Committee Study, p. 59.
*3 percentage points or more.

TABLE 4-3

Cabinet Committee Study, Appendix Table 15, p. 58

Classification of 213 comparable industries by level of 4-firm concentration for 1947, 1954, 1958, 1963 and 1966

Year	*Number of industries in which percent of production accounted for by 4 largest companies was—*			
	75 to 100 percent	*50 to 74 percent*	*25 to 49 percent*	*0 to 24 percent*
A. 213 industries:				
1947	30	41	75	67
1954	25	46	73	69
1958	25	46	76	66
1963	22	51	78	62
1966	22	51	80	60
B. 132 producer-goods industries:				
1947	21	30	51	30
1954	17	34	48	33
1958	16	32	52	32
1963	12	36	54	30
1966	12	36	53	31
C. 81 consumer-goods industries:				
1947	9	11	24	37
1954	8	12	25	36
1958	9	14	24	34
1963	10	15	24	32
1966	10	15	27	29

Source: "Annual Survey of Manufactures: 1966 Value-of-Shipments Concentration Ratios by Industry." U.S. Bureau of the Census; and "Industry Classification and Concentration," Federal Trade Commission, 1967.

In the same period, declines in 4-firm concentration were strongest in industries with undifferentiated products.

Changes in 4-Firm Concentration, 1947-1966

Type of Industry Products	*Percent of Industries Where Concentration*		
	*Increased**	*Little Change**	*Decreased**
Highly Differentiated	14	0	3
Moderately Differentiated	21	9	6
Undifferentiated	12	7	9

*3 percentage points or more.
Source: Cabinet Committee Study, p. 59.

The decline in 4-firm concentration in producer goods industries appeared noteworthy at the time because it involves key capital-intensive industries which have traditionally contributed to higher concentration levels; of this group, concentration failed to decline from 1947 to 1966 only in motor vehicles and parts. From 1966 to 1970, however, concentration increased in most of these industries and the overall record from 1947 to 1970 shows a less pronounced decline:

SIC #	Industry Name	Four Largest Companies — Percent of Shipments 1947	1954	1966	1947-66	1970	1966-70	1947-70
2911	Petroleum refining	37	33	32	−5	33	+1	−4
3312	Blast furnaces and steel mills	50	55	49	−1	47	−2	−3
3722	Aircraft engines and parts	72	54	58	−14	68	+10	−4
3717	Motor vehicles and parts	56	75	79	+23	91	+12	+35
2812	Basic chemicals—alkalies and chlorine	70	69	63	−7	71	+8	+1
2813	Industrial gases	83	84	72	−11	75	+3	−8
2821	Plastic materials and resins	44	47	32	−12	29	−3	−15

Source: Hearings before Subcommittee on Antitrust and Monopoly of the Senate Committee on the Judiciary, 91st Cong., 2d Sess., on Economic Concentration, Part 8, p. 5296 (1970) ("Economic Concentration Hearings"); U.S. Department of Commerce, Bureau of the Census, Annual Survey of Manufactures, 1970.

Professor Willard F. Mueller[4] asserts that the increase between 1947 and 1968 in 4-firm concentration ratios in ninety-five industries in contrast to declines in only seventy-five and no significant change in thirty-nine indicates a continuing rise in market concentration. On the other hand, offsetting changes of this order of magnitude may, as persuasively, be regarded as indicative of general stability, and most observers have so characterized the problem.

In manufacturing, the percentage of value added in industries with 4-firm concentration ratios of more than 50% increased from 1947 to 1963 and has declined since then:

Year	*Percentage*
1947	24.4%
1954	29.9
1958	30.2
1963	33.1
1966	28.6
1970	26.3*

*Using 1967 value added figures.
Source: F.M. Scherer, Industrial Market Structure and Economic Performance (Rand McNally & Co., 1970), p. 62.

It is of note that the relative stability in market concentration levels was maintained in the face of intensive merger activity during this period. A major factor contributing to this result was the success of antitrust enforcement in restricting horizontal mergers. These declined to low levels in the late 1960s when merger activity was at its height. In 1967, they accounted for

[4] Willard F. Mueller, A *Primer on Monopoly and Competition* (New York, N.Y.: Random House, Inc., 1970).

17% of all acquisitions of assets and in 1968 for only 4%. Acquisition patterns, however, then changed, and by 1972, horizontal mergers were responsible for 30% of the assets involved in acquisitions.

Professor Morris A. Adelman also advances the explanation that with larger industries and faster growth, concentration tends to decrease. While the bigger market makes for economies of scale and bigger companies, this is more than offset by the increased room for rivals. Adelman concludes that the correlation between rapid growth and lower concentration is somewhat stronger (though not very marked) than the stereotype of the big company with the big market share. He points to fifty-two product classes in 1963 with $1 billion in sales or more, in which only three products had a 4-firm concentration ratio of 80% and sixteen a 4-firm concentration ratio of 50% or more. He contrasts this with the other extreme of ninety-six product classes with sales of less than $50 million, in which fourteen products had a 4-firm concentration ratio of 80% and forty-seven a 4-firm ratio of over 50%.

C. THE CAUSES OF MARKET CONCENTRATION

A comparison of the United States with other developed countries indicates that there are fundamental economic factors at work which seem to contribute to high or low concentration in particular industries in industrialized economies generally. Professor Mueller notes steels, chemicals, autos, matches, and liquid detergents are highly concentrated in all or mostly all western nations while services and trades are generally unconcentrated.

Professor Caves has prepared a tabulation of industries ranked according to the degree of concentration in the United States, Canada, and the United Kingdom that shows a significant degree of uniformity. It strongly indicates that common factors of market structure are responsible:

Rank of Selected Industries in Order of
Decreasing Seller Concentration, 1963

*United States**	*Canada**	*United Kingdom***
1. Tires	1. Tires	1. Petroleum refining
2. Railway rolling stock	2. Railway rolling stock	2. Pipe
3. TV sets	3. Cement	3. Tires
4. Petroleum refining	4. Pipe	4. Cement
5. Fertilizer	5. TV sets	5. Railway rolling stock
6. Cement	6. Petroleum refining	6. TV sets
7. Cotton mills	7. Fertilizer	7. Fertilizer
8. Steel pipe	8. Cotton mills	8. Canning
9. Wire	9. Paint	9. Bread
10. Paper boxes	10. Canning	10. Wire
11. Bread	11. Paper boxes	11. Paint
12. Canning	12. Heating equipment	12. Paper boxes
13. Paint	13. Bread	13. Heating equipment
14. Heating equipment	14. Wire	14. Furniture
15. Furniture	15. Printing	15. Cotton mills
16. Printing	16. Furniture	16. Printing

*Based on concentration ratios for largest eight firms.
**Based on concentration ratios for largest five firms.
Source: United States—*Concentration Ratios in Manufacturing Industry, 1963* (same as Table 1-1). Canada—G. Rosenbluth, "The Relation between Foreign Control and Concentration in Canadian Industry," *Canadian Journal of Economics,* Vol. III (February 1970), Table I. United Kingdom—Board of Trade, *Report on the Census of Production, 1963,* Vol. 131 (London: HMSO, 1969), Table 5.
Richard Caves, *American Industry: Structure, Conduct, Performance* (Englewood Cliffs, N.J.: Prentice-Hall, Inc., 3d ed. 1969), p. 19.

Phlips' study of concentration in the Common Market also reached the same conclusion provided that adjustments were made for relative size; countries of comparable size tended to have comparable market organization.

The economists point to the following factors as possible explanations of high concentration: barriers to entry; absolute costs based on patents, know-how, trade secrets, control over sources of supply, or high cost of capital; economies of large-scale production, innovation and invention; large-scale promotion and distribution leading to product differentiation; mergers and acquisitions; predatory business practices; and finally the environment created by public policy.

High entry barriers can arise from such factors as requirements of minimum scale, *i.e.* the minimum share of the existing market that must be acquired, technology requiring heavy capital outlays, high distribution and advertising costs, or governmental restrictions. These make for concentration. Scarcity of sellers is not a necessary characteristic since relatively large numbers of small firms may also be present.

Professors Mueller and Blair contend that economies of large-scale production do not explain concentration in many industries. Professor Mueller points out that the existence of multi-plant operations in concentrated industries must indicate that some cause other than large-scale production economies is responsible. Thus, in motor vehicles and parts in 1966, 4-firm concentration amounted to 79%, but the largest eight plants contributed only 16% of the total. Mueller concludes that modern technological imperatives do not make for increased concentration.

Blair similarly asserts that except in certain defense industries, the relative importance of the large plants has tended to decline and that concentration is increasingly a function of multi-plant operations rather than plant size. He attributes this to new technologies that have reduced the plant size required for optimal efficiency. A study by Ralph L. Nelson, referred to by Blair, indicates the lack of correlation between concentration and large plants. In most industries of high concentration, the leading firms tended to operate many large plants.

Mueller also asserts that economies of scale in research and innovation are not responsible for concentration. Although there is some evidence suggesting that relatively large size, if not giant size, leads to increased innovation, there appears to be little empirical demonstration of any necessary relation between concentration and innovation. Judge Richard W. McLaren, while Assistant Attorney General, Antitrust Division, summarized:

> The bulk of the available evidence runs counter to the hypothesis that high concentration, huge size and substantial market power are prerequisites for research and innovation. Indeed, some of the most careful studies find that, if anything, market power and the security of bigness . . . may have a stultifying effect. (Staff Report of Antitrust Subcommittee of House Judiciary Committee. Investigation of Conglomerate Corporations (1971), at p. 58).

The Federal Trade Commission, Bureau of Economics reached similar conclusions.

Thus, Professor Caves reports that competitive pressures provide a large share of the incentive to innovate. Between 1899 and 1955, labor productivity rose most sharply in those industries where the levels of concentration declined. Once made, innovations spread quickly through less concentrated industries.

Large-scale promotion and distribution would appear, however, to make for high concentration, particularly in consumer goods industries, because of the heavy cost of establishing product differentiation. Professor Blair has shown the relationship between television advertising and the increase of concentration in certain consumer goods industries. Where only the largest firms can afford such outlays, concentration results. As Mueller points out, the staggering cost of frequent style changes has contributed to the high concentration in automobiles. In 1973 for example, General Motors, Ford, and Chrysler charged off $1,736 million as special amortization for tools and dies related to model changes.

Mueller finally points to mergers as the most important single cause of market concentration, asserting that most big businesses owe their relatively large size to merger-accelerated growth.

The Federal Trade Commission has classified mergers in the following groups:

- *Horizontal* (combination of companies making the same or closely related products in the same market).
- *Vertical* (a combination of companies with a buyer-seller relationship).
- *Conglomerate market-extension* (a combination of companies making the same or closely related products for sale in different geographical markets).
- *Conglomerate product-extension* (a combination of companies making products which do not compete, but which are related in production or distribution).
- *Other conglomerate* (where the companies lack any buyer-seller relationships and their products are not functionally related).

Horizontal and vertical mergers declined sharply in the 1960's as a result of the strengthening of Section 7 of the Clayton Act in 1950 while conglomerate mergers dramatically increased as a less vulnerable alternative for acquisition-minded firms. By 1971 and 1972, there had been an abrupt reversal. Horizontal mergers substantially increased. Conglomerate product-extension mergers continued to be important, while conglomerate market-extension mergers almost disappeared, and vertical mergers remained at a low level:

	Percent of Assets				
Type of Large Merger	*1948*	*1960-1963*	*1968*	*1971*	*1972*
Horizontal	38.8%	16.9%	4.0%	23.2%	30.0%
Vertical	23.8%	20.2%	7.0%	0.4%	7.6%
Conglomerate					
Market-Extension*		8.0%	5,9%	2.2%	0
Product-Extension	37.5%	37.8%	39.0%	30.8%	44.5%
Other Conglomerate		17.1%	43.6%	43.4%	17.9%
	100.0%	100.0%	100.0%	100.0%	100.0%

*One may question whether market-extension mergers may properly be regarded as "conglomerate" acquisitions.

Sources: FTC Merger Report; Economic Concentration Hearings, Part 8, p. 4715 (1970); FTC Statistical Report, Large Mergers in Manufacturing and Mining (1972), Table 14.

During 1967-68, conglomerate mergers of all types represented 301 of 361 "large" acquisitions involving $17.9 billion of assets of a $20.8 billion total. Although mergers have contributed to increased *aggregate* concentration, the preponderance of conglomerate mergers over horizontal mergers has let most authorities to disagree with Blair and Mueller and conclude that mergers have not made for increased *market* concentration in the economy as a whole.

D. MARKET CONCENTRATION AND THE MEGACORPORATIONS

Notwithstanding the lack of association between aggregate concentration and general market concentration levels, there is a troublesome interrelationship between the megacorporations and market concentration. The Cabinet Committee Study reports that in 1963 the 200 Largest were particularly active in thirty-seven more highly concentrated industries and much less important in ninety-eight less concentrated industries.

Level of 4-Firm Concentration, 1963	*Number of Industries*	*Share of the 200 Largest*
75% and over	6	87%
51% – 75%	31	63%
25% – 50%	59	31%
25% and under	39	14%
	135	100%

Source: Cabinet Committee Study, p. 92.

109 of these 135 industries involved producer goods with the 200 Largest responsible for a 34% share. In the twenty-six consumer goods industries, the market share of the 200 Largest increased with product differentiation, ranging from a high of 73% in highly differentiated consumer goods industries to 25% in undifferentiated industries.

The Federal Trade Commission, *Economic Report on Corporate Mergers* ("FTC Merger Report") noted the increasing role of the 100 Largest industrials in market leadership, largely as a result of mergers. Each of the 100 Largest (ranked by value added) held at least one of the four top positions in 1,052 different 5-digit product classes in 1963. Seventy of the 100 Largest were in one of the top four positions in at least four separate industries [see Table 4-4].

The FTC Merger Report found a close relation between the 200 Largest and the industries showing an increase in market concentration. Thus, from 1947 to 1966 in the industries where companies in the 200 Largest accounted for 70% or more of value added, market concentration tended to increase an average of 7.6%, where other factors were held constant. In contrast, in industries where the 200 Largest accounted for only 20% of value added, concentration decreased by about 7.3%. In commenting on these statistics, Professor Turner pointed out that superior efficiency or performance rather than anticompetitive market power might well account for the differential. Professor Jules Backman has suggested that the analysis itself is misleading.

In the industries in which the members of the 200 Largest were primarily engaged in 1963, the 200 Largest were responsible for $77.9 billion or 40.5% of the $192.1 billion of value-added for the group. In some industries, the

TABLE 4-4

Investigation of Conglomerate Corporations (1971),
Table 4-1, p. 22

The Number of Leading Industry Positions Held By Companies Ranking Among the 100 Largest Manufacturers

	Number of companies	
Number of leading positions held [1]	*1958*	*1963*
20 or more	2	3
10 to 20	5	14
7 to 9	14	21
4 to 6	22	32
4 or more total	43	70
2 or 3	34	23
Only 1	18	7
No leading positions	5	0
Total	100	100

[1]Four leading producing positions of 4-digit census product industries.

Source: Concentration Ratios in Manufacturing Industry, 1963, Part II, Subcommittee on Antitrust and Monopoly, U.S. Senate, 90th Cong., 1st sess., table 21, p. 284.

share of the firms within the 200 Largest reached major proportions; these included motor vehicles and equipment with 83.2%, blast furnaces and steel mills with 77.2%, tobacco products with 82.5%, and more than 50% in chemicals and petroleum products [See Table 4-5]. These are major industries with which the megacorporations have traditionally been associated. Professor Donald Turner thus concludes that insofar as the economy is generally concerned, he finds no significant link between the 200 Largest and undue concentration.

A connection between size and market concentration is not inevitable. A First National City Bank study points out that the largest industrial firms, in terms of absolute size, are found in petroleum, automobiles, and steel. While the automobile industry is highly concentrated, petroleum and steel are in the medium-concentration classification. Some industries such as shoe machinery and chewing gum are highly concentrated in the hands of firms that do not rank among the giants.

Professor Adelman agrees that size alone does not convey an inherent advantage in view of the general stability in the level of industrial concentration. He suggests that bigness is much more important sociologically or politically than in terms of its economic or market significance. He urges that size be studied directly and not confused with concentration as a market phenomenon.

Senator Philip Hart of Michigan who has been in the forefront among political figures concerned with concentration has similarly stated that the economic aspects are less disturbing than the power of economic concentration in social and political areas.

E. CONCENTRATION AND PROFITS

A number of studies have found a correlation between market concentration and profit levels although some economists dispute their significance. Others who recognize the existence of some correlation assert that facts other than collusive behavior, such as high entry barriers, may be responsible.

The Cabinet Committee Study reported that some of the studies showed that profit rates tended to be 50% or more higher in highly concentrated industries in comparison with moderately concentrated industries. The close interrelation between entry barriers and concentration was noted by the Cabinet Committee Study which suggested that concentration ratios might reflect or act as a proxy for entry barriers.

The Report of the White House Task Force on Antitrust Policy ("Neal Report" 1968) similarly concluded that there was "a close association between high levels of concentration and persistently high rates of return on capital . . . that suggests . . . the absence of fully effective competition."

Others have found less positive relationships. The Stigler Task Force on Productivity and Competition to President Nixon (1969) reported:

Numerous statistical studies have been made of the relationship between concentration and rates of return on investment, and these studies generally yield positive but loose relationships. Concentration is not a major determinant of differences among industries on profitability, although it may sometimes be a significant factor.

TABLE 4-5

Economic Concentration Hearings, Part 8, p. 4668

Major Industry Groups and Selected Enterprise Industry Categories Share of Value Added By Companies Among 200 Largest Primarily Engaged Therein, 1963

Group or category	(2) Number of companies among 200 largest primarily engaged therein	(3) Total value added by group (or category), (Million)	(4) Value added in group (or category) by companies among 200 largest primarily engaged therein (Million)	(5) 200 largest as percent of total (4÷3)
20 Food and kindred products	29	$ 21,825	$ 5,555	25.4
21 Tobacco products	6 [1]	1,681	1,387 [1]	82.5
22 Textile mill products	4 [1]	6,123	907 [1]	14.8
27 Printing and publishing	6	10,476	789	7.5
28 Chemicals and allied products	31	17,586	9,125	51.9
28A Basic chemicals, plastics and synthetics	16	9,037	5,664	62.7
28B Drugs	3	2,087	1,125	40.1
28C–E Cleaning and toilet goods, paints and miscellaneous chemicals	7	5,742	1,449	25.2
29 Petroleum and coal products	10	3,713	2,143	57.7
30 Rubber and plastics products	4	4,654	1,348	29.0
32 Stone, Clay and Glass	8	7,044	1,303	18.4
33 Primary metal products	18	15,261	7,350	48.2
33A Blast furnaces and steel mills	13	7,699	5,941 [2]	77.2
33E Nonferrous primary metals	5	4,096	1,409 [2]	34.4
34 Fabricated metal products	6	11,791	944	8.0
35 Machinery, excluding electrical	12	17,311	2,451	14.2
36 Electrical machinery	19	17,010	6,677	35.7
37 Transportation equipment	30	24,690	18,309	74.2
37A Motor vehicles and equipment	9	12,781	10,636 [3]	83.2
37B All other transportation equipment	21	11,911	7,673 [3]	64.4
Total	200	192,103	77,857	40.5

[1]Includes companies among 200 largest primarily engaged in leather and leather products.

[2]Shipments of primary metals by designated companies among the 200 largest.

[3]Shipments of transportation equipment by designated companies among the 200 largest.

Source: Columns (2) and (4): Table 24, "Concentration Ratios in Manufacturing Industry," 1963, Part II; Column (3): Table 23, ibid.

Professor Adelman also observed that there is only a weak relation between concentration and profitability, *i.e.* the "odds are only a little over 50-50 that a more concentrated industry will be more profitable than a less concentrated one." Similarly, a study by the UCLA Graduate School of Business found that the relationship between the concentration of an industry and profit rates of the companies in the industry was weak. Like the Cabinet Committee Study, it suggested that concentration rates may act as a proxy for other factors such as barriers to entry, which may explain variation in profit rates on grounds other than collusive behavior.

Contrary to the Neal Report, Professor Yale Brozen found no "persistent" relation between high concentration and abnormal profits. He observed that over the long run, the rates of return in concentrated industries, which may enjoy high profits for a time, tended to move down toward average levels. He suggested that while concentration may lead to excess profits where high entry barriers exist, such exercises of monopoly power were relatively modest and irregular.

In reviewing the literature on market concentration, Professor Harold Demsets has contrasted the earlier studies by such scholars as Bain, Kilpatrick, Stigler, and Collins and Preston which found small but significant correlations between profit and concentration and the later studies particularly by Brozen which either cast doubt on this conclusion or alternatively did not confirm it. Brozen found a positive correlation between concentration and profit rates for large firms but not for small firms. According to Demsets, the omission of small firms in the earlier studies apparently was responsible for the positive correlation which they reported.

Demsets found a correlation between high rate of return and higher concentration in the case of firms of large size. Firms with assets over $50 million in industries with a 4-firm concentration ratio of 60% or more earned an average rate of return of 20.3% and those in industries with a 4-firm concentration ratio of 50% or more earned an average 13.2%. These totals were well above the rates of return in smaller size categories. He found no correlation in the case of smaller firms in the same industries. Demsets attributed these results to the increased efficiency or competitive superiority of the large firm, rather than to collusive behavior, pointing to the failure of the rates of return for the various classes of firms of smaller asset size to increase with the concentration level in their industry. He deemed small-firm performance relevant because even though small firms might not be parties to collusive efforts, they would benefit from the higher prices resulting from any such efforts.

Other authors have similarly asserted that the existence of higher profits in more concentrated industries may be more consistent with such factors as efficiency, the age of an industry, its technology, or capital requirements than with collusion.

F. CONCENTRATION AND PRICES

Professor Gardiner Means has asserted for four decades that high concentration leads to market power reflected in prices that are "administered" rather than produced by market forces. In 1935, Means contended that "administered prices" were kept from falling in oligopolistic industries and advanced the theory as an explanation for the continuance of depressed economic conditions and unemployment. Subsequently in the 1950's, Means argued that "administered prices" increased at a faster rate than competitive prices and were responsible for inflation.

Like so many questions of this nature, the economists disagree vigorously over the soundness of the Means contention and the empirical data advanced in its support.

In a study of 1953-59, DePodwin and Selden criticized, among other things, Means' reliance on unadjusted price data of the Bureau of Labor Statistics, which they asserted mistakenly utilized reported or "catalogue" prices rather than actual prices, describing them as often far more flexible and substantially lower. Thereafter, Professor Leonard Weiss introduced demand and cost data in his analysis of the correlation between concentration and prices for 1953-63. He found a small positive correlation for 1953-59 but no significant correlation for 1959-63. A First National City Bank study found no correlation between 1967-70 price changes and 4-firm national concentration ratios in 85 well-defined industries, ranging from 15% for hardwood flooring to 94% for electron tubes. The Bank study concluded there was no demonstrable link between concentration and market power.

Louis Phlips studied data in Belgium, The Netherlands, and France in 1958-1965 to test the Means concept, utilizing Weiss' approach. He found no verification for the administrative inflation hypothesis on prices.

Professor Demsets similarly concluded that there is not any broad statistical support for the Means assertion that inflation and market concentration are linked, relying on the foregoing studies by DePodwin and Selden, Weiss, and Phlips. Demsets notes that the discussions attempting to link inflation or price inflexibility to market concentration have been largely concerned with price behavior and monopoly power. He questions the implicit assumption that market concentration is a measure of monopoly power. Dr. Bock also concluded that there is no empirical proof that pricing in concentrated industries is more akin to monopoly or oligopoly pricing than competitive pricing. Along with Demsets, she notes that it appears possible to come to sharply different conclusions on the causes and effects of concentration.

G. MARKET CONCENTRATION AND ANTITRUST POLICY

In Antitrust Policy: Economic and Legal Analysis, (1959) Kaysen and Turner recommended that the antitrust laws prohibit "unreasonable market power." Where a single company accounted for 50% or more of sales or where 4-firm concentration exceeded 80% in a market for five years, they recommended that divestiture be required in the absence of proof of economies arising from size, patents, extraordinary efficiencies, or certain other factors.

The Neal Report in 1968 in similar vein recommended deconcentration in industries in which 4-firm concentration exceeded 70%. The proposed goal was to reduce the shares of firms with 15% or more each to 12% or less. Exceptions were similarly suggested in cases of demonstrated economies of scale, declining industries, or likely losses in efficiency. By this time, however, both Kaysen and Turner had cooled on the desirability of using market concentration data as mechanical guides for divestiture under the antitrust laws.

The Stigler Report to President Nixon released shortly thereafter took issue with the Neal Report, asserting that the correlation between concentration and profitability was weak. It concluded that "present knowledge" did not justify use of the antitrust law to deconcentrate highly oligopolistic industries.

Market concentration, always an important factor, has become increasingly significant in antitrust litigation. A study by Dr. Bock reports that whereas concentration was alleged in only 60% of the complaints filed prior to 1966, such allegations were present in more than 96% of the cases in 1966-1968.

In 1968, the Department of Justice used market concentration and the market share of the companies in question as the basis of published guidelines to its policy in enforcement of the antitrust laws. In the case of horizontal mergers, for example, the Department of Justice utilized a 4-firm concentration ratio of 75% as the dividing line.[5]

[5]Where this existed, the Department stated that it would usually contest a horizontal merger if the combining businesses were responsible for the following market shares.

Acquiring Firm	*Acquired Firm*
4%	4% or more
10%	2% or more
15% or more	1% or more

Where the 4-firm concentration ratio in the industry was less than 75%, the Department stated that it would usually contest a horizontal merger where the following market shares were involved:

Acquiring Firm	*Acquired Firm*
5%	5% or more
10%	4% or more
15%	3% or more
20%	2% or more
25%	1% or more

In 1973 and 1974, Senator Philip Hart introduced and held hearings on a proposed Industrial Reorganization Act (93d Cong., S. 1167). Among other things, the proposed Act provided that a 4-firm concentration ratio of 50% in any level of commerce in any section of the country in any year was presumptive evidence of the existence of unlawful monopoly power and required divestiture in the absence of proof that such power was due to patents or that divestiture would result in a loss of "substantial economies." The same presumption of unlawful monopoly power would arise in the case of corporations with average earnings in excess of 15% per annum after taxes on net worth over five consecutive years.

In addition, the Industrial Reorganization Commission to be established under the Act would be directed to study the structure, performance, and control of seven concentrated industries: chemicals and drugs, electrical machinery and equipment, electronic computing and communication equipment, energy, iron and steel, motor vehicles, and nonferrous metals. Even in the absence of monopoly power as defined above, the Commission would be charged to develop a plan of reorganization for each such industry to accomplish the maximum feasible number of competitors and the minimum feasible degree of vertical integration without the loss of substantial economies and to accomplish the maximum feasible degree of ease of entry.

It is obvious that the doctrine of market concentration has moved into a central place in political consideration of antitrust policy.

Professor Demsets is troubled that the doctrine that market concentration provides a reliable index of market power is gaining influence in both the courts and the Congress at a time where the balance of evidence, as he evaluates it, no longer clearly supports that doctrine.

H. SUMMARY

Market concentration in the economy as a whole is "remarkably stable" despite the increase in aggregate concentration and the increases in market concentration in those industries in which the 200 Largest are particularly active. The Neal Report did not regard this relative lack of change in overall market concentration as comforting. It pointed out that neither antitrust enforcement nor market forces had been able to accomplish any reduction and that "the problem is not one which will disappear with time."

BIBLIOGRAPHY

Adelman, Morris A., "The Two Faces of Economic Concentration", *The Public Interest,* Fall, 1970, p. 117.

Bain, Joe S., *Barriers to New Competition.* Cambridge, Mass.: Harvard University Press, 1956.

Bain, Joe S., *Industrial Organization.* New York: John Wiley & Sons, 1968.

Blair, John M., *Economic Concentration,* op. cit.

Bock, Betty, *Dialogue on Concentration, Oligopoly and Profit: Concepts vs. Data.* New York: The Conference Board, Report No. 556, 1972.

Bock, Betty, *Mergers and Markets: 7.* New York: The Conference Board, Studies in Business Economics, No. 105, 1969.

Boyle, Stanley E. "The Average Concentration Ratio: An Inappropriate Measure of Industry Structure", *Journal of Political Economy* LXXXI, No. 2 (1973), 414.

Brozen, Yale, "The Antitrust Task Force Deconcentration Recommendation", *Journal of Law and Economics,* XIII, No. 2 (1970), 279.

Brozen, Yale, "The Persistence of 'High Rates of Return' in High Stable Concentration Industries", *Journal of Law and Economics,* XIV, No. 2 (1971), 501-512.

Brozen, Yale, "Bain's Concentration and Rates of Return Revisited", *Journal of Law and Economics,* XIV, No. 2, (1971), 351-369.

Cabinet Committee on Price Stability, Staff of, *Industrial Structure and Competition Policy,* op. cit.

Caves, Richard, *American Industry: Structure, Conduct, Performance,* op. cit.

Collins, Norman R. and Preston, Lee E., *Concentration and Price-Cost Margins in Manufacturing Industries.* Berkeley: University of California Press, 1968.

Collins, Norman R. and Preston, Lee E., "Price-Cost Margins and Industry Structure", *Review of Economics and Statistics,* LI, No. 3 (1969), 271.

Demsets, Harold, *The Market Concentration Doctrine.* Washington, D.C.: American Enterprise Institute for Public Policy Research, 1973.

Department of Commerce, Bureau of the Census, "Concentration Ratios in Manufacturing", 1967 *Census of Manufactures,* Special Report Part 1 (1970), Part 2 (1971), Part 3 (1971). Washington, D.C.: Government Printing Office, 1970 and 1971.

Department of Commerce, Bureau of the Census, *Concentration Ratios in Manufacturing Industry,* 1963. Report prepared for Subcommittee on Antitrust and Monopoly of Senate Committee on the Judiciary, Parts I and II. Washington, D.C.: Government Printing Office, 1966 and 1967.

DePodwin, Horace J. and Selden, Richard T., "Business Pricing Policies and Inflation", *Journal of Political Economy,* LXXI, No. 2 (1963), 116.

Federal Trade Commission, *Economic Report on Corporate Mergers, op. cit.*

______, Statistical Report, *Large Mergers in Manufacturing and Mining* (1972).

Hamberg, D., "Invention in the Industrial Research Laboratory," *Journal of Political Economy,* LXXI, No. 2 (1963), 95.

Hearings on Economic Concentration, Subcommittee on Antitrust and Monopoly, Senate Committee on the Judiciary, Eighty-Eighth, Eighty-Ninth, Ninetieth, and Ninety-First Congress, Parts 1 to 8A. Washington, D.C.: Government Printing Office.

Hearings on Investigation of Conglomerate Corporations, Subcommittee on Antitrust, House Committee on the Judiciary, 92d Cong., 1st sess., Washington, D.C.: Government Printing Office, 1970.

Hearings on The Industrial Reorganization Act, Subcommittee on Antitrust and Monopoly, Senate Committee on the Judiciary, 93d Cong., 1st sess., Part 1. Washington, D.C.: Government Printing Office, 1973.

House of Representatives, Subcommittee on Antitrust, House Committee on the Judiciary, 92d Cong., 1st sess., *Staff Report on Investigation of Conglomerate Corporations.* Washington, D.C.: Government Printing Office, June 1, 1971.

Kaysen, Carl and Donald F. Turner, *Antitrust Policy: Economic and Legal Analysis.* Cambridge, Mass.: Harvard University Press, 1959.

Kilpatrick, Robert W., "Stigler on the Relationship Between Industry Profit Rates and Market Concentration", *Journal of Political Economy,* LXXVI, No. 3 (1968), 479.

MacAvoy, Paul W., James W. McKie, and Lee E. Preston, "High and Stable Concentration Levels, Profitability, and Public Policy: A Response", *Journal of Law and Economics,* XIV, No. 2 (1971), 493-500.

McGee, John S., *In Defense of Industrial Concentration.* op. cit.

Mann, H. Michael, "Seller Concentration, Barriers to Entry, and Rates of Return in Thirty Industries, 1950-60", *Review of Economics and Statistics,* XLVIII, No. 3 (1966), 296.

Mueller, Willard F., *A Primer on Monopoly and Competition,* op. cit.

Neal, Philip et al., Report, White House Task Force on Antitrust Policy, *Antitrust Law and Economics Review,* Vol. 2, No. 2 (1969), 11.

Phlips, Louis, *Effects of Industrial Concentration: A Cross-Section Analysis for the Common Market.* Amsterdam: North Holland, 1974.

Scherer, F. M., *Industrial Market Structure and Economic Performance.* New York: Rand McNally & Company, 1970.

Stigler, George, et al., "Report of the Stigler Task Force on Productivity and Competition", *Antitrust Law and Economics Review,* Vol. 2, No. 3 (1969), 13.

Weiss, Leonard, "Average Concentration Ratios and Industry Performance", *Journal of Industrial Economics,* XI, No. 3 (1963), 237.

______, "Business Pricing Policies and Inflation Reconsidered", *Journal of Political Economy,* LXXIV, No. 2 (1966), 177.

Weston, J. Fred and Stanley I. Ornstein, op. cit.

CHAPTER FIVE

Ownership and Control: Dispersal of Individual Shareholdings and Growing Concentration of Institutional Ownership

Unlike other industrialized countries, American corporations have experienced a meteoric increase in the number of shareholders and a widespread dispersal of stock ownership throughout the American population. This widespread distribution of individual stock ownership has become so pronounced that it has led to general acceptance of the concept of the separation of ownership and control in the large corporation, which has been part of the conventional wisdom of our times since the publication by Berle and Means of *The Modern Corporation and Private Property* in 1932. The conventional view now appears outdated. Indeed, Berle himself in 1959 predicted that the separation of ownership and control was only a transitory stage that would ultimately be followed by the massive accumulation of stock by institutional investors, particularly pension funds, that would unite ownership and control. Massive institutional ownership has since occurred to an impressive degree and may be expected to increase further. What remains is the question whether the financial institutions will exercise the *potential* influence or even control that they will increasingly possess.

A. INCREASE IN NUMBER OF SHAREHOLDERS AND ATOMIZATION OF HOLDINGS

As we have already seen, individual stock ownership in American corporations has increased remarkably although growth has come to an end, at least for the time being. Stock ownership has increased from about 6.5 million Americans in 1952 to approximately 31,000,000 in 1973, to include about one adult in four [see Table 5-1]. With the stock market decline in 1973-74, individual stock ownership decreased somewhat.

Most of the individual 30,520,000 shareholders classified in the 1970 New York Stock Exchange Census held a relatively small amount of shares. 12,509,000 (or 40.99%) had portfolios of under $5,000 and 18,907,000 (or

TABLE 5-1
Number of Individual Shareholders of Record and Relation to United States Population

Year	*Total Number of Shareholders (millions)*	*United States Population (millions)*	*Shareholder Percentage*
1952	6.49	156.4	4.2%
1956	8.63	168.1	5.2%
1959	12.49	177.1	7.1%
1962	17.01	185.7	9.2%
1965	20.12	193.5	10.4%
1970	30.85	204.9	15.1%
1971	32.50	207.0	15.7%
1972	31.70	208.8	15.2%
1973	30.90	211.7	14.6%

Source: *New York Stock Exchange 1973 Fact Book,* Shareholder Census, 1970, Statistical Abstract, 1973.

61.95%) had portfolios of under $10,000. This wide distribution among shareholders with small portfolios compares with a relatively small number of shareholders with portfolios of significant size. Only 2,934,000 (or 9.61%) had portfolios of $50,000 and over [see Table 5-2].

TABLE 5-2
Classification of Individual Shareholders of Record By Size of Portfolio, 1970

Size of Portfolio	*Number of Individual Shareholders*	*Percent of Total*
Under $5,000	12,509,000	40.99%
$5,000 to $9,999	6,398,000	20.96%
$10,000 to $24,999	5,853,000	19.19%
$25,000 to $49,999	2,826,000	9.26%
$50,000 and over	2,934,000	9.61%
	30,520,000	100.00%
Not Classified	330,000	
	30,850,000	

Source: New York Stock Exchange Shareholder Census, 1970.

If we assume that the average portfolio size in each class was equal to the median of the classification (i.e. the average size of all portfolios under $5,000 was $2,500 and the average size of all portfolios from $5,000 to $9,999 was $7,500), an indicated $79.3 billion aggregate value was held by the 18,907,000 individual shareholders with portfolios of under $10,000 during early 1970. Sixty-two percent of all shareholders thus held only 12% of total individual portfolios of $682.8 billion. Although 12% represents a small proportion of all stockholdings, the $79.3 billion total is an impressive illustration of the substantial absolute amount of shareownership among small shareholders in the United States.

The modest 12% share of the 18,907,000 smaller holders contrasts with the substantial share of total individual portfolios owned by the 2,934,000 large shareholders with portfolios of $50,000 or more. If we assume, as above, that the average portfolio in each class in the New York Stock Exchange Census was equal to the median of the classification, this would indicate the following distribution for portfolios of under $50,000:

Portfolio Size	*Number of Individual Shareowners*	*Total Estimated Portfolio Value*
Under $5,000	12,509,000	$ 31.3 Billion
$5,000 - $9,999	6,398,000	48.0 Billion
$10,000 - $24,999	5,853,000	102.4 Billion
$25,000 - $49,999	2,826,000	106.0 Billion
Total		$287.7 Billion

If this $287.7 billion estimate for all portfolios under $50,000 is deducted from the $682.8 billion total value of individual portfolios, it indicates an estimated value of $395.1 billion for the 2,934,000 shareholders with portfolios of $50,000 and over. In other words, on the foregoing assumptions, approximately 9.6% of all shareholders (or a little over 1% of the population) owned approximately 58% of total individual portfolios. This likely understates the degree of concentration. Of the 2,934,000 individuals with portfolios of $50,000 or more, 1,536,000 persons, or more than half, had household incomes of $25,000 or less. It is likely that the remaining 1,398,000 individuals (or about 0.6% of the population) with incomes over $25,000 owned a disproportionately large amount of the total portfolios of the group.

This is supported by a 1972 study by Oliver Quayle and Company commissioned by the New York Stock Exchange. This study showed that only 9% of all investors held stocks or mutual fund shares in excess of $100,000 and only 4% in excess of $500,000.

B. PEOPLE'S CAPITALISM

The New York Stock Exchange has described the foregoing development as "People's Capitalism," presumably to indicate widespread ownership of American industry by the American people generally. It is apparent that this description is far from accurate.

Although there has been progressive fragmentation of stockholdings with wider and wider distribution among the American public, it does not represent any significant redistribution of corporate wealth. Sixty-two percent of all stockholders own less than $10,000; their stockholdings do not represent interests of such significance as to overshadow their other interests. In General Motors, for instance, seventy-eight percent of all shareholders own 100 shares or less.

The mere fact of shareownership is not significant in and of itself. As J.A. Livingston puts it, "Shareholders are not shareholders. They are something else instead." Shareownership for the individual attains a meaningful relationship only when it represents an economic interest of sufficient importance to compete effectively with his conflicting interests. Before "People's Capitalism" can have economic or psychological validity, the shareholder must be so identified with his holding that he thinks as a shareholder rather than as an employee or consumer or whatever other role he may perceive for himself. Furthermore, with shareholders behaving as temporary investors rather than as owners in the traditional sense and with the high mobility of portfolio composition reflecting the absence of pressures (other than taxes and brokerage commissions) against switching from one equity to another or to bonds, the description of individual shareownership distribution as "People's Capitalism" seems no more apt than the Communist predilection for describing totalitarian states of the left as "People's Democracies."

C. STUDIES OF THE SEPARATION OF OWNERSHIP AND CONTROL

The widespread growth of individual ownership and the increasing atomization of holdings have contributed to intense interest in the phenomenon of the separation of corporate ownership and control and its consequences. Commencing with the classic work of Berle and Means, *The Modern Corporation and Private Property* (1932), there have been a number of studies of the separation of shareholder ownership and corporate control in the major American corporations. Berle and Means have been followed by the 1940 report of the Temporary National Economic Commission and studies by Robert A. Gordon, Don Villarejo, Ferdinand Lundborg, Robert J. Larner, Jean-Marie Chevalier, and others.

Robert J. Larner[1] provides the best basis for comparison with Berle and Means. Larner made a comprehensive empirical view of the extent of separation of ownership and control as of 1963, employing the definitions, procedures, and classifications used by Berle and Means in their 1929 study.

[1]Robert J. Larner, *Management Control and the Large Corporation* (New York: Dunellen Publishing Company, Inc., 1970).

TABLE 5-3
Summary According to Type of Ultimate Control of the
200 Largest Nonfinancial Corporations, 1963 and 1929

Type of Control	*Number of Corporations*				*Proportion of Companies by Industrial Groups*			
1963	Total	Industrials	Public Utilities	Transportation Companies	Total %	Industrials %	Public Utilities %	Transportation Companies %
Private Ownership	0	0	0	0	0.0	0	0	0
Majority Ownership	6	4	1	1	3.0	3	2	4
Minority Control	18	18	0	0	9.0	15	0	0
Legal Device	9	6	0	3	4.5	5	0	12
Management Control	167	89	58	20	83.5	76	98	83
Total	200	117	59	24	100	100	100	100
1929								
Private Ownership	12	8	2	2	6	8	4	5
Majority Ownership	10	6	3	1	5	6	6	2
Minority Control	46½	34½	7½	4½	23	32	14	11
Legal Device	41	14½	19	7½	21	14	36	18
Management Control	88½	43	19½	26	44	40	38	2
In Receivership	2	—	1	1	1	0	2	2
Total	200	106	52	42	100	100	100	100

Robert J. Larner, *Management Control and the Large Corporation* (New York: Dunellen Publishing Company, Inc., 1970), Table 1, p. 12.

Sources: 1963, Appendix A (Appendix A lists the 500 Largest nonfinancial corporations of 1963, giving for each its size and rank in assets, its classification by type of control, and the source and reasons for its classification); 1929, Berle and Means, *The Modern Corporation and Private Property,* p. 115.

The Berle and Means study included the 200 Largest nonfinancial corporations in 1929 and the Larner study looked at the corresponding group in 1963. Each ranked corporations by size of assets and included public utilities and transportation companies as well as industrial firms. Because size of assets rather than sales or value-added was used as the basis for ranking, industrials are under-represented and utilities and transportation companies are over-represented. Each defined control as the power to select the board, and corporations were classified as privately owned, controlled through ownership or legal devices, or management-controlled. The Berle and Means study showed widespread separation of ownership and control in 1929, and Larner found a dramatic increase by 1963.

Larner concluded that 84% of the companies (and 84% of the assets) of the 200 Largest nonfinancials were management-controlled in 1963 in comparison with 44% of the companies (and 58% of the assets) of the 200 Largest nonfinancials in the Berle and Means study. Looking solely at the industrials in the group, management control climbed from 40% to 76% of the companies [see Table 5-3].

Larner's study included all 500 Largest nonfinancial corporations, not merely the 200 Largest. With the addition of the 300 next largest corporations, the percentage of industrial concerns under management control dropped from 76% to 67%. As might be expected, corporate size contributes to increased separation of ownership and control. After a point, the immense resources required become simply too much for continued ownership control [see Table 5-4].

D. EROSION OF FAMILY CONCENTRATIONS

The increasing separation of individual ownership and control reflects, along with other factors, the continued decline of concentrated family holdings in the major corporations. In the intervening four decades since the Berle and Means study, there has been great erosion of family concentrations. Death taxes and the ability of the security markets to absorb major stock offerings have contributed to substantial sales of many of the well-known family holdings.

Notwithstanding the continuing reduction of family concentrations, Larner reported that in 1963, control by a single family was apparent in at least twenty of the very large nonfinancial corporations, with control by a group of several families existing in a number of other companies.

Thus, Larner lists fifteen major nonfinancials as still under single family control as of 1963 [see Table 5-5].

In addition, five other companies, classified as management-controlled, were described as "controlled or strongly influenced" by a single family

TABLE 5-4

"500 Largest" in 1963 Divided by Rank into Ten Groups and Number of Management-Controlled Firms in Each Group

Firms Ranking	*Number of Management-Controlled Firms*
1 through 50	42
51 through 100	39
101 through 150	45
151 through 200	41
201 through 250	37
251 through 300	42
301 through 350	38
351 through 400	29
401 through 450	32
451 through 500	32
Total	377

Robert J. Larner, *Management Control and the Large Corporation* (New York: Dunellen Publishing Company, Inc., 1970) Table 5, p. 21.

Source: Appendix A (Appendix A lists the 500 largest nonfinancial corporations of 1963, giving for each its size and rank in assets, its classification by type of control, and the source and reasons for its classification).

TABLE 5-5

1963 Rank (According to Sales)	*Company*	*Family*
#3	Ford Motor	Ford
9	Gulf Oil	Mellon
10	E.I. Du Pont de Nemours	Du Pont
52	Dow Chemical	Dow
56	Reynolds Metals	Reynolds
32	Firestone	Firestone
60	Sun Oil	Pew
129	Kaiser Aluminum & Rubber	Kaiser
1 (merchandising)	Great Atlantic & Pacific Tea	Hartford
32 (utilities)	Duke Power	Duke
49	General Tire & Rubber	O'Neil
16 (merchandising)	May Department Stores	May
175	Joseph E. Seagram & Sons	Bronfman
317	Schenley Industries	Rosenstiel
160	Kaiser Industries	Kaiser

Robert J. Larner, *Management Control and the Large Corporation* (New York: Dunellen Publishing Company, Inc., 1970), Appendix A.

represented within the management but owing only a very small fraction of the voting stock. These five companies are listed below.

1963 Rank According to Sales	*Company*	*Family*
#18	IBM	Watson
64	Inland Steel	Block
96	Weyerhauser Paper	Weyerhauser
11 (merchandising)	Federated Department Stores	Lazarus
90	J.P. Stevens	Stevens

Professor Eisenberg points out that as one moves to the larger group of the 500 Largest industrials, the number of family concentrations increases as corporate size decreases. In 1967 *Fortune* estimated that family concentrations of 10% or more existed in as many as 150 of the 500 Largest. In the megacorporations with their giant size, the number shrinks to the limited group described by Larner. In time, the list of family-controlled enterprises may be expected to shrink further. As we have already noted, a number of giant American companies—several with sales in excess of $1 billion—are still privately owned (e.g. Cargill, Continental Grain, Deering-Milliken, Hallmark, Hearst Publishing and United Parcel). Eventually, these, too, may be expected to become public companies, initially under family or group control, but in all likelihood ultimately indistinguishable in the widespread distribution of their stock from the family companies which underwent the same transformation earlier.

E. WHAT IS "CONTROL"?

The commonly accepted definition of "control" which Berle and Means and Larner adopt is the power to select or change the board of directors, but when does such "control" exist? Some quantitative yardstick of "control" is necessary. The Berle and Means study required 20% or more stock ownership before classifying a corporation as minority controlled. This is unrealistically high.

The Securities Exchange Act of 1934 and the Investment Companies Act of 1940 have both employed 10% as the standard for determining control for certain purposes of the statutes. The Investment Companies Act uses 25% for other purposes and the Internal Revenue Code, 20%. A 10% standard was originally used in the 1969 Williams Act regulating tender offers as the basis for reporting the acquisition of corporate stock, but in 1972 this was reduced to 5%. The Staff Report for the Subcommittee on Domestic Finance of the House Committee on Banking and Currency, *Commercial Banks and*

Their Trust Activities: Emerging Influence on the American Economy (1969) also considered 5% as the critical level but noted that in appropriate cases even 1% or 2% ownership could provide tremendous influence.

Larner uses 10% as the basis for classification of a corporation as minority-controlled. In view of the substantial increase in the distribution of shares and the great increase in the aggregate market value of the stock of the megacorporations which occurred in the thirty-five years between 1929 and 1964, Larner's use of a 10% standard for "control" does not materially affect the comparability of his study and the Berle and Means analysis. Indeed, Jean-Marie Chevalier goes further and uses 5% for purposes of his analysis.

For purposes of ascertaining the extent of the separation of ownership and control, the definition of "control" as the power to select or change the board is dangerously ambiguous because it fails to distinguish between the level of ownership required for *retention* of control and the substantially increased level of ownership needed for *acquisition* of control, particularly in the face of management hostility. It also ignores different types of struggles for corporate power in which sharply different percentages of stock may be required for successful exercise or assumption of "control." Control ample for one of these power states may be entirely inadequate for others.

The use of the inflexible 5%, 10%, or 20% yardsticks to measure control is, therefore, unrealistic. "Control" must be related to the circumstances under which it is sought to be exercised. The amount of voting strength required for "control" will increase as one progresses through the following stages:

(a) Retention of control by management or minority in the absence of any external threat.
(b) Retention of control by management or minority owners in the face of an external threat represented by the hostile acquisition of a significant minority of shares.
(c) Retention of control by management or minority owners in the face of an external threat represented by a tender offer for shares, typically at a substantial premium above the market.
(d) Assumption of control in the face of management opposition by an external group through the acquisition of a minority of shares by purchase or tender offer and the institution or potential threat of institution of a proxy fight.

Further, it is obvious that the power to select or change the board is affected not only by ownership of a requisite amount of the voting power but by possession of the corporate electoral machinery. This is an immense advantage to management in tests of strength with external forces. It also presents a dramatic illustration of the problems that may face stockholders in "control" in the event that they have a falling out with management and decide to exercise their "control" to change the board and oust the management. Thus, in the celebrated Standard Oil of Indiana controversy of 1929, John D. Rockefeller, Jr. was acknowledged as possessing "control." He held directly or indirectly 14.9% of the voting stock. The chairman of the board, Colonel Robert W. Stewart, had apparently been involved in the Teapot Dome Scandal, and Rockefeller decided to remove him. Stewart declined to be removed, and a proxy contest developed. Notwithstanding the size of the Rockefeller holding and the tarnish of the scandal, Stewart's control of the electoral machinery led to a tense struggle before Rockefeller finally won with 59% of the shares outstanding and 65% of the votes cast.

To the extent that Berle and Means as well as Larner employ a single inflexible yardstick to measure "control" for differing power states, they obviously are unrealistic. On the other hand, if one accepts their studies as dealing with "control" in hand, in the absence of any external threat, the 5% or 10% standard is entirely acceptable. It becomes questionable if one introduces the element of an external threat or if one is concerned with an attempt to assume control rather than to maintain existing control.

Finally, there is the basic underlying problem of determining the "control group" whose shares may be properly aggregated. Neither Berle and Means nor Larner sufficiently considers the difficulties of uncovering the behind-the-scenes alliances which can accumulate the necessary critical mass. Where groups are formed for the purpose of acquiring control through a tender offer, the Williams Act fortified by judicial decisions has required disclosure of the ownership of the group. However, when a tender offer is not involved, there is little available information which throws light on anything but the most obvious set of interrelationships. "Group" for purposes of the Larner study thus shrinks to families and "associates."

Larner employs the definition of "associate" used by the Securities and Exchange Commission for purposes of disclosure in proxy statements and prospectuses.[2] This includes only the most obvious alliances, ignoring many of the combinations of forces which in fact produce control. Thus, both the Berle and Means and Larner studies may be expected to understate the extent of minority control.

F. RADICAL CRITICISMS

In contrast to Berle and Means and Larner, neither Villarejo nor Lundborg agrees that separation of ownership and control is characteristic of the

[2]"The term associate used to indicate a relationship with any person means (1) any corporation or organization . . . of which such person is an officer, director, or partner or is, directly or indirectly, the beneficial owner of 10 percent of more of any class of equity securities; (2) any trust or other estate in which such person has a substantial beneficial interest or as to which such person serves as trustee or in a similar fiduciary capacity; and (3) any relative or spouse, or any relative of such spouse who has the same home as such person, or who is a director or officer of the issuer or any of its parents or subsidiaries." (Securities and Exchange Commission Rule 14a-1).

large corporation. Villarejo combines the holdings of all insiders and of financial institutions, assumes they act in concert, and concludes that "the propertied rich, both own and control the giant enterprises of the nation." Lundborg follows much the same pattern. Larner is properly critical of Villarejo and Lundborg because of the absence of any evidence that the insiders and the institutions in fact act in concert.

Larner's criticism is entirely valid if concerted action is looked upon as representing a consensual arrangement for common action where there is a common intent to join forces to accomplish an agreed objective. Concerted action, however, need not reflect formal agreement. It may arise as an objective phenomenon produced by congruent pressures leading to common patterns of conduct. Thus, one may inquire whether the existing pattern of management control with the acquiescence and support of the institutions does not constitute a *modus vivendi* representing an accommodation of the interests of these groups. Such a *modus vivendi* is strengthened by the fact that the various persons involved, whether in the corporation or the financial institution, are in a sense all members of the same club. There is a widespread identity of social origins, status, values, and outlook. A *modus vivendi* between various groups with a common social background and eonomic outlook accommodating their respective economic interests is, however, a radically different relationship than intentional joint action. It rests on sociological and psychological factors rather than on an economic alliance or other intentional association to achieve common objectives.

Larner's study thus may be accepted as establishing the spread of the separation of ownership and control insofar as *individual* stockholdings are concerned. The major corporations have become so large that not even the wealthiest families can retain control via stock ownership, except in an isolated and shrinking number of cases. Larner, however, dismisses the implications of *institutional* ownership. This is a grave error, which we will now proceed to review.

G. INSTITUTIONAL OWNERSHIP

Since World War II, there has been an astronomic increase both in the size and concentration of stock ownership in the large financial institutions, particularly the trust departments of commercial banks and to a lesser extent, investment companies, insurance companies, and state and local government pension funds.

Total institutional assets in 1972 reached \$957.6 billion of which \$389.7 billion represented common stocks:

	Total Assets	*Total Common Stock (billions)*	*Total NYSE Common Stock*
Private Noninsured Pension Plans	$150.0	$111.8	$ 95.8
Investment Companies	79.6	64.0	57.6
Life Insurance Companies	239.4	21.4	20.3*
Property-Casualty Insurance Companies	75.9	18.0*	19.7*
Personal Trust Funds	170.0	113.0	NA
Common Trust Funds	15.5	7.3	6.4
Mutual Savings Banks	100.6	2.5	1.8
State and Local Pension Funds	72.1	13.7*	17.4*
Foundations	39.5	28.0	18.7
Educational Endowments	15.0	10.0	8.7
Other Nonprofit Institutions	NA	NA	11.8
Total	$957.6	$389.7	$258.3

*Discrepancy unexplained.
Sources: *SEC Statistical Bulletin* (1973), p. 867; NYSE Fact Book, 1973.

Financial institutions have steadily increased their holdings of the stocks listed on the New York Stock Exchange from $9.7 billion in 1949 to $258.3 billion or 29.6% of all NYSE stocks in 1972. These totals do not include the largest class of institutional holdings—personal trusts. With the addition of bank-administered personal trust funds, foreign institutions, nonregistered mutual funds, private hedge funds, and nonbank trusts, the Exchange has estimated that total institutional holdings at the end of 1972 exceeded 45% of the NYSE stocks. In the four years prior to 1973, the institutional share increased by about 25%.

Professor Robert M. Soldofsky's study[3] of ownership by institutional investors of all stocks—whether or not listed on the New York Stock Exchange—estimated that the value of total institutional stock holdings, which he estimated at $177.1 billion in 1968, would increase to an estimated $5.06 trillion or 55.2% of total market value by the year 2000 [see Table 5-5].

The concentration of securities in institutional hands has led to increasing institutional domination of the securities markets. In a ten-year period, the share of institutional investors in the total volume of trading on the Exchange rose from 29.2% of total value in 1961 to 52.4% in 1971. With transactions

[3]Robert M. Soldofsky, *Institutional Holdings of Common Stock 1900-2000: History, Projection, Interpretation*, Michigan Business Studies 18, No. 3 (Ann Arbor, Mich.: Bureau of Business Research, Graduate School of Business Administration, The University of Michigan, 1971).

TABLE 5-6

Projected Market Values for Stock Holdings of Financial Institutions

Financial Institution	*Market Value (In Billions)*			*Percentage of Total Market Value*			*Growth Rates (Percentage per Year*	
	1968	*1980*	*2000*	*1968*	*1980*	*2000*	*1968-80*	*1981-2000*
Noninsured corporate pension funds	$ 56.0	$269	$2,362	7.3	13.7	25.8	14.0	11.5
Investment companies	59.6	258	1,730	7.8	13.1	18.9	13.0	10.0
State and local pension funds	4.8	37	357	0.6	1.9	3.9	17.0	12.0
Life insurance companies	12.8	46	171	1.7	2.3	1.8	13.5	6.8
Property and casualty insurance companies	14.7	37	118	1.9	1.9	1.3	8.0	6.0
University and college endowments	9.0	28	190	1.2	1.4	2.1	10.0	10.0
Foundations	15.8	28	74	2.1	1.4	0.8	5.0	5.0
Common trust funds	4.4	11	53	0.6	0.6	0.6	9.0	8.0
Total institutional holdings	$177.1	$ 714	$5,055	23.2	36.3	55.2	12.3	10.3
Market value of all outstanding stock	$761.3	$1,966	$9,161				8.0	8.0

[a]Data from U.S., Securities and Exchange Commission, *Statistical Series,* Release No. 2358, May 1, 1969, p. 5, Table 3.

[b]For widely held companies only includes both common and preferred stocks.

Source: Robert M. Soldofsky, *Institutional Holdings of Common Stock, 1900-2000: History, Projection, Interpretation* Michigan Business Studies 18, No. 3, Ann Arbor, Mich.: Bureau of Business Research, Graduate School of Business Administration. The University of Michigan, 1971) Table 39, p. 209. Copyright by The University of Michigan; reproduced with permission.

by Exchange members excluded, institutional investors were responsible for 68.2% of the value of transactions in 1971. In some securities it has been estimated that institutions generally account for 90% of the trading volume and that the Morgan Guaranty Trust Company with the largest bank trust department alone represents more than 20%.

This has led in turn to a substantial lack of liquidity in the market place. Price swings have grown wider and more frequent. The size of institutional transactions has dwarfed the resources of the NYSE specialists. "Crossing" transactions between institutions, where both the buyer and seller are identified in advance, or "block positioning," where a broker acquires a large block from one institution and finds others to buy it, have developed as alternative marketing methods. The problem is aggravated by the frequency of common investment attitudes among institutions. This is the product of a number of factors. Common investment principles applied by persons of similar background, training, and experience not surprisingly lead to common conclusions. Further, investment officers of different institutions exert a reciprocal reinforcing influence upon each other. Institutional investment patterns develop, and there is pressure (and protection) for investment officers to follow the conventional wisdom. As a result of such factors, many institutions tend to invest in many of the same securities and to buy or sell at the same time.

Such lack of liquidity may have a profound influence on the extent to which institutions will continue to regard themselves as temporary investors ready to sell in the event of unfavorable developments. If institutions are "locked in" and unable to liquidate their holdings, they come under obvious pressures to reconsider their relationship to the stocks and companies in their portfolios. This possibility was noted in 1964 by Daniel J. Baum and Ned B. Stiles in *The Silent Partners—Institutional Investors and Corporate Control,* but there is little indication in the intervening decade that such lack of liquidity has become acute or that such reconsideration has in fact occurred.

H. INSTITUTIONAL CONCENTRATION

With the tremendous growth of the common stock investments of financial institutions, a high degree of concentration of institutional holdings in many major American corporations has inevitably resulted. The 1971 Institutional Investor Study Report of the Securities and Exchange Commission ("Institutional Investor Study"), covering more than 200 major financial institutions, including the 50 largest bank trust departments, disclosed that as of September 30, 1969, financial institutions held surprisingly high percentages of the outstanding shares of major American corporations, including the ten largest American corporations (ranked by market value):

1969 Rank by Market Value	*1969 Rank by Sales*	*Company*	*Institutional Holdings* Percentage of Stock	Number of Institutions
#1	#5	International Business Machines	43.1%	81
2	1 (Utilities)	American Telephone and Telegraph	10.0%	130
3	1	General Motors	20.0%	79
4	2	Exxon	30.0%	101
5	27	Eastman Kodak	41.0%	102
6	1 (Retailing)	Sears Roebuck	45.3%	106
7	8	Texaco	30.0%	62
8	4	General Electric	30.0%	69
9	71	Xerox	52.8%	76
10	10	Gulf Oil	50.0%	102

Other prominent corporations in which institutional holdings were concentrated included:

1969 Rank by Size of Sales	*Corporation*	*Percentage of Outstanding Shares Held by Institutions Surveyed*
174	Merck	50.9%
172	Avon Products	47.6%
94	American Home Products	35.0%
28	Proctor & Gamble	34.5%
59	Minnesota Mining & Manufacturing	33.2%

In Larner's study of 1963, all but three of the foregoing fifteen companies were classified as management-controlled. Sears Roebuck was described as owner-controlled, Minnesota Mining & Manufacturing as controlled by owner-directors, and Avon Products was not listed.

The concentration of institutional holdings in major portfolio companies is startling. Further, as we will examine the causes for such concentration, we will see that this trend may be expected to continue and these already impressive totals become even more substantial.

An analysis of the Institutional Investor Study's findings with respect to International Business Machines illustrates the extent of concentration:

Number of Institutions	*Percentage of I.B.M. Stock Held*
3	10%
6	15%
10	20%
18	25%
30	30%
47	35%
81	43.1%

These shares were held primarily by banks with investment fund complexes, insurance companies, and self-administered funds following in that order.

If collusion or concerted action by institutions is the concern, the fact that ten institutions held 20% of I.B.M. may be more significant than the fact that eighty-one institutions held 43.1%.

The Institutional Investor Study concluded that findings such as these demonstrated a major concentration of portfolio company ownership in financial institutions generally. This development is doubly compounded. The institutional holdings are concentrated in a relatively small number of institutions. Further, the portfolios of these institutions are concentrated in a limited number of major American companies. Thus, Baum and Stiles refer to a New York Stock Exchange 1964 Study that found that institutional investors had only 1.8% of their portfolios invested in the 500 smallest companies listed on the Exchange which had total market values of $50 million or less. The 500 companies almost entirely ignored by the institutions accounted for about 40% of the total number of shares listed on the Exchange. As a result, the Institutional Investor Study concluded that these leading financial institutions may have the economic power to control or influence corporate affairs and that this represented a most formidable potential counterforce to corporate management hegemony.

As already noted, Berle foresaw this development almost two decades ago. In *Power Without Property,* he predicted the gradual evolution of the separation of ownership and control from minority ownership and control to management control and ultimately to control by fiduciary institutions. Berle recognized that the growth of pension funds and their increasing investment in equity securities were events of great significance and pointed out that if these continued, "the pension trusts . . . may well have the prevailing control-stockholding position and the capacity to make it absolute." However, Robert J. Larner's 1963 survey updating the Berle and Means study failed to recognize the fundamental implications of institutional ownership. Larner was aware of the concentration in bank trust departments but observed that since the banks did not always have full voting power, its significance was exaggerated. In contrast, Jean-Marie Chevalier concluded that the large corporations were entering the stage of institutional control, asserting that the commercial banks hold "a potential power which they will find difficult not to exert."

The data to update the 1969 recapitulation of the Institutional Investor Study with respect to the concentrated holdings of the nation's largest bank trust departments is not entirely available. However, as a result of increased voluntary disclosure by many of the institutions involved and data released in the 1973 hearings before the Subcommittee on Financial Markets of the Senate Committee on Finance on the Impact of Institutional Investors in the Stock Market headed by Senator Lloyd Bentsen ("Bentsen Hearings"), it is possible to recapitulate the major holdings[4] of the 13 largest bank trust departments in 1973.

This tabulation reveals not only high concentration but high concentration in the very largest corporations. The recapitulation of only the largest holdings of this relatively small number of institutions discloses that they held 5% or more of nine of the ten Largest, fourty-seven of the 100 Largest, and eighty of the 200 Largest, industrials and 10% or more of six of the ten Largest and thirty of the 100 Largest [see Table 5-7].

Concentration ratio	*10 Largest*	*100 Largest*	*Second 100 Largest*	*Third 100 Largest*	*Fourth 100 Largest*	*Fifth 100 Largest*	*Total 500 Largest*
1% – 5%	1	25	24	2	2	—	53
5% – 10%	3	17	15	4	2	4	42
10% – 15%	4	16	9	8	—	2	35
15% – 20%	1	9	4	—	1	1	15
20% – 25%	1	4	1	—	2	—	7
over 25%	0	1	3	2	2	—	8
Totals:							
1% and over	10	72	56	16	9	7	160
5% and over	9	47	32	14	7	7	107
10% and over	6	30	17	10	5	3	65

Among the more prominent companies, the largest holdings of these thirteen banks included:

Avon	32.01%
Polaroid	25.21%
Xerox	25.06%
Merck	23.62%
American Home Products	20.72%
International Business Machines	20.64%

One of the most interesting items disclosed by the tabulation is the relatively high concentration of holdings in other banks. Thus, four major banks (First National City, U.S. Trust, Chase Manhattan, and Bank of America) hold more than 10% of the stock of J.P. Morgan, Inc. The twelve banks (other than First National City) held 16.50% of the stock of First National City.

Since the tabulation includes only the largest holdings of the thirteen banks and not their total holdings, it obviously understates the level of concentration in these institutions. This understatement is compounded by the

[4]These range from the twenty largest to the one hundred largest portfolio holdings in terms of size.

fact that in the case of some banks, the data disclosed included only the twenty largest holdings.

A careful review of the largest holdings of these major trust departments indicates the limitations on the extent of institutional concentration. Impressive as the aggregate totals are, a high degree of concerted action among the group is required to achieve a level that could represent potential control. It indicates that a community of values, outlook, and objectives rather than deliberate, concerted action is the likely avenue of institutional influence.

In certain industries, institutional concentration is especially pronounced. A 1974 study by the Civil Aeronautics Board made at the request of Senator Lee Metcalf of the largest thirty stockholders of American certified air carriers disclosed that 30% or more of the stock of seven major carriers was held by financial institutions:

Carrier	*Number of Institutions*	*Percentage of Outstanding Shares Held*
Northwest	22	56.3%
National	18	56.0%
TransWorld	18	45.7%
United	24	45.5%
Delta	21	37.73%
Flying Tiger	14	34.98%
American	18	33.60%

Source: Civil Aeronautics Board Report, *Thirty Largest Stockholders of U.S. Certified Air Carriers and Summary of Stock Holdings of Financial Institutions* (1974), Appendix A.

As impressive as these totals are, it is important to note that it is the aggregate position of the financial institutions rather than the holdings of individual institutions that is of overriding importance. This means that power resides in the institutions collectively; they must act in concert to be effective. In isolated cases, a particular institution may possess a significant voice, but this is not typical. Thus, a study of the nation's twenty-five largest bank trust departments by the Subcommittee on Financial Markets of the Senate Committee on Finance found that 5% or more of the outstanding shares of only six of the 200 Largest industrials and nineteen of the 500 Largest was held by any single bank; in only two instances did more than one bank hold 5% of the stock of the same company. Further, as we will see, fiduciary ownership does not necessarily mean voting power. Although the trust departments of the commercial banks possess full voting power over most of the shares held by them, there is a significant minor fraction over which the institution shares voting power with a cotrustee or over which it has no voting power at all.

TABLE 5-7
Portfolio Concentration of the 13 Largest Bank Trust Departments and Investment Companies, 1973

Rank	1973 Largest Industrials [Ranked according to sales]	Morgan Guaranty	Bankers Trust	First National City	(A) United States Trust Co.	Chase Manhattan	(B) Manufacturers Hanover	Mellon National	(C) First National, Chicago	(D) Continental Illinois	Bank of America	(E) Harris Trust	(F) Chemical Bank New York Trust	(G) Girard Bank	Total 13 Largest Banks	All Investment Companies	Total 13 Largest Banks and All Investment Companies	
1.	General Motors	1.68%	.50%	.89%	.66%	.50%	.53%	.27%	.62%	.37%	.20%	.20%	.34%	.03%	6.79%	2.60%	9.39%	1.
2.	Exxon	1.52	.91	.98	1.41	2.90	1.01	.58	.51	.42	.40	.53	.74	.03	11.94	4.80	16.74	2.
3.	Ford	2.83		.90	.18	.50			1.02		.30	.51	.46		6.70	7.20	13.90	3.
5.	General Electric	.62	1.05	2.44	1.54	1.50	.84	.47	.76	.44	.50	.27	.63	.03	11.09	2.80	13.89	5.
6.	Texaco	2.08	1.01	1.19	1.02	.77	1.15	.25	.74	2.08	.20	.52	.32	.04	11.37	4.70	16.07	6.
7.	Mobil Oil	3.60	6.56	.75	.71	3.70		.29			.37	.79	.54	.06	17.37	4.90	22.27	7.
8.	IBM	4.65	2.80	2.31	3.07	1.70	1.55	1.00	.68	.58	.40	.59	1.29	.02	20.64	4.90	25.54	8.
9.	I. T. & T.	1.99			1.68	3.30		.84				.67			8.48	6.28	14.76	9.
10.	Gulf Oil	.06			.38	.14		12.03				.30	.22		13.13	1.93	15.06	10.
11.	Standard Oil (California)	1.80	1.46	.31	.86	2.80		.25		.23		.29	.73	.05	8.78	4.80	13.58	11.
14.	Westinghouse	3.45		2.10	.84	.34		1.11				.07			7.91	5.67	13.58	14.
15.	Standard Oil (Indiana)	.18	.77	.55	.76	3.00		.20	8.89	.94	.50	.56	.43		15.78	2.60	19.38	15.
16.	E.I. DuPont de Nemours	.50	.78	.74	1.37	1.10		.20			.20	.08	.36		5.33	4.20	9.53	16.
17.	G. T. & E.	.11		2.23	.30	.13					.40	.12			3.29	6.80	10.09	17.
19.	Goodyear Tire	3.77			.51	.18						.10	.57		5.13		5.13	19.
21.	Continental Oil	.09	3.52		.82	.27		2.67				.68			3.05	9.70	17.75	21.
24.	Bethlehem Steel				.26										.26	12.50	12.76	24.
25.	Eastman Kodak	3.59	1.43	2.14	2.15	1.00	1.23	.85	.25	1.13	.30	.42	.64	.02	15.15	2.70	17.85	25.
26.	Atlantic Richfield	.17	2.41	4.31	.53	2.80	2.06	.68	1.70		.70	.87	.46	.06	16.75	8.30	25.05	26.
28.	Union Carbide	.31			.48	1.89					1.20	.17			4.05	8.57	12.62	28.
30.	Procter & Gamble	5.06		.39	2.18	.90				.98	.30	.19	.37		10.37	1.58	11.95	30.
31.	Kraftco	2.54			.19	.38		1.42	1.92			.10			6.55		6.55	31.
34.	Caterpillar Tractor	2.03		4.25	1.65	1.21		1.58	5.53		.30	.28	.26		17.09	3.16	20.25	34.
38.	Dow Chemical	1.55	1.48	.26	1.57	1.20				.34	.60	.66	.21		7.87	3.70	11.57	38.
39.	McDonnell Douglas		17.37		.06										17.43		17.43	39.
40.	Phillips Petroleum	.05			2.13	.85		.29		.25	.40	.03			4.00	6.00	10.00	40.
41.	Xerox	5.22	2.19	6.07	3.35	1.90	1.79	.33	1.17	1.21	.40	.45	.98		25.06	7.10	32.16	41.
43.	Beatrice Foods			1.27	.12	1.52				1.14		2.08			10.73		10.73	43.
45.	Monsanto	.27			1.24	1.42						.22			3.15	9.09	12.24	45.
50.	Minnesota Mining & Mfg.	1.45	1.63	2.43	2.92	.56	1.00	.43	1.26	1.26	.40	.64	.57	.04	14.59	3.00	17.59	50.
52.	Singer				7.01	.25							.79		8.05		8.05	52.
53.	Ralston Purina	6.08			.15			2.74							8.97		8.97	53.
54.	Honeywell	.62		4.70	2.50	1.90						.21	.82		10.75		10.75	54.
55.	Armco Steel				.23			10.34							10.57		10.57	55.
[illegible]	[illegible]				.43	1.66				1.85					3.94	9.07	13.01	56.

57.	International Paper	7.27			1.44	4.80						.24	.47	14.22	11.00	25.22	57.
58.	Weyerhaeuser	.15	1.60		3.84	1.07			1.08			.92		8.66	5.90	14.56	58.
61.	Bendix			13.08	.11							.30		13.49		13.49	61.
62.	Sperry Rand	2.51			.85	4.50								7.86	14.60	22.46	62.
63.	Georgia-Pacific	.08			.61	1.40						.01		2.10	5.35	7.45	63.
64.	Champion Internat.	5.88			.31									6.19		6.19	64.
65.	Colgate-Palmolive	.06		2.17	1.14	1.64		2.76				2.50		10.27		10.27	65.
67.	TRW	.42		6.22	.11			3.15	8.34			.02		18.26		18.26	67.
68.	Aluminum Co. of America				.44	2.01		7.47					1.38	11.30	12.20	23.50	68.
69.	Coca-Cola	4.53		3.73	1.39	.49		.74		.60	.20	.04	.43	12.05	1.80	13.95	69.
71.	Burlington Ind.	9.56			.70	.76						.06		11.08		11.08	71.
72.	Uniroyal				.37								5.78	6.15		6.15	72.
76.	Consolidated Foods				2.70					3.33				6.03		6.03	76.
77.	Cities Service	.24			.47	.48								1.19	5.79	6.98	77.
78.	Deere	.77			.82			1.08					1.16	3.83	12.90	16.73	78.
80.	Amerada Hess				.88	2.78								3.66	11.74	15.40	80.
83.	Textron	.28		3.81	.05			3.47				.62		8.23		8.23	83.
87.	American Home Prod.	6.11	2.29	1.17	2.52	.80	1.21	1.60	.53	2.60	.60	.98	.31	20.72	2.68	23.40	87.
92.	Philip Morris	11.11	2.01	2.64	1.90					1.77		.92	1.36	23.57	17.50	41.07	92.
93.	Pepsi Co.	8.39	5.00		.53	1.86				3.13		.36		20.44	7.63	28.07	93.
94.	Warner-Lambert	.81	2.36		2.84	1.68		1.35		1.28		.06	.92	10.97	7.50	18.47	94.
95.	Allied Chemical	.42			.82	2.70							.80	2.15	13.70	15.85	95.
97.	Whirlpool	3.31		4.82	1.45	.11						.20		19.12		19.12	97.
99.	Johnson & Johnson	2.95	2.53	3.62	1.67					.72		.37	.55	16.65	2.13	18.78	99.
101.	Getty Oil	.09			1.02							.03		1.88	6.50	8.38	101.
102.	General Mills	.53		1.22	.85	.74						2.86		6.76		6.76	102.
104.	Marathon Oil	2.04			.78	1.30						.72		4.88	9.67	14.55	104.
109.	PPG Industries				.49									5.85		5.85	109.
110.	Standard Oil (Ohio)	.61		.68	2.38	.78		4.58						4.95	7.77	12.72	110.
111.	American Cyanamid	4.15			.51	1.28					1.80			12.98		12.98	111.
116.	Motorola			5.63	.11							2.34		13.82	8.70	20.52	116.
118.	Norton-Simon	3.15			.88	3.74						.18	1.52	9.90		9.90	118.
120.	Kennecott Copper	6.18			.60	1.70			2.47			1.21	1.10	9.09	9.04	18.13	120.
122.	Crown Zellerbach	.44	5.54		.09							.16		10.63	16.53	27.16	122.
123.	Bristol-Myers	2.08			5.46	4.40						.33		9.94	9.27	19.21	123.
124.	Standard Brands	.22			1.06	2.07								5.99		5.99	124.
126.	American Metal Climax				1.63									1.63	9.70	11.33	126.
131.	Texas Instruments	.14	5.63	7.04	.74	2.70								16.25	9.70	25.95	131.
132.	Pfizer	2.98			2.50	.72						.19		6.39	6.00	12.39	132.
136.	Burroughs	.19	2.31		2.51	.60		1.66		1.00	.50	1.58	.19	10.54	12.60	23.14	136.
137.	Olin	5.71												5.71		5.71	137.
138.	H.J. Heinz	.53			5.24	.50		20.88			1.80			28.95		28.95	138.
143.	Ill. Central Ind.				5.86									5.86		5.86	143.
144.	Allis-Chalmers				.74									.74		.74	144.
145.	Hercules	.08			.47	2.58						3.43		6.56	12.16	18.72	145.

TABLE 5-7 cont.

Rank	1973 Largest Industrials [Ranked according to sales]	Morgan Guaranty	Bankers Trust	First National City	United States Trust Co. (A)	Chase Manhattan	Manufacturers Hanover (B)	Mellon National	First National, Chicago (C)	Continental Illinois (D)	Bank of America	Harris Trust (E)	Chemical Bank New York Trust (F)	Girard Bank (G)	Total 13 Largest Banks	All Investment Companies	Total 13 Largest Banks and All Investment Companies	
146.	Avon Products	7.87	4.82	5.36	4.99	1.70	2.69	1.76		1.82	.20	.28	.52		32.01	5.20	37.21	146.
148.	St. Regis Paper				.14	2.37									2.51	17.90	20.41	148.
151.	Merck	4.25	4.08	5.10	2.45	2.20	1.36	1.32		1.58	.40	.16	.72		23.62	3.20	26.82	151.
154.	Anheuser-Busch	6.44			3.03			1.03				.18	.88		11.56		11.56	154.
157.	Amer. Smelting	.17			.76	.26									1.19		1.19	157.
158.	Gillette	3.88			.33	.19						.41			4.81	8.45	13.26	158.
159.	Jim Walter	1.65			.96				9.40						12.01		12.01	159.
163.	Dresser Ind.				.34	.27		2.27					5.31		8.19		8.19	163.
164.	Zenith Radio				.15				6.20			.26			6.61		6.61	164.
168.	Dart Industries				.37	3.40		4.20							7.97		7.97	168.
169.	Quaker Oats				2.28	.30		4.23				.20			7.01		7.01	169.
173.	Eli Lilly	3.37	3.61	3.01	.84	.98	2.29	.46		1.11		.30	.26		16.23	3.20	19.43	173.
176.	Phelps Dodge	2.46			.83										3.29	19.50	22.79	176.
179.	Corning Glass Works	.23		7.73	1.41	1.69						.26			11.32		11.32	179.
180.	Emerson Electric	1.09	3.68	3.38	3.38			2.18				.97			14.68		14.68	180.
184.	American Broadcasting	4.23			1.14										5.37		5.37	184.
189.	Squibb	9.44	5.45		2.86								.75		18.72	6.33	25.05	189.
190.	Carrier	9.62			.54	.22						.30			10.46		10.46	190.
192.	Heublein	9.34			2.76							3.36			15.46		15.46	192.
197.	Kellogg				.04							52.20			52.24		52.24	197.
203.	Pillsbury	2.88			7.50										10.38		10.38	203.
204.	Sterling Drug	2.32	4.83		1.58						1.70				13.70		13.70	204.
205.	Armstrong Cork	5.95		4.27	.85	.13			3.14			.11			11.18		11.18	205.
226.	Jos. Schlitz Brew.	4.98			.12							1.55			6.65		6.65	226.
228.	Northrop	8.81			.35										9.16		9.16	228.
229.	Times Mirror	3.62			4.13							.01			10.76		10.76	229.
230.	Anderson, Clayton	13.26						3.00							13.26		13.26	230.
234.	Cummins Engine	6.27													6.27		6.27	234.
235.	Polaroid	10.66	3.94		1.03					3.03		1.38	1.22		25.21	10.90	36.11	235.
241.	Hewlett-Packard	.05		4.79	.41	2.83		1.12		1.44		.12			10.89	5.22	16.01	241.
249.	Upjohn	3.75	2.60	1.73	1.27	.50	3.48					1.51	.98		12.64	8.70	21.34	249.
259.	Schering-Plough	6.21	2.76	1.96	3.93					.43	.70	1.29	1.08		25.21	6.50	31.71	259.
293.	Revlon	4.34			.69										6.64		6.44	293.
294.	Richardson-Merrill	9.73			4.68	1.41									14.41		14.41	294.
308.	G.D. Searle				.81					1.80		30.60			33.41	10.05	43.46	308.
313.	Chesebrough-Ponds	15.00		3.09	.41	.20				4.20					23.16		23.16	313.
337.	Black & Decker	5.34	1.20		9.73	.46						.11			16.93		16.93	337.

341.	General Amer. Transp.	.44			.62			.55							8.28		8.28	341.
343.	AMP	11.29	3.51	2.81	.71				7.22	1.21		.72	5.91		29.53	9.21	38.74	343.
395.	Baxter Labs.	4.06	4.37	3.08	2.96							.46			22.88	8.22	31.10	395.
396.	Pabst Brewing				4.70		5.43		2.52			5.21			9.91		9.91	396.
407.	V.F. Corp.	6.27													6.27		6.27	407.
428.	Hobart Mfg.	1.59		7.07											8.66		8.66	428.
447.	Masonite	11.61			.47							3.23			15.31		15.31	447.
463.	Gardner-Denver				.34						3.50	.58			12.08		12.08	463.
468.	Lubrizol	6.25		1.90	.81				7.66						8.96		8.96	468.
475.	Digital Equipment	2.79		2.47	.23							.79			6.28	21.50	27.78	475.
488.	Ferro	11.44			2.16										13.60		13.60	488.
	Perkin-Elmer	1.03		6.44	5.40										12.87		12.87	
	Dr. Pepper	2.85			1.27					4.75					8.87		8.87	
	Halliburton	8.15	2.61		.58					1.50	.60		1.86		16.56	7.40	23.96	
	Nalco Chemical	.23			1.44	.06		1.20		2.84		.34			15.32		15.32	
	Syntex		2.17		.33			10.47					1.82		4.32	21.90	26.22	
	Quaker State Oil	.37								5.36					5.73		5.73	
	Dun & Bradstreet	6.41			9.30					3.37		.97			20.05		20.05	
	American Hospital Sup.	1.15		5.98	1.98							.15			16.08		16.08	
	Hughes Tool				1.30	2.49			4.33			6.36	6.74		14.40		14.40	
	Tampax	1.83			3.19							2.49			7.51		7.51	
	Walt Disney	13.50	3.90	3.48	.69							.57			25.86		25.86	
	McDonalds	10.94	2.74	1.96	.66					2.16		.10			22.84	15.80	38.64	
	Marriott	4.31		3.10	.20	.80		2.92							14.20		14.20	
	Economics Labs.	5.11		3.42	19.24	2.46		1.82							27.77		27.77	
	Louisiana Land & Exp.	8.02		.88	2.96	4.00		2.59					.53		13.91	9.80	23.71	
	Inter. Flavors & Frag.	5.13		.99	8.85	.70		.82		1.42					17.67		17.67	
	Colonial Penn			1.93	.99										2.92	18.24	21.16	
	Doubleday			30.33		.28		1.00							30.33		30.33	
	MGIC Invest.	10.64			.52							2.49	.75		14.40	16.36	30.76	
	Lowes Cas.	11.50			.80										12.30		12.30	
U1.	AT&T	.18	1.78	.20	.26	.50		.15	.10	.07	.10	.25	.25		3.84	2.50	6.34	
U4.	Southern Co.	.13		2.55	.89	2.43						.07			6.07		6.07	
U7.	So. Calif. Ed.	.41		2.72	.51	.25					1.60	.30			5.79		5.79	
U12	Virginia Electric			5.20	1.05	1.82						.03			8.10		8.10	
U14.	Consumers Power			3.17	.57	1.27						.30			5.31		5.31	
U15.	Middle South Util.	1.73		3.57	.94	.27			4.79			.37		.27	11.94		11.94	
U17.	Florida Power & Light	.61		3.25	2.53	2.56						.48	.63		10.06		10.06	
U18.	Texas Utilities	1.36		2.15	1.80	2.02			3.79			.49	.82	.24	12.67		12.67	
U23.	United Tele. Comm.			4.25	6.26						2.20				12.71		12.71	
U28.	Continental Tele.	.50		4.98	.22	4.05									9.75		9.75	
U30.	Carolina Power			4.62	.91	1.30									6.83		6.83	
U34.	Central & S.W.	1.67			1.68				4.75			1.79			9.89		9.89	
U39.	Houston Light	1.54			1.31				4.74			.35		.51	8.45		8.45	
U50.	Northern Ind.			3.90	1.45							2.03			7.38		7.38	
	50 Largest Banks																	
B1.	Bank America	1.71			.21	.64		1.54	1.35	1.30	1.90	.26			8.91		8.91	
B2.	First National City	5.21	1.01	2.40	2.14	.67	1.52	1.20	.52	1.58	.20	.85	1.60		18.90	4.90	23.80	
B3.	Chase Manhattan	.46			.89	.43			1.95		.70	.87	.34		5.64		5.64	
B4.	J.P. Morgan			3.96	2.43	2.80				.67	.60		1.54		12.00		12.00	

TABLE 5-7 cont.

Rank	1973 Largest Industrials [ranked according to sales]	Morgan Guaranty	Bankers Trust	First National City	United States Trust Co. (A)	Chase Manhattan	Manufacturers Hanover (B)	Mellon National	First National, Chicago (C)	Continental Illinois (D)	Bank of America	Harris Trust (E)	Chemical Bank New York Trust (F)	Girard Bank (G)	Total 13 Largest Banks	All Investment Companies	Total 13 Largest Banks and All Investment Companies
B9.	Continental Ill.	.91			.47	.23				4.85		.20			6.66		6.66
B10.	First Chicago	.46		2.01	1.24	.30			12.97			.10			17.08		17.08
B19.	N.W. Bancorp.	5.31			.84			4.25				1.09			11.49		11.49
B20.	First Bank System	4.10		2.63				4.51	2.76			.23			14.23		14.23
B22.	First Inter. Bancshares	1.62		3.60											5.22		5.22
	50 Largest Financials																
F1.	Aetna Life & Cas.	.46			.51	.19							1.06		2.22	14.50	16.72
F2.	Travelers	2.89		2.69	.87	.13						.40			6.98	15.10	22.08
F3.	Amer. Express	6.45	2.11	1.70	3.53	.81				1.70		.03			16.33		16.33
F15.	Household Finance	.22			.38			1.65	5.10	2.93		.05			10.33		10.33
F21.	U.S. Fidelity & Guar.				.23	1.25					2.30		1.88		5.66		5.66
F27.	Chubb	.58		4.16	2.24	1.25									8.23		8.23
F36.	General Reinsurance	6.90	6.63	1.30	6.00	.19		11.83							32.85		32.85
	Conn. General	6.54			1.75	.13		4.28					.84		13.54		13.54
	50 Largest Retailing																
R1.	Sears	3.52	.69	1.53	1.79	.50	.58	.77	.47	.92	.30	.23	.42		11.72	1.40	13.12
R3.	A & P				11.35										11.35		11.35
R4.	J.C. Penney	5.99	1.29	4.04	1.77	.80		.35		1.45	.30	.61	.53		17.13		17.13
R5.	S.S. Kresge	7.12		4.29	1.89	3.10		1.96		.51		.27			19.14	7.00	26.14
R7.	Marcor			4.20	1.61	2.04						1.61			9.46		9.46
R9.	Federated Dept.	3.35		2.39	.91	.16			8.01		1.00	.15	.52		16.49		16.49
R26.	Assoc. Dry Goods	6.09		4.91	.85				6.17						18.02		18.02
R31.	Broadway-Hale	2.54							4.94						7.48		7.48
R33.	ARA Services	7.42			.21				4.49			1.21			13.33		13.33
	50 Largest Transportation																
T1.	UAL	2.04			.13												6.39
T5.	Southern Pacific	.18		1.32	.39	11.00										8.61	10.50
T5.	American Airlines	2.89			.21	.15											14.50
T10.	Union Pacific	.12			.50	5.00						.40				12.70	14.17
T13.	Delta Airlines				.26	4.22					.70					14.50	22.15
T17.	Consolidated Freights	9.19										2.39					9.19
T18.	N.W. Airlines	1.87			.71	8.10						.47				25.93	37.08

(A) As of July 31, 1973
(B) As of January 8, 1974
(C) As of June 30, 1973
(D) As of June 29, 1973
(E) As of October 1, 1973
(F) As of September 28, 1973
(G) As of September 30, 1973
All other institutions as of December 31, 1973.

I. THE FORCES BEHIND INSTITUTIONAL CONCENTRATION

At least four major factors have produced this remarkable concentration of control in the financial institutions: the extraordinary growth of pension and welfare funds, the substantial accumulation of individual savings represented by investments in investment companies and insurance policies, the change in prevailing concepts of prudent trust investment leading to the substantial investment of trust funds generally in common stocks, and finally, the concentration of the vastly increased volume of institutional funds in a relatively limited number of companies, embracing many of the largest corporations in the nation.

1. The Extraordinary Growth of Pension and Welfare Funds

The growth of private pension and welfare funds is a post-World War II phenomenon. The private plans originally tended to be insured plans in which pension obligations were satisfied by the purchase of annuities from life insurance companies. In such insured plans, pension fund assets ultimately became a part of insurance company assets and represented in insurance company portfolios. Noninsured plans in which pension trust fund assets were invested directly by the fund trustee gradually became more popular, largely because of the greater opportunity to have pension fund resources invested in common stocks. In 1950 the assets of insured and noninsured plans were about equal. By the end of 1972, noninsured plans were almost three times as large as insured plans. Insured plans had total assets of $56.3 billion for the benefit of 12,435,000 million participants while noninsured plans had $154.1 billion of assets and involved 25 million participants.

The massive accumulation of resources by noninsured pension funds and their emergence as one of the major aggregations of capital in the nation has been a notable development. Further, since these noninsured funds are most often managed by the trust departments of commercial banks, the tremendous resources involved have been responsible for the emergence of the trust departments of commercial banks as the largest single class of institutional investor.

2. Changes in Investment Policy and Concentration in Common Stocks

Prior to World War II, trust investments were overwhelmingly represented by fixed-income securities, and equity investments were relatively unimportant. Thus, under almost all state statutes dealing with "legal investments" for fiduciaries, investment in equities was either prohibited or limited to a negligible percentage of the portfolio (in the absence of express authorization in the instrument establishing the estate or trust.) Similarly, statutes rigorously restricted stock investments by life insurance companies to negligible fractions of their total portfolios.

As a result of the continued inflationary pressures since World War II, investment limited to fixed-income securities exposed trust principal to continual erosion in terms of purchasing power. The various state statutes regulating "legal investments" for fiduciaries were progressively amended to increase the portion of the trust principal which could be invested in common stocks. In New York, for example, the prewar prohibition against any equity investments (in the absence of express authorization in the governing instrument) was repealed in 1950 and equity investments were authorized up to 35% of the portfolio. This ceiling was increased to 50% in 1965. In 1970 the ceiling was eliminated entirely and a general investment standard of the "prudent man" was substituted. New York life insurance companies were not allowed to invest in common stocks until 1951 when a 2% overall limit was established. This was later increased to 5%, and all limitations were removed for their pension fund accounts.

The change in investment philosophy of institutional money managers as a result of the greater total yields available in common stocks and inflationary pressures was as important as legislative action. Even prior to the amendments of the statutes, it is more than likely that wide investment discretion had already been permitted under many pension trust instruments.

As a result, the percentage of pension trust portfolios invested in common stocks increased from about 10% in 1945 to 74.5% of market value and 63.7% of book value in 1972 [see Table 5-8]. Since securities convertible into common stocks are not treated as common stocks, the foregoing actually understates the importance of equity securities in the trust portfolios. The decline in stock market values in 1973 and 1974 resulted in a change in investment policies and a movement away from common stocks.

3. Increase in Individual Savings Represented by Common Stocks

The patterns of investment on the part of individuals changed markedly after World War II. Individual savings invested directly or indirectly in common stocks increased tremendously. The number of individuals who owned stocks increased from 6.5 million in 1945 to 30.9 million in 1973. The total value of individual investment portfolios increased from $110.4 billion in 1945 to $907.5 billion in 1972. The same change in investment attitudes was also reflected in the great growth of mutual funds which provided a method for individuals to own common stocks indirectly and to obtain the benefit of professional management. Thus, stocks held by mutual funds increased from

TABLE 5-8
Private Noninsured Pension Funds
(book value, billions)

Year	*Common Stock*	*Total Assets*	*Common Stock as Percentage of Total Assets*
1973	$79.21	$124.36	63.7%
1972	74.58	117.53	63.5%
1971	62.78	106.42	59.0%
1970	51.74	97.01	53.3%
1969	47.86	90.58	52.8%
1968	41.74	83.07	50.2%
1967	34.95	74.24	47.1%
1966	29.07	66.17	43.9%
1965	25.12	59.18	42.4%

Source: *S.E.C. Statistical Bulletin*, Apr. 3, 1974, Vol. 33, No. 14, p. 406.

$7.4 billion in 1956 to a year-end peak of $59.8 billion in 1972 before declining to $42.7 billion in 1973 and even lower in 1974 as a result of the market slump.

4. Concentration of Trust Investments in Relatively Few Corporations

As we have already noted and will later explore in greater detail, the bulk of noninsured pension trust funds is managed by a handful of major commercial banks.

As a result, pension trust funds along with other funds managed by banks or under institutional management generally reflect comparable investment attitudes and have been concentrated in a relatively small number of giant companies. Concentration in institutional hands has been compounded by concentration in the selection of portfolio securities.

J. THE EXTENT OF INSTITUTIONAL CONCENTRATION

1. The Predominance of the Trust Departments of Commercial Banks

The trust departments of the commercial banks have emerged as the most important class of institutional investors. It is estimated that as of the end of 1972, 3,800 trust departments held total assets of $403.6 billion of which $134.5 billion represented employee benefit trusts and $16.0 billion employee benefit agency accounts. Common stock investments accounted for $276.7

billion or about 68% of total assets. This represents about 67% of the total common stock investments of all financial institutions in 1972.

In 1972 the *ten* largest bank trust departments held assets of $135.7 billion of which $76.5 billion represented pension and other employee benefit funds.

	Total Trust Assets	*Pension and other Employee Benefit Funds*
Morgan Guaranty	$ 27.2 billion	$16.9 billion
Bankers Trust	19.9	15.1
First National City	17.2	9.3
U.S. Trust	17.0	3.0
Manufacturers Hanover	10.9	6.2
Mellon	10.5	4.6
Chase Manhattan	9.2	6.0
First National of Chicago	8.4	5.4
Continental Illinois	8.2	4.0
National Bank of Detroit	7.2	5.0
	$135.7 billion	$76.5 billion

The foregoing figures represent enormous increases since 1967. Total trust assets increased by 58% and employee benefit accounts by 62% in the five-year period. The industry leader, Morgan Guaranty, almost doubled in size.

The Bentsen Hearings disclosed that the ten largest banks held almost 30% of Polaroid, almost as much of Xerox, more of Avon Products, and nearly 40% of Walt Disney.

A 1973 study by the American Bankers Association of the twenty-five largest holdings in the portfolios of fifty-two major trust institutions with trust assets in excess of $1 billion each revealed heavy concentration in favored securities:

Corporation	*Number of the 52 Trust Departments in which among 25 Top Holdings*
International Business Machines	52
Eastman Kodak	51
General Motors	51
Exxon	49
General Electric	48
Sears Roebuck	41
Xerox	38
Texaco	33
Minnesota Mining & Manufacturing	32

Aside from heavy concentration in the highly favored issues, there was substantial diversification. Thus, only eighty-seven securities appeared on three or more lists. The thirty-first most popular stock, for example, appeared on only ten lists. Furthermore, the American Bankers Association Study found that the trust departments of major size (assets of $750 million or more) held stocks in an average of 2,567 corporations. Nevertheless, concentration in institutional favorites is a reality. The Bentsen Hearings disclosed that a single security, International Business Machines, represented 8% of the trust assets of Morgan Guaranty, 9% of the trust assets of Chemical Bank New York Trust Company, and almost 10% of those of The Bank of New York.

The regulatory restrictions on bank activities under the National Banking Act or the various state statutes relate largely to the solvency of the institutions and do not apply to the management of fiduciary accounts. Thus, the largest source of institutional concentration has been unregulated. There is no statutory or administrative restriction on the percentage of stock of any company which a bank trust department may hold in its fiduciary accounts or the percentage of trust assets which may be invested in any single portfolio company. Accordingly, as noted, ownership in portfolio companies favored by the banks as promising investments has reached high levels.

The concentration of such holdings in a relatively limited number of companies, the continued interest of the banks in further purchases for the investment of new funds, and the resulting high price/earnings ratios for the favored few aroused considerable attention in 1972-73 in what was called the "two-tier structure" in the stock market. This was the curious phenomenon of a small group of stocks, almost exclusively institutional favorites, selling at relatively high price/earnings ratios, while the rest of the market sold at unusually low price/earnings ratios. Although most of this differential was eliminated in the 1973-74 decline, some difference in price/earnings ratios has continued.

In recognition of this phenomenon, Senator Bentsen's subcommittee in 1974 recommended enactment of statutory restrictions on the extent of institutional ownership in any portfolio company as well as periodic reporting requirements. It should be noted, however, that the primary motivation of the subcommittee for limiting concentration in a relatively small group of portfolio companies was its desire to develop greater buying support for equity securities generally rather than concern with the existence of potential control by banks and other financial institutions over portfolio companies.

Bank investment policies for trust accounts are subject to the traditional legal limitations on trustees to act prudently. While this may tend to restrict the amount of investment of any single trust account in any single portfolio company, the "prudent investment" rule has only remote application to the aggregate amount of investments of all the trust accounts of a bank in a particular portfolio company. It is, of course, conceivable that the lack of liquidity resulting from an outsized aggregate position in a particular portfolio company might result in loss in the event that the bank decided to dispose of the holding and thus raise a question whether the "prudent investment" rule had been violated. This possibility, however, appears to be a legal restraint of relatively remote significance and clearly has not operated to prevent substantial concentration in particular securities. Furthermore, in many trust agreements, the bank or other trustee is released from normal fiduciary standards and is liable only for willful wrongdoing or gross negligence.

2. Investment Companies.

Although much less important than bank trust departments, investment companies are major institutional investors, representing about one-quarter of the total holdings of all financial institutions. As part of the pattern of the diversion of individual savings to common stock investment, investment companies, in spite of the scandals and abuses of the 1920's, grew from $3.2 billion in 1945 to $79.6 billion in 1972 [see Table 5-9]. Professor Soldofsky was encouraged to estimate that total investment company assets would increase to $258 billion in 1980 and $1,730 billion in 2000, but it is very doubtful that these estimates will be realized.

TABLE 5-9
Investment Companies
(billions)

Year	*Common Stock*	*Total Assets*	*Common Stock as Percentage of Total Assets*
1972	$64.0	$79.6	80.4%
1971	57.9	72.3	80.1%
1970	48.4	61.5	78.7%
1969	49.8	61.8	80.6%
1968	57.0	69.5	82.0%
1967	49.2	58.4	84.2%
1966	36.2	45.3	79.9%
1965	40.0	47.0	85.1%

Source: *S.E.C. Statistical Bulletin,* 1973, p. 867.

Investment companies were adversely affected by individual investor disenchantment with the stock market as a result of a 1973-74 decline of more than 35% in the Dow Jones industrial averages. At their year-end peak in 1972, mutual funds had $59.8 billion of assets held for the benefit of 10,635,000 accounts, representing an estimated 8,500,000 individual shareholders and 260,000 institutions. With the depressed conditions in stock market prices, the confidence of individual investors in equities was badly shaken, and redemptions after 1972 substantially exceeded sales. By May 1974 reflecting major declines in market values and aggregate net redemptions of $3.1 billion in excess of sales, net assets had declined to $41.1 billion.

Investment companies are divided into two classes:

(a) *Open-end companies.* These companies are better known as "mutual funds". They dominate the industry and engage in a continuous offering of additional shares to investors. They also redeem outstanding shares from existing holders at the net asset value of the fund on the date of redemption.

(b) *Closed-end companies.* These companies have a fixed number of outstanding shares. Like any other corporation there may be occasional offerings of additional shares to investors. While the company may repurchase outstanding shares, the shareholder has no right of redemption. The shareholder desiring to dispose of his shares must do so by selling them on the securities markets, as in the case of other types of corporate shares. For this reason, the larger closed-end companies are listed on the New York Stock Exchange. The market value of closed-end investment companies usually reflects a significant discount from net asset value, although on occasion certain popular companies have sold at a premium.

Investment companies—whether open-end or closed-end—are further divided into two types: "diversified" and "nondiversified." Open-end diversified companies dominate the four classes of investment companies. In 1968, for example, they represented 87% of the assets of all investment companies.

The Investment Companies Act requires that 75% of the assets of "diversified" investment companies must comply with the limitation that not more than 5% of total assets may be invested in the securities of any one company nor represent more than 10% of the voting securities of any company; the remaining 25% is not restricted. Although "nondiversified" companies may exceed such limitations, important income tax advantages are lost. Almost all open-end and closed-end investment companies holding almost half of total closed-end assets are registered as diversified companies.

The Internal Revenue Code adopts the same 5% and 10% limitations for 50% of the assets of investment companies as the basis for qualification as "regulated investment companies" required for favorable tax treatment;[5] the remaining 50% is free of restrictions (except that not more than 25% of total assets may be invested in securities of any one company or any two controlled companies in the same or similar business). Professor Soldofsky points out that a number of states, including Ohio, Wisconsin, and

[5]A regulated investment company which distributes at least 90% of all interest, dividends, and short-term capital gains as dividends to shareholders escapes federal tax liability on the distributed amounts; the company also escapes federal tax on all long-term capital gains distributed to shareholders. Shareholders are taxable on the long-term capital gains at capital gains rates and on the other distributions at ordinary rates. They thereby achieve the doubly happy result of avoiding tax at the corporate level and of capital gains treatment on long-term capital gains at the shareholder level. These advantages create substantial pressures on investment companies to achieve "diversified" status.

California, apply the 5-10% limitations on all investment company assets, superseding the 25% "free assets" clause in the Federal act.

Among other things, the Investment Companies Act of 1940 has accomplished complete disclosure of investment portfolios so that, unlike the trust departments of commercial banks, full portfolio information of investment companies is available on a quarterly basis. It is worth noting that there is no opposition whatsoever by the industry to such disclosure or any contention that it weakens the competitive position of companies or violates confidentiality. The industry does not appear to have suffered from the "fish bowl" climate in which it has been operating. The trust departments of those commercial banks that are still reluctant to release detailed information on their portfolios might well study the experience of the investment companies.

Although during the consideration of the Investment Companies Act of 1940, the Congress discussed the establishment of a $150,000,000 maximum size for diversified investment companies, this provision was not included in the statute as finally enacted. Similarly, the Act does not restrict the indirect control exercised by investment management companies. Such companies are not prohibited from managing more than one investment company, and there is no restriction on the aggregate amount of voting stock or securities in portfolio companies held by the different investment companies managed by any single management company. Thus, the statutory restraints do not prevent the concentration of investments by investment companies as a whole in a relatively small group of portfolio companies. Investment company portfolio concentration arises in two ways.

First, a number of giant mutual fund complexes are managed by a single investment advisor. In 1968 the largest single complex, run by Investors Diversified Services, included five separate funds with net assets of $6.7 billion. The four largest complexes managed an aggregate of $17.1 billion in 25 different funds or approximately 30.9% of total fund assets; the ten largest complexes controlled about $28.9 billion or 52.2% of mutual fund assets. Although allowance must be made for the different investment objectives of the various funds within the same complex, it is apparent that to the extent that investments with the same characteristics are sought by more than one fund within the group, the common investment advisor will tend to utilize the same securities in the various funds which it manages.

Second, as in the case of the banks, concentration also results from common investment behavior of different investment advisors. Certain industries or companies become widely favored, and "fads" in investments develop. Movement of investment money into certain securities contributes to market activity and rising prices, which in turn attracts further investment interest. A "following" develops in which new institutional purchasers are encouraged by the disclosed purchases of other institutions. A common pattern of investment interest emerges. The net result of this pattern is a significant concentration of investment company holdings in selected companies.

While the favored portfolio securities are often companies of very substantial size, they rarely include the largest companies in the nation. The heaviest investment company concentration tends to involve so-called "special situations." Thus, the ten companies with the heaviest concentration as of December 31, 1973 included the following:

Company	*Percentage of Stock Held by Investment Companies*	*Number of Investment Companies Involved*
Norton Simon	64.2%	46
McDonald's	36.7%	79
Great Western Financial	30.5%	37
Northwest Airlines	25.8%	34
Weyerhauser	25.1%	45
Walter Kidde	24.4%	12
Digital Equipment	21.9%	62
Trans World Airlines	20.0%	26
CMI Investment	19.2%	16
American Broadcasting	18.9%	30

Source: Wiesenberger, *Investment Companies* (1974 ed.) pp. 97-99.

In spite of such heavy positions in the foregoing companies, investment companies as a group do not have major positions in the largest of the megacorporations. The following table shows the relatively small percentages owned by investment companies as of December 31, 1973 in the ten Largest NYSE companies (ranked according to market value of their shares).

Company	*Percentage of Stock Held by Investment Companies*	*Number of Investment Companies Involved*
International Business Machines	4.9%	404
American Telephone & Telegraph	2.5%	193
General Motors	2.6%	179
Exxon	4.8%	231
Sears Roebuck	3.8%	97
Eastman Kodak	2.7%	191
General Electric	2.8%	167
Xerox	7.1%	193
Texaco	4.7%	149
Minnesota Mining and Manufacturing	3.0%	96

It should be noted that the stock held by investment companies in the major corporations in contrast to the "special situations" not only represents much smaller percentages but the smaller aggregate holdings are spread much more widely among the institutions in question.

3. Insurance Companies.

Insurance companies fall into two classes—life insurance and property and casualty—which are subject to different systems of regulatory controls over investments and which therefore present different investment patterns.

Life insurance. The life insurance industry is by far the largest branch of the insurance industry. Total assets in 1973 aggregated $252.1 billion of which the five largest companies alone accounted for approximately $108 billion (or 40%).

New York has exercised decisive influence over the regulation of life insurance investments since its regulations apply not only to companies organized under the laws of New York but to all life insurance companies doing business in the state. According to Soldofsky, New York-licensed companies hold four-fifths of the assets of the life insurance industry.

Following the celebrated Armstrong investigation of 1905 in which Charles Evans Hughes was counsel, New York prohibited all stock investments by life insurance companies. The prohibition against preferred stock was removed in 1928. In 1951, life insurance companies were authorized to invest up to 2% of total assets in common stock; in 1957, this maximum was increased to 5%[6] (or 50% of capital and surplus or policy holder surplus, if smaller). The Insurance Law was subsequently amended to provide separate investment rules for pension fund accounts with no ceiling on common stock investments for such accounts.

With changing statutes and investment attitudes, stock ownership by life insurance companies increased to a significant level—$26.8 billion in 1973—which, however, represented only 10.6% of their total portfolios [see Table 5-10]. Of the $26.8 billion total stockholdings, the five largest companies held about $10.4 billion (or about 40%). Prudential, the leader, had $4.4 billion of its $34.9 billion total assets invested in common stocks.

Property and Casualty Insurance Companies. These companies represent a much smaller portion of the industry with total assets of $75.9 billion in 1972 in contrast to life insurance company assets of $239.4 billion at that time. On the other hand, they have been subject to much less severe statutory restrictions, and approximately 25% of their total assets has been invested in common stocks [see Table 5-11]. As a result, for many years, the common stock investments of the relatively small property and casualty insurance industry exceeded the common stock investments of the much larger life insurance industry. Life insurance company equity portfolios, however, increased at a much greater rate and by 1970 exceeded the common stocks held by the property and casualty companies.

[6] In addition, there is a free assets clause under which companies may invest up to 2% of assets without restriction, including common stocks.

TABLE 5-10
Life Insurance Companies
(billions)

Year	*Stock*	*Total Assets*	*Stock as Percentage of Total Assets*
1973	$26.3	$252.1	10.6%
1972	21.4	239.4	8.9%
1971	16.8	222.1	7.6%
1970	11.9	207.3	5.7%
1969	10.3	197.2	5.2%
1968	10.0	188.6	5.3%
1967	7.8	177.8	4.4%
1966	6.0	167.5	3.6%
1965	6.3	158.9	4.0%

Sources: *1973 Life Insurance Fact Book, Federal Reserve Bulletin,* July 1974; S.E.C. Statistical Bulletin, 1973, p. 867.

TABLE 5-11
Property-Casualty Insurance Companies
(billions)

Year	*Stock*	*Total Assets*	*Stock as Percentage of Total Assets*
1972	$18.0	$75.9	23.7%
1971	14.6	67.3	21.7%
1970	11.7	58.6	20.0%
1969	11.9	52.4	22.7%
1968	13.2	51.2	25.8%
1967	11.7	46.6	25.1%
1966	9.9	42.3	23.4%
1965	10.9	41.8	26.1%

Source: *S.E.C. Statistical Bulletin,* 1973, p. 867.

The New York statute restricts portfolio concentration in the securities of any single company to a maximum of 2% of an issuer's stock for both life insurance and property and casualty insurance companies. Although the portfolios of the individual insurance companies are thus limited, the cumulative holdings of the entire industry increase the total portfolio concentration of financial institutions generally.

4. Noninsured Private Pension and Welfare Funds.

Noninsured private pension and welfare funds have grown enormously from a mere $2 billion with $212 million in common stocks in 1945 to $154.3 billion ($117.5 billion book value) in 1972 of which $113.4 billion ($74.6

billion book value) was invested in common stocks for the benefit of approximately 25 million participants. With the market decline in 1973, the total value of noninsured private pension funds dropped to $129.9 billion ($124.4 billion book value) of which $88 billion ($79.2 book value) was invested in common stocks.

With pension fund receipts continuing to outdistance payments, the increase in noninsured pension funds shows no signs of abating. According to the *Federal Reserve Board-Federal Deposit Insurance Corporation Study of Trust Assets of Insured Commercial Banks-1972,* employee benefit trusts managed by banks were increasing at about 20% per annum in the period from 1970-1972. Professor Soldofsky estimated on the basis of much lower growth rates that total pension fund assets would increase to $269 billion in 1980 and to $2.362 trillion by the year 2000.

The Federal Employee Retirement Income Security Act of 1974 introduced a fresh element with its restrictions on forfeiture of participants' interests and a consequent increase in the financial costs incurred by the employer. This may well retard the growth rate in fund assets. Further, the erosion of equity values in the 1973-74 market decline swept away, at least for the time being, billions of dollars of market value.

The New York Stock Exchange statistics disclose a comparable increase in NYSE-listed stock held by nongovernmental pension funds from $500 million in 1949 to $104.5 billion in 1972. By 1973, these pension funds held 12.1% of all NYSE stocks. This statistic, however, obscures the concentration significance of pension fund holdings because the 12.1% is related to the aggregate value of the approximately 1,500 listed companies on the Exchange. In fact, pension fund equity investments are not made across the board in NYSE-listed securities but are concentrated in a limited number of selected stocks. The pension fund share of that selective group of stocks must substantially exceed 10%.

This process of pension-fund concentration is compounded three-fold. First, most pension fund trust assets are held by relatively few funds. Professor Soldofsky estimated that in 1968, 16.8% of the funds with assets over $20 million owned 83.6% of all pension fund assets. Second, the bulk of pension trust funds are managed by a small number of major banks. In 1972 ten major banks controlled an estimated 70% of all corporate trusteed funds. Third, this small number of bank trustees tend to invest in similar securities. The compounded result is a concentration of trust assets in relatively few funds managed by a small number of banks tending to follow the same investment philosophy and to invest in a relatively small group of the same portfolio companies. The inevitable product is a high degree of concentrated ownership of the megacorporations.

Although the overwhelming bulk of pension fund assets is under the investment control of the major banks, there are a number of major noninsured funds which are not managed by banks. This restricted group includes the giant funds of concerns such as General Electric, Sears Roebuck, and United States Steel, each of which has assets in excess of several billion dollars and a number of union-administered funds, which tend to be smaller.

While the extent of pension-fund concentration has attracted considerable attention, a factor of even greater significance is concentration of the management (and in most cases, the voting) of such funds in the trust departments of a relative handful of major commercial banks, together with the other personal and corporate trust portfolios managed by such banks.

The absence of regulation or effective disclosure with respect to pension fund portfolios is a striking feature of the past. As we have seen, the banks which manage most of the funds are not subject to regulatory restrictions or controls over their management or investment policies. Although the Federal Pension and Welfare Plans Disclosure Act (repealed in 1974) required disclosure of total assets and aggregate holdings of pension funds, the statute required no information as to the composition of the portfolio. This constitutes a severe barrier to any comprehensive analysis of the overall impact of the pension funds with respect to portfolio concentration. The information that is available arises from the salutary voluntary disclosures of an increasing number of the major banks led by the First National City Bank and Morgan Guaranty Trust and information obtained and made available by Senate Subcommittees headed by Senators Bentsen, Metcalf, and Muskie. The recalcitrance of some of the remaining banks to make full disclosure led to the introduction of legislation by Senator Bentsen in the 1974 Congress applicable to all banks and other financial institutions and to a 1974 decision by the Comptroller of the Currency applicable to the national banks under his supervision to make disclosure of bank investment holdings and transactions mandatory. Details on the portfolios of pension and welfare funds which are not managed by banks are not available.

The Federal Employee Retirement Income Security Act of 1974 (which repealed the Pension and Welfare Plans Disclosure Act) requires annual disclosure of all investment assets, but reporting under this statute will not begin until 1976. Aside from disclosure, the 1974 Act restricts investment in employer securities and property to 10% of the assets of the fund and requires diversification of the portfolio, but it contains no restriction whatsoever over the amount of investment in portfolio companies.

Tax exemption is an essential element of the pension or welfare fund. The provisions of the Internal Revenue Code governing the qualification of such funds as tax-exempt constitute the other source of statutory restriction on their portfolios. These restrictions are expressed almost entirely in terms of self-dealing. So long as securities of the employer corporation establishing the welfare fund are not involved, the Code imposes no controls. Even where employer securities are involved, the statute deals only with the terms, not the relative or absolute size, of the investment. The Code establishes no ceiling on the percentage of fund assets that may be invested in any single company or on the percentage of the stock of any company that may be owned by any fund.

5. State and Local Government Pension Funds.

Pension funds for state and local government employees represent an increasingly important source of common stock investments. As recently as 1965, these funds held aggregate common stocks of only $1.4 billion, but by 1972 their common stock portfolios amounted to $13.7 billion, or 19.0% of their total portfolios [see Table 5-12].

TABLE 5-12
State and Local Government Pension Funds
(billions)

Year	*Stock*	*Total Assets*	*Stock as Percentage of Total Assets*
1972	$13.7	$72.1	19.0%
1971	10.8	64.8	16.7%
1970	7.6	58.0	13.1%
1969	5.5	51.2	10.7%
1968	3.8	46.2	8.2%
1967	2.6	41.5	6.3%
1966	1.9	36.9	5.1%
1965	1.4	33.1	4.2%

Source: *S.E.C. Statistical Bulletin,* 1973, p. 867.

Professor Soldofsky believes that in coming years, state and local government pension funds will experience the greatest growth rates of all financial institutions and estimates that their stock holdings will increase to $37 billion in 1980 and $357 billion in 2000. This growth has been encouraged by the progressive liberalization of statutory restrictions which had originally prohibited equity investments or restricted them to a negligible portion of the portfolio of the funds. New York now permits 10% and California, 15% of such portfolios to be invested in common stocks.

Soldofsky estimates that by 1980 state and local funds will have significant levels of concentration in portfolio companies. He is particularly concerned at the prospect of such shares being voted by political appointees. The introduction of political considerations in the investment, sale, and voting of corporate stock has important implications with respect to political influence over major corporations. This possible future development represents, however, a markedly different problem than the current concentration of stock of portfolio companies in the banks or private financial institutions.

6. Tax-exempt Institutions

Foundations, private universities, and churches have a surprisingly large amount of wealth, but the total, large as it may be from some points of view, is relatively small in comparison with other institutional investors.

Although the New York Stock Exchange provides data on the holdings of listed shares of tax-exempt institutions, accurate statistics on total assets and total stock of these institutions are not available. Information about church wealth is particularly weak. The extent of the total security investments of foundations, universities, and churches has been estimated as follows:

	Year of Data	*Portfolio Assets (billion)*	*Common Stocks*
Foundations	1972	$39.5	$28.0
Universities	1972	15	10.0
Churches	1969	3	N.A.

Sources: *SEC Statistical Bulletin*, 1973, p. 867; Martin A. Larson, Church Wealth and Business Income (Philosophical Library 1965).

The holdings of nonprofit institutions in NYSE stocks increased ten-fold from $3.2 billion in 1949 to $39.2 billion in 1972 [see Table 5-13].

TABLE 5-13
NYSE-listed Common Stocks Held by Nonprofit Institutions (billions)

	Universities	*Foundations*	*Other Non-Profits*	*Total*
1972	$8.7	$18.7	$11.8	$39.2
1971	7.8	14.3	10.1	32.2
1970	6.9	12.2	9.0	28.1
1969	6.8	13.9	8.9	29.6
1967	6.0	11.3	8.6	25.9
1962	3.5	6.7	5.0	15.2
1959	3.0	5.4	4.4	12.8
1949	1.1	1.1	1.0	3.2

Source: NYSE, *1973 Fact Book.*

Foundations. Foundations are important institutional investors but occupy a relatively minor position in comparison with investment companies and insurance companies, let alone bank trust departments. According to the 1971 Foundation Directory, the most recent study, there were 5,454 foundations (with assets of $500,000 or grants of $25,000 in the year of record) with total assets of $25.18 billion. The 20,000 small foundations had little aggregate significance. The Peterson Commission on Foundations and Private Philanthropy ("Peterson Report") pointed out that the estimates of foundation portfolios were understated because they were based on cost rather than market. For example, the Peterson Report noted that the assets of the Irvine Foundation, which were carried at $6 million for book purposes, had a market value of $100 million or higher.

There was a high degree of concentration. The sixteen leading foundations held $11.03 billion (or 44%) of all foundation assets. Of these, two (Ford with $3.4 billion and Johnson with $1.2 billion) were over $1 billion and 6 others were larger than $500 million. Within this group, 71% of total assets was represented by stock. Table 5-14 sets forth the growth of foundation portfolios.

TABLE 5-14

Foundations
(billions)

Year	*Stock*	*Total Assets*	*Stock as Percentage of Total Assets*
1972	$28.0	$39.5	70.9%
1971	24.5	36.5	67.1%
1970	21.6	32.0	67.5%
1969	19.6	29.5	66.4%
1968	21.6	31.5	68.6%
1967	19.8	29.9	66.2%
1966	18.3	28.3	64.7%
1965	19.1	28.7	66.6%

Source: *S.E.C. Statistical Bulletin,* 1973, p. 867.

There is greater significance to foundation stockholdings than their absolute size. Contributions of "control" stock to tax-exempt foundations have been a well-recognized method of simultaneously perpetuating family control of corporations and sidestepping federal estate tax. The 1971 Staff Report on the Fifteen Largest United States Foundations by the Subcommittee on Domestic Finance of the House Committee on Banking and Currency ("Foundation Study") regarded the use of foundations to maintain control of business enterprises as one of the major inducements for their creation. The great foundations have typically been founded with substantial endowments consisting primarily of the shares of the family company which made the donors wealthy. The Peterson Report found that "control" stock represented 44% of the contributions to all foundations and a remarkable 70% of all contributions to foundations with assets of $100 million or more.

According to the Foundation Study, in 1968 major foundations held dominant positions in seven major corporations as a result of controlling blocs of stock contributed by their founders.

Foundation	*Company*	*Market Value of Common Stock Held*	*Percentage of Common Stock*
Duke	Duke Power	$498,592,575	56%
Lilly	Eli Lilly Co.	579, 058,795	23%
Pew	Sun Oil Co.	431,084,475	21%
Kellogg	Kellogg Co.	388,897,160	50%
Kresge	S.S. Kresge Co.	240,116,550	18%
Hartford	Great Atlantic & Pacific Tea	296,810,175	33%
Moody	American National Insurance	171,075,889	35%

In addition, the Danforth Foundation held $97.4 million or 23% of Ralston Purina Stock, and Ford Foundation held $1.7 billion market value of *nonvoting* Class A stock of Ford Motor Company. Although the Foundation stock was nonvoting, the Ford family retained Class B stock which involved only 6.6% of the equity but entitled the family to 40% of the voting power of the company. The common stock held by the public carried the remaining 60% of the voting power. The Foundation holdings thus permitted the continuation of family working control. The avoidance of the potential heavy estate taxes that would have otherwise been payable on the death of family members meant that the shares could be kept in the Ford Foundation instead of being sold to the public to raise funds for the payment of death taxes. The Foundation gradually reduced its Ford holdings and in 1974 sold all its remaining Ford stock back to Ford Motor Company under the pressures of the Tax Reform Act of 1969.

Universities. Universities are less significant than foundations. Their aggregate portfolios are much smaller, and the pattern of "control stock" ownership is entirely absent. According to a 1973 study of the National Association of College and University Business Officers, the aggregate market value of securities held by American colleges and universities in their endowment funds was between $15 and $16 billion. Of this, approximately two-thirds or about $10 billion was in common stock [see Table 5-15].

Harvard University has the largest university portfolio by far. On June 30, 1973 its portfolio was valued at $1.36 billion, of which $853 million was invested in common stocks. Yet, its largest single equity holding, International Business Machines, with a market value of $77.8 million was only an insignificant 0.17% of the total shares outstanding. Although it was reported to be a major shareholder in Middle South Utilities, its holding of 555,000 shares amounted to only 1.375% of the shares outstanding.

In areas of social reform in general and "public interest" shareholder proposals in particular, universities, churches, and foundations play

TABLE 5-15
Educational Endowments
(billions)

Year	*Stock*	*Total Assets*	*Stock as Percentage of Total Assets*
1972	10.0	15.0	66.7%
1971	8.3	13.6	61.0%
1970	7.5	13.0	57.7%
1969	7.4	13.0	56.9%
1968	8.0	13.6	58.8%
1967	7.6	13.1	58.0%
1966	6.1	11.1	55.0%
1965	6.9	11.7	59.0%

Source: *S.E.C. Statistical Bulletin*, 1973, p. 867.

important roles. This, however, arises from their public significance which makes their attitudes newsworthy, not from their economic position.

Churches. Church wealth is much more difficult to ascertain. Martin A. Larson estimated total church assets in 1969 at $164 billion of which securities constituted only $3 billion (Jewish congregations excluded). It is obviously not a significant element from the financial point of view. On the other hand, even more than the universities and foundations, church groups assert a moral influence over corporate policy that has been increasing and may be expected to become even more influential in the future.

Although universities' and churches' investments are not subject to restrictive federal or state statutes or constraints—other than general rules applicable to investments by fiduciaries generally—the Tax Reform Act of 1969 imposed restrictions on so-called private foundations. These included for the first time a mild limitation on concentration of foundation assets in particular securities. Subject to certain exceptions, no tax-exempt private foundation may own more than 20% (or a lesser amount after deduction of shares held by certain disqualified persons) of the voting shares of any company.

Except for the so-called one-stock foundations, it is plain that the tax-exempt philanthropic, educational, and religious institutions do not significantly contribute to overall concentration of institutional investments leading to control of portfolio companies.

7. Voting Power and Institutional Concentration.

Ownership of equity securities in and of itself, without regard to voting rights, may create the power base of institutional influence over the policies of portfolio companies. Management will obviously listen carefully to the suggestions of an institutional investor holding substantial amounts of the corporation's common stock, without inquiring whether the institution's role is restricted to portfolio management or whether it includes voting power as well. Nevertheless, the ultimate exercise of control—selection or change of the Board of Directors—rests on voting power. The tabulations of equity ownership in selected giant corporations by institutional trustees give a distorted picture when they are not correlated with voting power.

The locus of voting power depends on the terms of the trust instrument. In many cases the institutional trustee has sole voting power; in others it shares voting power with co-fiduciaries; and in still others, it has no voting power at all.

It is unfortunate that only a few of the major banks have disclosed information with respect to voting power. Most major banks which provide information on their portfolio holdings have not disclosed the extent to which they either share voting power with others or have no voting power over trust investments. It is characteristic of the continuing penchant for secrecy that this information, which could only be helpful from the bank's point of view, is withheld from the public.

The report of the Subcommittee on Domestic Finance of the House Committee on Banking and Currency, *Commercial Banks and Their Trust Activities: Emerging Influence on the American Economy* (1968), disclosed that forty-three banks managing 13,598 employee plans had sole voting rights over stock investments in 11,087 or about 81.5% of the accounts. The Institutional Investor Study similarly concluded that banks had sole voting rights over about 75% of the stock held in employee benefit accounts and also had sole voting power over about 55% of the stock held in personal trust and estate accounts.

A review of the voting power distribution of the First National City Bank over its 100 Largest holdings at the end of 1973 reveals the extreme limits over which sole voting power may vary:

Percent of Sole Voting Power	*Number of Portfolio Companies*
Over 90%	10
80% – 90%	8
70% – 80%	31
60% – 70%	20
50% – 60%	8
40% – 50%	4
30% – 40%	4
20% – 30%	5
10% – 20%	4
Under 10%	6
	100

It is apparent that with respect to any particular security, the extent of sole voting power can range from 100% to zero and that an individual analysis will be required in every case.

There is a further limitation on the banks' voting power over portfolio securities in corporate trust accounts that arises from the realities of the situation, whatever the provisions of the trust agreement. The trustee is appointed and usually subject to removal by the corporate employer. In matters in which the corporation is interested, it may be expected that its views will carry heavy weight with the bank.

In the case of other financial institutional investors, the problem of shared voting power does not arise. In the very limited area of "public interest" shareholder proxy proposals, there may be some exceptions. At least one major investment company, Dreyfus Leverage Fund, consulted its shareholders for guidance on voting its General Motors shares on the proposals of Campaign GM. Similarly, many universities, including Harvard, Yale, Princeton, Stanford, Cornell, and Boston University, have established advisory committees with faculty, student, and on occasion alumni representation to advise trustees on voting on "public interest" proposals. The responsibility for a decision, however, remains with the trustees. This development is not particularly significant at the present time in view of the relatively small size of the overall holdings of the institutions involved and because the "public interest" proposals in question do not typically relate to fundamental financial matters or the election of the Board as a whole. It may have more significance in the future if the increasing politicization of the corporation leads to the nomination of "public interest" directors or competing slates.

8. "Pass-through" Voting in Employee Benefit Plans

Employee stock purchase, profit-sharing, savings, and self-administered noninsured pension plans present a different picture where shares of the employer corporation are concerned. In a significant number of cases, such funds are the largest single holder of the employer corporations's stock.

Under such plans the employer stock is held in an employee trust fund and voted by the trustees administering the fund. These trustees are typically the trust departments of major commercial banks, which are sensitive to the wishes of the employer corporation, or in some cases, individuals associated with the senior management of the employer company.

In view of the evident conflict of interest involved in voting company shares for the election of directors by trustees, who have either been selected by directors or are themselves directors, it has become increasingly common for the trustees of such funds to "pass through" the voting rights to the beneficiaries (or the vested beneficiaries) of the plan in question. The Bankers Trust Company's *1972 Survey of Savings and Thrift Plans* and the Gilbert

Brothers' *Annual Report* for 1972 list a total of 152 major corporations with employee benefit plans holding employer stock, which utilize "pass through" voting in whole or part. These impressive totals reflect the wise policy of the New York Stock Exchange Department of Stock List, which since 1961 has pressed corporations to authorize "pass through" voting where 1% or more of the outstanding stock is held by a trust fund for employees. The New York Stock Exchange action followed Congressional exposure of abuses in this area and the adoption of pass-through voting procedures by Exxon in 1957 and Sears, Roebuck in 1958.

Sears, Roebuck and Company is perhaps the most well-known example of this development. As of December 31, 1972, 30,735,251 shares (or approximately 20% of the outstanding stock) with a market value of $3.5 billion were held by the Sears Savings and Profit Sharing Pension Fund for the benefit of 224,142 employee participants, subject to "pass through" voting. This is in addition to substantial shares previously distributed to employees upon retirement; for example, in 1972 alone, almost 3,200,000 shares (or approximately 2% of the outstanding shares) were so distributed. It should be noted that employees retiring with 25 to 30 years of service during 1972 received on the average a distribution of $114,832 in cash and Sears stock.

Under the Sears' "pass through" program, proxy materials are mailed by the trustee of the Sears plan to all beneficiaries with five years of service or more. The beneficiaries have proportional voting rights that reflect their length of service and vote their respective interests by completing a ballot that is returned to Price, Waterhouse and Company, accountants for Sears. Price, Waterhouse preserves the confidentiality of each participant's vote and certifies only the aggregate totals to the trustees who vote the shares held by them accordingly. Shares not voted by the beneficiaries are voted in the proportions represented by the voted shares.

Other corporations with employee benefit plans with major holdings of employer stock that provide for "pass through" voting include:

Company	*Number of Shares Held by Fund*	*Number of Outstanding Shares, 1973*	*Percentage of Outstanding Shares, 1973*
Bendix	1,331,000	12,135,000	10.6%
Broadway-Hale Stores	1,828,024	16,665,000	10.9%
Burlington Industries	2,832,000	27,262,000	10.7%
Caterpillar Tractor	2,717,700	57,173,000	4.7%
Ford	9,170,619	*	*
General Dynamics	1,200,000	10,464,000	11.4%

*Data are as of March 31, 1972. Only 7,469,000 of the shares or 11.1% were vested and voted on a "pass through" basis. As noted, the Ford common shares possess only 60% of the total voting power.

Company	Number of Shares Held by Fund	Number of Outstanding Shares, 1973	Percentage of Outstanding Shares, 1973
General Motors	10,231,467	285,922,900	3.6%*
International Harvester	1,664,216	27,772,000	6.2
McDonnell Douglas	4,720,839	37,156,000	12.5
Phillips Petroleum	5,484,091	75,386,711	7.0*
TRW	1,323,638	75,709,000	5.1
Textron	2,952,322	27,284,000	10.8*
United States Steel	5,953,347	54,169,462	11.0*

*1972 Data.

Some of the larger holdings may possess the potential concentrated power to influence corporate policy, provided that the participants concerned are prepared to vote in concert. Although this potential power has never been exercised, its very existence is a factor of significance. It seems likely that sooner or later unions in one or more of these enterprises will endeavor to induce members to vote their shares for shareholder proposals furthering union objectives or to elect representatives to the board. If such unions can successfully mobilize their member-participants, particularly where cumulative voting is applicable, the balance of power in industrial relations in such concerns could be profoundly affected.

In summary, the heavy concentration of institutional stock ownership is startling and may be expected to increase substantially. In the next chapter, we consider the significance of this development.

BIBLIOGRAPHY

American Assembly, *The Future of Foundations,* Englewood Cliffs, N.J.: Prentice-Hall, Inc. 1973.

Bankers Trust Company, *1972 Study of Employee Savings and Thrift Plans,* New York, 1972.

Baum, David J. and Ned B. Stiles, *The Silent Partners: Institutional Investors and Corporate Control.* Syracuse, N.Y.: Syracuse University Press, 1965.

Berle, Adolf A. Jr., *Power Without Property,* op. cit.

Berle, Adolf A. and Gardiner C. Means, *The Modern Corporation and Private Property,* op. cit.

Chevalier, Jean-Marie, *"The Problem of Control in Large American Corporations",* The Antitrust Bulletin, XIV (1969), 163.

Civil Aeronautics Board, *Thirty Largest Stockholders of United States Certified Air Carriers and Summary of Stock Holdings of Financial Institutions,* Washington, D.C.: Government Printing Office, 1974.

Commission on Foundations and Private Philanthropy Report and Recommendations, *Foundations, Private Giving and Public Policy.* Chicago: University of Chicago Press, 1970.

Eisenberg, Melvin, "The Legal Roles of Shareholders and Management in Modern Corporate Decision Making", op. cit.

Enstam, Raymond A. and Harry P. Kamen, "Control and the Institutional Investor" 23 *Business Lawyer* 289 (1968).

Federal Reserve System—Federal Deposit Insurance Corporation, *Trust Assets of Insured Commercial Banks—1972.*

Gilbert, Lewis and John Gilbert, *Thirty-Fourth Annual Report on Stockholder Activities at Corporation Meetings.* New York: 1973.

Gordon, Robert A., *Business Leadership in the Large Corporation.* Berkeley: University of California Press, 1961.

Harbrecht, Paul J., *Pension Funds and Economic Power.* New York: Twentieth Century Fund, 1959.

Hearings on Financial Markets before the Subcommittee on Financial Markets, Senate Committee on Finance, 93d Cong., 1st sess. Parts 1-2 and Appendix, 1973. (The Impact of Institutional Investors in the Stock Market) Washington, D.C.: Government Printing Office, 1973.

Hearings on Stockholders Investment Act of 1974 before Subcommittee on Financial Markets, Senate Committee on Finance, 93d Cong., 2d sess. Feb. 5, 6, 1974. Washington, D.C.: Government Printing Office, 1974.

Hone, Philip, "Pass Through Voting: An Analysis," *Profit Sharing,* Vol. 17 (1969), 22.

House Subcommittee on Domestic Finance, House Committee on Banking and Currency, 92d Cong., 1st sess., *Staff Report on the Fifteen Largest United States Foundations: Financial Structure and the Impact of the Tax Reform Act of 1969.* Washington, D.C.: Government Printing Office, 1971.

House Subcommittee on Domestic Finance, House Committee on Banking and Currency, *Staff Report on Commercial Banks and Their Trust Activities: Emerging Influence on the American Economy,* 90th Cong., 2d sess. Washington, D.C.: Government Printing Office, 1968.

Larner, Robert J., *Management Control and the Large Corporation.* New York: Dunellen Publishing Co. Inc., 1970.

Livingston, J.A., *The American Stockholder.* Philadelphia and New York: Lippincott, 1968.

Lundberg, Ferdinand. *The Rich and the Super-Rich.* New York: Bantam Books, 1969.

New York Stock Exchange, *1970 Census on Shareownership,* op. cit.

Securities Exchange Commission, *Institutional Investors Study Report,* House Doc. No. 92-64, Parts 1-6, 92d Cong., 1st sess. Washington, D.C.: Government Printing Office, 1971.

Securities Exchange Commission, *Public Policy Implications of Investment Company Growth,* House Report No. 2337, 89th Cong., 2d sess. Washington, D.C.: Government Printing Office, 1966.

Senate Committee on Finance, 93d Cong., 1st sess., Staff Briefing Material, *The Role of Institutional Investors in the Stock Market.* Committee Print, July 24, 1973. Washington, D.C.: Government Printing Office, 1973.

Senate Subcommittees on Intergovernmental Relations and Budgeting, Management and Expenditures of Senate Committee on Government Operations, 93d Cong., 1st sess., *Disclosure of Corporate Ownership,* Committee Print, December 27, 1973. Washington, D.C.: Government Printing Office, 1973.

Soldofsky, Robert M., *Institutional Holdings of Common Stock 1900-2000: History, Projection, Interpretation.* Michigan Business Studies 18, No. 3. Ann Arbor, Mich.: Bureau of Business Research, Graduate School of Business Administration, The University of Michigan, 1971.

Solomon, Lewis D., "Institutional Investors: Stock Market Impact and Corporate Control", 42 *George Washington Law Review* 761 (1974).

Temporary National Economic Committee. *The Distribution of Ownership in the 200 Largest Nonfinancial Corporations.* Monograph No. 29. Washington, D.C.: Government Printing Office, 1940.

Villarejo, Don, *Stock Ownership and the Control of Corporations.* Somerville, Mass.: New England Free Press.

Wrightman, Dwayne, "Pension Funds and Economic Concentration", *Quarterly Review of Economics and Business,* VII, No. 4 (1967), 29.

CHAPTER SIX

Institutional Investors: Possible Future Center of Control

A. POWER OF INSTITUTIONAL INVESTORS: POTENTIAL AND REALITY

In Chapter 6, we reviewed the generally accepted concept of the separation of ownership and control as a result of widespread distribution of stock ownership. We noted that, although such widespread distribution has in fact occurred with respect to individual investors, there has been a dramatic increase in the concentration of stock ownership among institutions of all types, particularly in the trust departments of commercial banks. This concentration is even more significant because of the further concentration of institutional holdings among a relatively small number of securities on the Exchange. As we have seen, this compounded concentration has resulted in institutional holdings of significant size in most, although not all, of the megacorporations.

In the Institutional Investor Study, the Securities and Exchange Commission concluded that as a result of the concentration of institutional ownership, financial institutions possessed the economic power to control or influence corporate affairs. At the same time, the Institutional Investor Study concluded that there was no evidence that the potential power of institutional investors to control or influence corporate decision-making had in fact been exercised in a significant way.

1. The United States Experience.

In the United States, only scattered and relatively unimportant overt examples are available of institutional use or attempted use of power over portfolio companies.

The Institutional Investor Study documented a series of corporate takeovers where institutional support for the "raider" represented a significant element of the take-over campaign. Such institutional investor participation in take-overs usually involved purchases of the target corporation's shares on the market with the advance knowledge that a tender offer was contemplated. Prior to the tender, the acquired shares were "warehoused" in the institution's portfolio and were ultimately sold to the "raider" when the contemplated tender offer took place. In these cases, however, the objective of the institution was not to achieve influence or control over its policies but to gain the anticipated increase in the price of the shares resulting from the "raider's" attempted take-over of the target company.

The Institutional Investor Study also noted that institutions on isolated occasions deviated from their policy of invariably voting their shares in support of management. On such issues as alteration of preemptive rights of shareholders, stock option plans, or particular acquisitions or mergers, institutions have voted on occasion against management's recommendation but never with a commitment to opposition that extended to the board. In other cases institutions have abstained; abstention may be the equivalent of opposition where proposals require the approval of a specified percentage of outstanding shares. A *Fortune* survey of 1967 reported thirty-three occasions during the previous year in which bank trust departments had cast antimanagement votes.

The crux of the matter is that the occasions where institutions have not agreed with management are rare and even in these cases, the institutions have not vigorously resisted the proposal. In fact, according to a study of the proxy voting practices of commercial bank trust departments by Herman and Safanda, some of the antimanagement votes of trust departments were deliberately made only "for the record" to serve as a demonstration of ostensibly independent responsible behavior.

Herman and Safanda further emphasize the role of institutional proxy voting as part of a system of reciprocal business dealings between the bank and the portfolio company and the mutual desire for preservation of business relationships. In particular, they point to cases of intervention by the commercial department bank officers handling the account of a portfolio company to overrule a proposed antimanagement vote by the trust department on such matters as defensive measures against takeover through insertion of discriminatory voting requirements in the certificate of incorporation. J.A. Livingston gives a similar example in *The American Stockholder* (1958) pertaining to the Montgomery Ward proxy contest. Opposition to management is apparently regarded by the commercial bank officer as an antagonistic act that will tend to offset all of the acts of goodwill undertaken by the bank to strengthen customer relationships. Why provide a good customer with hard-to-get tickets to "hit" shows or "big games" and then vote against its proposal at the shareholders' meeting? It is apparent that the professed insulation of the trust departments and commercial departments of the bank is less than perfect. In the resulting conflict of interest, accommodation of the bank customers who are also portfolio companies may take precedence over fiduciary obligations. This is apt to be particularly true where there is a director interlock between the bank and the portfolio company.

Public instances of institutional pressure are few. Professors Marvin Chirelstein and Victor Brudney present an interesting case study involving General Public Utilities. In this instance, a company proposal for the substitution of periodic stock dividends for cash dividends as a method of raising new capital was withdrawn largely because of institutional opposition, apparently arising from the increased record keeping for fiduciary accounts that would result. Baum and Stiles speculate that institutional pressures were responsible for the resignation of Sewell Avery as chairman of Montgomery Ward and that the promise of such resignation was the price of institutional support for management in the face of the attempted take-over by Wolfson. They concluded, "Institutional power, perhaps long dormant, was ultimately forced to exert itself in order to preserve a valued investment."

Institutional attitude towards so-called "public interest" shareholder proposals which present no threat to management control have been only somewhat less inhibited. After an uneasy start, the institutions, like management, have come to recognize that the issues at stake are not vital to continued control of the enterprise. Both the Investment Companies Association and meetings of bank trust officers have, at least for the record, recognized an institution's fiduciary obligation to take an independent look at "public interest" proposals rather than automatically supporting management.

As "public interest" proxy contests have continued, a tiny but increasing number of institutional investors have supported some shareholder proposals in areas of public policy concern. These have included an isolated number of financial institutions, including Aetna Life and Casualty Insurance Company, Teachers Insurance and Annuity Association-College Equities Retirement Fund, First Pennsylvania Bank and Trust Company, and the Dreyfus Leverage Fund. Much more frequent support has come from universities, foundations, church funds, and state and local governmental pension funds. Except perhaps for church activities where the institution is itself acting as a social activist, these occasional institutional votes in support of isolated shareholder proposals in no sense represent opposition to management policy as a whole. Thus, it is not without significance that institutional support, such as it is, has been particularly evident in the case of proposals for increased disclosure, where no challenge to corporate substantive conduct, even in a narrow area, is involved.

With the intensification of public interest in environmental problems, a number of lenders and investors announced that they would not purchase securities or make loans to corporations that they deemed polluters. These included such groups as the state banking associations in Maine and Vermont, the mutual funds managed by Investors Diversified Services, and Phoenix Mutual Life Insurance Company. Similarly, a number of mutual funds (Dreyfus Third Century, Social Dimensions, Pax, and First Spectrum) were organized with portfolio investment policies restricted to "socially responsible" corporations. Two comments are in order. Although widespread adoption of such policies could influence corporate policy by the threatened denial of access to the capital markets, these activities reflect the policies of potential investors or lenders. They do not represent the use of power by existing shareholders in their capacity as "owners" to determine corporate decision. Further, there is no demonstration that these isolated efforts have had any impact on availability of credit or on corporate behavior.

In *United Funds, Inc. v. Carter Products, Inc.*, CCH Fed. Sec. L. Rep. ¶91,288 (Md. Cir. Ct. 1963), a group of mutual funds which had acquired voting common stock of Carter Products, Inc., when it went "public" and was listed on the New York Stock Exchange unsuccessfully opposed a management proposal that the company authorize and sell shares of a new class of nonvoting common stock. Concerned about the likely loss of the listing of the voting common stock on the New York Stock Exchange as a result of the issuance of the nonvoting common, the funds obtained injunctive relief against the new issue. Although the funds were acting in concert as stockholders, the need to resort to legal remedies illustrates that they had no economic control over the enterprise. In fact the founder of the company at the time still retained a majority of the stock of the company and had insisted on the new stock issue in the form of nonvoting common so that his absolute control would not be affected.

Finally, the Commission's conclusion in the Institutional Investor Study that institutional investors have not significantly exercised their potential power of control must be restricted to public intervention. It is hard to believe that some measure of behind-the-scenes influence or "gentle persuasion" has not on occasion been exercised by institutions. The real extent to which behind-the-scenes influence may have played a major role in the retirement of chief executives, in the selection of successors, or in major corporate decisions concerning acquisitions and mergers or financing is not known. Although evidence is lacking, it taxes credulity to believe that such activity never takes place. The Institutional Investor Study agrees that the exercise of "backstairs" influence on occasion is probable.

2. The English Experience.

Unlike the United States, England has seen at least one highly visible example of the exercise of control by institutional holders.

In the thalidomide controversy in 1972 and 1973, the management of Distillers Company, Ltd., was extraordinarily unyielding in its resistance to mounting public pressures to settle on satisfactory terms the claims of the 451 horribly affected victims and their families, some of which had been in litigation for eleven or twelve years. The thalidomide controversy had been the subject of outraged debate in the House of Commons where 254 members called on the company to honor its "moral responsibilities." The Court of Appeal described the affair as a "national tragedy." Distillers responded by instigating an injunction proceeding to enjoin further discussion in the press (so long as the litigation was pending) and to stand pat on its previous £ 3.25 million settlement offer that had previously been rejected. As public outrage increased and the shares of Distillers fell to their low for the year, financial institutions became convinced that "the City had to act." Prudential Assurance, Distillers' largest shareholder with about 5% of the stock, was reported to feel it should become "fully involved." The investment banking advisors of the firm together with representatives of major institutional holders met with the senior management on January 4, 1973. On January 5, 1973 the company increased its settlement offer from £ 3.25 million to £ 21.75 million which led ultimately to settlement of the matter. There was no question but that the institutional investors had dictated the decision to the management.[1] In this isolated case involving a national *cause celebre,* institutional investors were prepared to act. Will less intense pressure in the future bring institutional intervention? This remains to be seen.

England provides another example of institutional intervention. In 1973 the Bank of England called upon institutional investors to exert influence on portfolio companies to modernize plant and technology and thereby improve the country's competitive position in the world market. It established an Institutional Shareholders Committee, including representatives of major institutional investors, to supervise this effort. Although this effort reflects official pressure directed toward advancement of the national interest and apparently restricted to modernization of production, it, nevertheless, casts the institutions into the role of influencing managerial decisions. One may well inquire whether such a process once commenced may not thereafter spread to other areas as well.

Finally, the Confederation of British Industry has urged institutional shareholders to "take a leading role" in participation in corporate meetings and thereby set an example to the whole body of stockholders.

B. RESTRAINTS ON INSTITUTIONAL INVESTORS

Institutional investors are subject to a number of restraints that thus far have inhibited the exercise of their potential power to affect corporate decision-making, or alternatively have restricted its exercise to activity which is not visible to the public. These include the prevailing views in the business

[1]After the settlement, institutional holders claimed recognition for their pressures on Distillers. Thus, Legal and General Assurance asserted that it was "the first City institution to urge Distillers to make a higher offer." Commercial Union Assurance's chairman similarly proclaimed that his company had "effectively" used its influence to secure action in settling the controversy.

and financial community as to the "proper" role of institutions, existing statutory restraints, and concern with potential statutory restraints.

1. Prevailing Institutional Views.

In the past the universally accepted policy in the financial communities both in the United States and England has been that institutional holders dissatisfied with the performance of a portfolio company sell their shares, rather than seek to change managerial policy or management. Thus, the senior officer in charge of the Morgan Guaranty trust department in 1973 testified before a Senate Subcommittee that he could not recall a single instance in which his institution tried to influence management when dissatisfied with a management decision. This has been described in the United States as the "Wall Street Rule" and in England as the "City Rule." This prevailing attitude reflects a number of factors.

[*a*] A major element is the view that the primary responsibility of the institutional investor was to achieve maximum performance consistent with the acceptability of risk for its shareholders, policy holders, or trust beneficiaries as the case might be. If performance of a portfolio company was inadequate, the institution switched its investment to a company with better prospects. Neither the law nor the financial community has recognized any responsibility of the institutional shareholder to its fellow shareholders, nor for that matter to any other groups which might be adversely affected by the inadequate managerial policies in question: employees whose jobs might suffer, consumers with unsafe or shoddy products, or communities facing plant relocation or burdened by pollution. The obligations of the institutional holder to its own constituency have been paramount. There was, therefore, no occasion for the institution to expose its constituents to the continued risks attendant upon a decision not to sell or to postpone a sale in order to participate in the solution of the problems of the portfolio company.

The prevailing view has two separate elements. First, it denies the existence of any duty on the part of the institution to be concerned with the impact of corporate performance on fellow shareholders or other affected groups. Second, it asserts that even if some such concern were to exist, the institution's primary and overriding obligation to its own constituency would require it to dispose of its shares rather than subject its constituency to the possibility of reduced return pending solution of the corporate problems in issue or to increased risk in the event that solution were not achieved.

[*b*] The financial institutions are evidently seriously concerned about the political consequences of any public demonstration of their potential power of control. Maintaining low visibility is an important objective. Thus, the same senior officer of the Morgan Guaranty also testified that his bank with the largest trust portfolio in the country was actively exploring ways of

divesting itself of the voting rights of the shares in its trust accounts. He added that the bank "would welcome being rid of the burden of voting our trust holdings and being rid of the notion that, through our trust holdings, we somehow desire to control corporate managements." Institutions are clearly well advised to avoid the stimulation of public concern with respect to the fundamental problem of institutional power in the society, the exposure to public criticism over their policy in any particular case, and the possible risk of governmental intervention.

[*c*] Institutional investors are reluctant to offend portfolio companies. In the case of institutions selling funds or services to businesses, such as banks or insurance companies, any vigorous utilization of their power as shareholders might well interfere with existing business relationships or anticipated business opportunities which after all constitute the primary objectives of the financial institution. Furthermore, in its continuing security analysis, the institutional investor relies on the cooperation of the portfolio companies with respect to current information concerning their progress and performance; ready accessibility of management for such information is regarded as essential. In spite of all the problems arising from use of "inside" information that have been presented by the almost explosive expansion of Section 10-b of the Securities Exchange Act of 1934, intimate access to current corporate information through liaison with management continues to be vitally important.

[*d*] A final factor has been the lack of institutional readiness to assume any responsibility for participation in a managerial decision that could involve the possibility of loss to the portfolio company. "Risk is the price of activity." The institutions have shrunk from activity and any assumption of risk, particularly because it would not be on behalf of those to whom they have traditionally regarded themselves accountable.

There is at least one major pressure pushing institutional holders in the other direction. The "Wall Street" or "City" Rule rests on the ability of the institutional investor to sell its shares. Liquidity, however, is threatened by the increasing concentration of institutional holdings in the shares of major corporations. The institution that decides to sell its shares in a company that has been an institutional favorite may discover an "air pocket" in the market and values disappearing. A number of horror stories of catastrophic declines in the price of securities illustrates the lack of reality in the values of some institutional favorites. Handleman lost 51% of its "value" in a single institutional trade. Levitz Furniture dropped from $47 to $33, or a loss of nearly 30% in a half hour of trading. Other declines in a single day include Seaboard Airlines, 50%; Westinghouse, 25%; Simplicity Pattern, 37½%; and Combustion Engineering, 36%.

The institutions may thus be "locked into" stocks which they cannot sell, except at heavy losses. Unable to dispose of their shares readily, the institutions may then be under pressure to concern themselves to a greater extent with respect to the management of troubled portfolio companies. This possibility was noted as long ago as 1959 by David Rockefeller, who pointed out that:

> . . . as holdings expand, institutions, as well as individuals, will feel obliged to take more active interest in seeing that corporations do indeed have good managements. This will be true especially if their holdings become so large that they cannot readily or quickly liquidate their investments, as is now their practice when they become dissatisfied with the management . . .

The Securities and Exchange Commission *Report on Public Policy Implications of Investment Company Growth* (1966) expressed some concern that the growing institutionalization of the market was leading to illiquidity. Similarly, in its evaluation of the thalidomide controversy, the Manchester Guardian regarded the "locked in" position of the major institutions in Distillers as the critical factor responsible for their intervention.

The significance of the lack of liquidity of institutional major holdings cannot be pushed too far. After all, the horror stories mentioned above demonstrate that some institutions will sell in spite of almost catastrophic declines. Institutional portfolio turnover is high, although declining:

Institutional Turnover
Common Stock Transactions

	1971	*1972*	*1973*
Private Noninsured Pension Funds	22.1%	19.7%	16.5%
Open-end Investment Companies	48.2%	44.8%	39.0%
Life Insurance Companies	31.0%	29.6%	24.8%
Property-Casualty Insurance Companies	23.2%	23.8%	20.3%

Source: S.E.C. Statistical Bulletin, April 3, 1974, p. 404.

Further, in 1971 three classes of institutions—pension funds, open-end investment companies, and insurance companies—bought and sold $92.3 billion of common stock on the New York Stock Exchange. These New York Stock Exchange statistics are particularly impressive because they do not include either the heavy volume of transactions consummated off the New York Stock Exchange or the transactions of other major classes of institutional investors, such as closed-end investment companies, state and local governmental pension funds, nonprofit institutions, common-trust funds, and bank-administered personal trust funds.

Increasing lack of liquidity may in time result in greater involvement of institutions in the affairs of portfolio companies, but the record to date hardly indicates that this development is inevitable.

2. Fiduciary Restraints.

The law has recognized the fiduciary obligations of a controlling shareholder to minority shareholders. These obligations prevent the controlling shareholder from taking advantage of its position and profiting at the expense of the minority, or even further from profiting by virtue of its position under circumstances where the minority is not injured and perhaps even where the minority is benefited. These are negative injunctions which the fiduciary must not transgress. By contrast there is no affirmative legal obligation requiring a shareholder with control or potential control to continue as a shareholder and to deal with existing corporate problems rather than to dispose of its shares. Baum and Stiles have sought to analogize the position of institutions to that of dominant shareholders and to assert the existence of their duties to other shareholders in the portfolio companies. There is no judicial support thus far for this view, and Baum and Stiles ultimately rely on the view that the "privilege of power carries with it the duty of responsibility"—a philosophical rather than a legal conclusion.

When the underlying problem relates to dishonest or highly inequitable conduct on the part of the portfolio company management, there is some support for the view that controlling shareholders are under a duty to take action. After all, a director, knowing of the existence of such conduct, may not properly resign. Since controlling shareholders have been held to have fiduciary obligations equivalent to those of directors, it is conceivable that in the future courts may apply the rule governing the conduct of directors to controlling shareholders as well. Controlling shareholders knowing of misconduct may be obliged to attempt to deal with it.

There are a number of problems with this view. First, a director has been elected by shareholders to a corporate office for a specified term. Having accepted the office, the director has implicitly undertaken not to abdicate the performance of his duties prior to the expiration of his term in the face of threatened or existing injuries to the corporation which are known to him. The shareholder, however, has not been elected to any corporate office.

Second, "controlling" shareholders have been held to have fiduciary obligations. Where, however, institutions are not represented on the Board, they have not attempted to influence Board decision, and where their power depends on their untested ability to act in concert, it is doubtful that the fact that they are major shareholders of itself will be deemed to constitute "control" giving rise to the existence of a fiduciary duty to other shareholders. "Potential control" may not be enough to create such a duty.

Finally, the duties of the director to remain and deal with known problems relate only to acts of dishonesty or unfairness giving rise to a cause of action on the part of the corporation. They do not include matters of business judgment. In the absence of such circumstances there is no indication that a director is not entirely free to resign, nor by extension that the controlling shareholders would not be free to sell.

3. Statutory or Administrative Restraints.

In Chapter 5 we reviewed statutory restraints on various classes of institutional investors. Those restrictions relate exclusively to limitations on the portfolio to the extent that they are not concerned with the solvency of the institution. They do not involve restrictions on the voting power of the shares in the portfolio. (An exception which is not relevant for our discussion is the situation where an administrative agency may require shares to be placed in a voting trust to achieve a regulatory objective.)

As we have seen, the regulatory framework applicable to investment companies, insurance companies and pension funds (effective in 1976) requires full disclosure of their portfolios. Although such compulsory disclosure does not appear to have had any significant impact on the investment policy of the institutions, it has a prophylactic effect further inhibiting institutions with significant positions in portfolio companies from attempts to utilize their disclosed power to influence management policy.

It is concern with potential additional statutory or administrative restraints rather than with existing restraints which is a limiting factor on the accumulation by financial institutions of controlling positions in portfolio companies. Institutions recognize the desirability of maintaining a "low profile" in the hope of avoiding further governmental regulation. While this restraining influence has contributed to the unreadiness of institutional investors to exercise their existing potential control over portfolio companies, it has not kept institutions from assuming such substantial investments in the major American corporations that they are now in a position to join forces and exercise control if they are so minded.

4. Concern with Market Performance.

Institutional investors have become increasingly aware of relative market performance. The prominence attained by performance-minded funds has created considerable pressure on institutional investment managers generally to defend their own performance records. A climate has developed where investment managers—whether managing pension funds, mutual funds, or university portfolios—are competing with each other as well as with the "averages" concerning the quality of their own professional performance. With performance evaluated on a comparative basis over periods as short as a calendar year or perhaps the even shorter period of a sudden market rise or decline, the pressures on institutional investment managers to sell shares of companies with problems and to move on to more promising investments become very strong indeed. With a heightened concern for comparative performance records, the institution all the more clearly emerges as an investor, and a temporary one at that, rather than as an owner. Responsibility for investment results overwhelms any incipient pressures for responsibility for direction of the portfolio company.

5. Summary.

In view of the foregoing factors, one may readily understand why institutional investors have not tended to exercise their potential power to influence or control the major corporations. Further, one would expect that this reluctance would continue as long as it is feasible for institutions to liquidate their holdings and terminate their interest in the troubled portfolio company.

The situation will not improve. Institutional accumulation of securities is continuing, and concentration in portfolio companies will inevitably increase. Thus far, lack of relative liquidity and heavy loss on sale have not kept institutions from liquidating positions in companies in which they have lost confidence. At some point, this may change, and we may see a departure from past practice and the beginnings of institutional involvement in the affairs of portfolio companies. On the other hand, this aspect of the problem may be expected to become overshadowed by public concern with the concentration of institutional power, and we are more likely to see instead the contrary pattern of a voluntary neutralization of voting power by the institutions themselves or the imposition of statutory or administrative regulation over institutional ownership and voting.

C. CONSEQUENCES OF POSSIBLE INSTITUTIONAL CONTROL

If the potential power of institutional investors over portfolio companies were exercised, what consequences would follow on the political level, on behavior of the firm, and on the accountability and legitimacy of the firm?

1. Political Consequences.

The development of the economic power of the megacorporations and their dominating position in the American and world economies are so striking that they are the very subject of this volume. If control of this awesome concentration of economic power was not diffused among the managements of the various giant corporations but was further concentrated in the hands of a relatively limited number of financial institutions and exercised by them, the result would likely be regarded as intolerable for a free society.

Immediate political pressures to subject the power of the financial institutions to public control would undoubtedly result. As noted institutions' awareness of the possibility of such a development may be regarded as one of the major factors that has restrained American institutional investors, at least on the public level, from exercise of their potential power over portfolio companies. The political consequences would be profound.

2. Behavior of the Firm.

If control shifted from management to institutional shareholders, the behavior of the firm might well be affected. If the separation of ownership and control really means that management determination of the objectives of the firm does not reflect single-minded dedication to the advancement of shareholder objectives, a shift in control from management to shareholders should theoretically mean a corresponding shift in firm objectives. Under this view profit-maximization, if not already the objective of the firm, would replace growth, a relative unreadiness for risk, a diversion of wealth from shareholders to management, and other non-stockholder-related objectives which, according to some critics, have been embraced by management seeking to advance its own interests. Dividend and capital investment policies might be revised. The advancement of shareholders' interests, as perceived by shareholders, would presumably be re-established as the goal of the enterprise. If, however, management objectives and shareholder objectives have been identical, or if not identical at least congruent, little change would follow.

3. Accountability.

Whatever one's conclusion concerning the impact on behavior of the firm, it is plain that the assumption of institutional control would automatically mean the creation of an agency to which management would become accountable. Instead of an enormous, unorganized, amorphous group of stockholders, manipulated by management for its own purposes through the proxy solicitation process, management would be supervised by institutional stockholders with the power to review, inspect, and question management decision and the performance of the firm, and to take such action as might seem appropriate, including change of the senior management and the board. The institutional shareholders would be looking over the shoulder of the board and management, and almost as important, the board and management would be under pressure to act as if the institutional shareholders were in fact looking over their shoulder. Accountability on the part of the board and management would have been restored.

Even in such event, one may still question whether the accountability of major business enterprise would have been re-established. To whom would the institutional shareholders be accountable? Who would guard the guardians? The assumption of institutional control might have major implications with respect to the behavior of the corporations. It would not dispose of the problem of lack of accountability. This would remain one of the major problems of our economic order. Institutional control would only push the problem of accountability back one level from the corporate board and management to the financial institutions themselves.

4. Legitimacy.

Whatever effect the exercise of institutional control over the giant corporations might have on the problem of accountability, the problem of the legitimacy of the corporation would remain.

One may, of course, argue that the concept of our corporate law is that the corporation is "owned" by its shareholders and that concern for the legitimacy of the modern corporation comes to an end when control is returned to the "owners" through the assumption of control by institutional shareholders. If, however, legitimacy is taken to refer to a system that commands widespread social support and is generally regarded as "proper," the assumption of control over the giants of American industry by a relatively limited number of financial institutions is not likely to represent a socially acceptable condition. For the very reasons which indicate that such concentration of power is not politically acceptable, one would conclude that the problem of legitimacy will remain.

One should recognize, however, that the separation of ownership and control and the emergence of an autonomous professional management able to take the long-term view, subject only to restraints to be described in a companion volume, may have contributed to the preservation of our present form of economic institutions. The available evidence suggests the possibility that shareholders might be more preoccupied with short-term results and less concerned with the long-run implications of corporate conduct than corporate managers, who recognize that their positions and power rest on an uneasy and uncertain public mandate and who are vitally concerned about the over-riding necessity of maintaining public support.

This is illustrated by the controversy over corporate contributions. It is noteworthy that corporate management generally has opposed shareholder proposals made by radicals of the right which suggest that charitable contributions be restricted to donations directly benefiting the corporation. It is even more noteworthy that despite management opposition and the absence of any organized campaign, these proposals have achieved the remarkably high total of almost 10% of the votes cast at recent annual meetings of stockholders of such megacorporations as Bethlehem Steel and American Telephone and Telegraph. In contrast, the highly organized "public interest" proxy contests instituted by social reform of church groups and featured by national publicity, intensive organization and solicitation, and the support on occasion of the nation's most prestigious universities, foundations, and church organizations have rarely attracted more than 2% to 4% of the votes cast. The sobering thought is that "shareholder democracy" may well involve appeal to the wrong constituency.

BIBLIOGRAPHY

Baum, David J. and Ned B. Stiles, *The Silent Partners: Institutional Investors and Corporate Control,* op. cit.

Chirelstein, Marvin and Victor Brudney, *Cases and Materials on Corporate Finance.* Mineola, N.Y.: The Foundation Press, 1973.

Galston, Clarence, "Fiduciary Responsibility of Institutional Investors" 1968.

Herman, Edward S. and Carl F. Safanda, "Proxy Voting by Commercial Bank Trust Departments," 90 *Banking Law Journal* 91 (1973).

Louis, Arthur M. "The Mutual Funds Have the Votes" *Fortune,* May 1967, p. 150.

Livingston, J.A., *The American Shareholder,* op. cit.

Lybecker, Martin E., "Regulation of Bank Trust Department Investment Activities", 82 *Yale Law Journal* 977 (1974).

Note, "Mutual Funds, Portfolio Companies and the Small Investor: The Role of Institutional Influence", 5 *Columbia Journal of Law and Social Problems* 69 (August, 1969).

Securities and Exchange Commission, *Institutional Investor Study Report,* op. cit.

Securities and Exchange Commission, *Public Policy Implications of Investment Company Growth,* op. cit.

Sunday Times, *The Thalidomide Children and the Law.* London: Andre Deutsch, 1973.

CHAPTER SEVEN

Management Power Arising from Separation of Ownership and Control and Its Consequences

The management of the major corporation typically has power that is rarely subject to challenge or restraint from shareholders. This power rests on three factors, the first two of which have already been discussed: 1) The widespread distribution of individual shareownership among approximately 31,000,000 Americans. 2) The unwillingness or inability of institutional shareholders to act in concert and exercise their potential power to influence or determine management policy, combined with their policy of selling shares rather than seeking to change management or corporate policy when dissatisfied. 3) Management control of the proxy solicitation machinery which we will review in this chapter.

A. SELF-PERPETUATING MANAGEMENT

Typically, management is assured of control of the large corporation, because the board of directors is a self-perpetuating oligarchy selecting itself and its successors, subject to automatic ratification at the ritual of the annual shareholders' meeting. Along with the widespread distribution of individual shareownership and the refusal of institutional investors to act as owners, management control of the corporate electoral machinery, and particularly of the proxy solicitation machinery, is an essential element in the maintenance of management hegemony. In effect, management operates a one-party political state, with its party and candidates financed at corporate expense. Organization of a contending party is lawful, but it must be accomplished at the personal expense of the opposition group. In brief, the contest is so unequal and unfair that proxy contests in the public corporation have always been confined to very few companies. This is largely the product of state corporation laws and the proxy rules of the Securities and Exchange Commission.

Under the present legal rules governing the corporate electoral process, the critical event is no longer the meeting of shareholders. In fact, attendance in person at the annual meeting is usually negligible. In Fuqua Industries, Inc., for example, only twelve holders attended the 1972 Annual Meeting which led the management to suggest that the annual meeting be eliminated entirely and corporate shareholder business be transacted entirely by mail. Similarly, it is worth noting that although the excitement and national interest generated by Campaign GM led to the attendance of 1600 persons at the 1972 General Motors Annual Meeting and of 1200 at the 1973 Annual Meeting, this attendance—large as it is by comparison with the meager attendance at the meetings of other giant corporations—is a tiny fraction of the 1,306,000 holders of record and estimated 1.75 to 2 million beneficial holders of General Motors shares.

The critical event in the shareholder voting process is the shareholder's execution of a proxy. Under the Securities and Exchange Commission rules (applicable to all but small or closely-held corporations), any solicited proxy—whether solicited by management or others—constitutes a binding instruction to the proxy holder on the manner in which the shares are to be voted. It thus represents the shareholder's exercise of his right to vote.

Every meeting involves the preparation and distribution to shareholders at corporate expense of the management proxy materials, consisting of the management proxy and proxy statement, setting forth the information which management deems useful in the presentation of its case and other relevant data required by the Securities and Exchange Commission. Although the proxy form required by the Commission provides appropriate spaces for holders to vote for or against the proposals on the agenda, all unmarked proxies that are signed and returned are voted in accordance with management recommendations. As a practical matter approval of management recommendations and nominees follows automatically.

There is no way under the present rules of the Commission or under existing state law by which opposing groups may have their nominees listed in the corporate proxy statement and upon the management proxy form, which for practical purposes is the electoral ballot. Insurgents are forced to act at their own expense with their own separate solicitation.

To attract attention to this inherently unfair situation, public interest groups have submitted shareholder proposals at the annual meetings of a number of major corporations calling for a change in the corporate bylaws to permit listing of any shareholder nominees for the board in the corporate proxy statement and proxy, along with the management slate of nominees. Other reformers have called for disclosure of the number of unmarked proxies. These efforts seek to accomplish through a change in the corporate organic instruments what the Commission has declined to require in its proxy rules. Although these proposals attracted the support of such institutions as Harvard, Yale, and the Ford Foundation, they were overwhelmingly defeated. It may be expected, however, that pressures for such change will continue.

In contrast to nominations for directors, Securities and Exchange Commission Rule 14a(8) (c) (with some exceptions), requires corporations to include shareholder proposals and a 200-word supporting statement in the management proxy statement and the proposals in the management proxy form. In this manner, the shareholder can circularize his proposals among the shareholders generally at corporate expense. Although such campaigns by public interest groups have attracted high public interest, thereby introducing the public into the corporate decision-making process, such proposals have never attracted a significant percentage of the vote[1] and except in isolated cases have typically received less than 5% of the vote. Among other reasons, this low percentage reflects the fact that the proxy is voted for such proposals only if expressly so marked. As noted, proxies returned without any specific vote are voted in accordance with the recommendations of management.

Although there are other restraints upon management that reflect shareholder pressures, they are less than wholly effective. The so-called "market for control," i.e. the possibility of take-over by proxy contest or tender offer, provides a significant pressure on management to be concerned with inadequate corporate performance that might be reflected in impaired market action of the shares and might encourage acquisition-minded groups to attempt to acquire a dominant interest. This pressure is affected by a number of other factors (for example, the substantial premium above market required for a successful tender offer; the difficulty, uncertainty, and expense of a proxy contest; the influence of many other elements affecting the market price of the shares) and is an imperfect discipline. Substantial management discretion independent of shareholder influence continues.

How then does management exercise the discretion which arises as a result of the separation of ownership and control and the ineffectiveness of other restraints? To what extent are the forces that facilitate management discretion and defeat accountability reflected in changed corporate policies or performance in such areas as profitability, dividend policies and reinvestment, and executive compensation?

B. IMPACT OF MANAGEMENT CONTROL

Larner properly terms the implications of management control with respect to the behavior of the firm a more fundamental matter than the separation of ownership and control.

[1]On isolated occasions involving noncontroversial items, management has adopted the shareholder proposal and its recommendation of favorable action has led to approval. These instances illustrate nothing other than the alertness of some corporate managements to seize an opportunity for "window dressing." An example is a 1974 proposal prohibiting discrimination for sex that was embraced by the Gulf Oil management, while it resisted other more telling proposals.

1. Profitability.

There is considerable literature on the consequences of management independence from shareholder control. Galbraith, Baumol, and Robin Marris, among others, contend that in place of maximizing profits for shareholders, management seeks to maximize growth in sales or growth in assets, is less inclined to take risks, and is more concerned with its own security and perquisites, subject to the constraint of a minimally acceptable profit level. Empirical studies, however, do not agree whether profit levels and profit fluctuations for firms under management control are lower than for firms under owner control.

Larner sought to relate profit rates to the size of the firm (as measured by assets) and concluded that there was little difference in the profitability of management-controlled corporations and owner-controlled corporations. Similarly, he did not find that management firms had less fluctuations in earnings and therefore were apparently taking less risks than owner-controlled firms. He suggested that the widespread extent of management stock options, stock ownership, and compensation plans related to profits made managers a subset within shareholders, rather than a separate group with interests in conflict with shareholders. Additionally, Larner concluded that the effects of separation of ownership and control on the profit orientation of firms were minor and did not justify the considerable attention in the literature which they have received.

There is disagreement on this issue. Although David Kamerschen reached a similar conclusion to Larner on the relation between profit rates and the nature of control of the firm, a study by Monsen, Chiu, and Cooley of a sample of seventy-two firms in twelve industries found that thirty-six owner-controlled firms had a 12.8% rate of return on equity while thirty-six management-controlled firms had only a 7.3% rate of return. It is apparent that economists are not yet in accord on whether behavior of the firm is affected by separation of ownership and control as far as profits are concerned.

2. Dividend Policies and Reinvestment

As previously discussed, there have been suggestions that in the management-controlled firm, management will attempt to increase internally generated funds as a method of lessening its need for issuance of additional securities and dependence on the capital markets. Dividends are a major element in reducing net internal cash flow. If the objectives of management are to promote its own interests and to strengthen its autonomy, one would expect this to be reflected in a reduction, or at the very least an absence of increase, in dividend distributions.

The facts, however, are to the contrary. From 1965 to 1973, annual dividend payments by American corporations increased from $19.8 billion to

$27.8 billion, with uninterrupted annual increases of approximately $1 billion per year, in spite of significant fluctuations in earnings. Aggregate dividends thus were not correlated with aggregate net income after tax. When earnings declined in 1969 and 1970, the ratio of dividends to net income after tax increased from 42.6% in 1965 to 62.9% in 1970, and when boom earnings in 1973 increased to $31.1 billion over the depressed 1970 level, the ratio sank back to 39.5%.

Dividend policy apparently serves management interests by contributing to improved market prices for the shares. Whether or not this reflects management objectives to render take-over or proxy contests less likely, to ease the sale of new securities, or to increase the value of stock-related compensation, it is entirely congruent with shareholder objectives. Whether management was in fact motivated to serve shareholders' interest or its own objectives which point in the same direction as the shareholders' is irrelevant.

The question then becomes whether dividends ranging from 39.5% to 62.9% of net earnings after taxes in the period from 1965 to 1973 would have been even more substantial in the event management was fully responding to shareholder interests. During this period, internally generated funds were inadequate to provide the capital funds required by corporations. This would appear to indicate that owner-managed firms would not have increased dividends further. However, this merely changes the area of the inquiry from dividend policy to capital investment policy. Were the capital programs of the major corporations during this period intended to fulfill management objectives which point in the same direction as the shareholders' is irrelevant. holders? Would owner-managed firms have maintained the same levels of capital investment? The evidence on this does not permit a satisfactory conclusion.

3. Executive Compensation.

Larner also studied the relation between the compensation and income of chief executive officers and the profitability, size, and growth of the firm. This involved such questions as: To what extent is compensation related to sales or growth? To what extent is it related to profits? What difference can be found in the compensation policies of owner-controlled and management-controlled firms?

Executive compensation includes cash salary, cash bonuses, and stock-related plans including stock-options, phantom option plans, and stock purchase plans.

Larner's study included stock-related elements and measured the total compensation package on an *after-tax* basis. He emphasized the importance of taking the entire compensation package into account, noting that deferred and contingent forms of compensation, particularly stock options, had increased in relative importance and by 1963 were nearly as large as salary and bonus. Larner also took dividends on employer stocks into account in order to obtain the full return to executives from their stock interests in the corporation. He thereby distinguished earlier studies which concluded that executive compensation tended to reflect firm size rather than profits. The earlier conclusions were reached on the basis of cash salary and bonuses measured on a *pre-tax* basis.

Studying the chief executives of ninety-four industrial corporations and including both capital gains and dividends on an after-tax basis in the computation of compensation, Larner concluded that dollar profit and rate of profit were the major variables in determining executive remuneration and that the nature and structure of rewards and incentives in management-controlled corporations were interrelated with pursuit of stockholders' interests.

Professor Lewellen similarly attributed considerable significance to the stockholdings of executives and to the interrelationship of the various elements of the compensation package to the price of the employer corporation's stock. While Professor Robert A. Gordon in an earlier study had concluded that the stock interest of executives in the employer corporation was not a significant factor, it turns out that Gordon had not taken dividends on the stockholdings into account.

4. Summary.

The differences in opinion among economists are significant. It is apparent that the separation of ownership and control has not led to such differences in corporate policies as to permit ready conclusions on whether management control has in fact led to different policies than stockholder control. Even if such writers as Larner, Kamerschen, and Lewellen are ultimately shown to be less than correct, the current differing conclusions would indicate that the deviations in the objective and behavior are not profound. If such authors ultimately prevail, separation of ownership and control would not have the economic significance that has so frequently been attributed to it, but it would continue to retain its significance with respect to such matters as the accountability of management and the legitimacy of the major American corporation as an institution.

BIBLIOGRAPHY

Blumberg, Phillip I., *Corporate Responsibility in a Changing Society,* op. cit.

Eisenberg, Melvin, "The Legal Roles of Shareholders and Management in Modern Corporate Decision Making", op. cit.

Galbraith, John K., *The New Industrial State,* op. cit.

Gordon, Robert A., *Business Leadership in the Large Corporation,* op. cit.

Hindley, Brian V., "Separation of Ownership and Control in the Modern Corporation", *Journal of Law and Economics,* XIII (1970), 185.

Kaysen, Carl, "Another View of Corporate Capitalism", *Quarterly Journal of Economics,* LXXIX, No. 1 (1965), 41.

Kamerschen, David R., "The Influence of Ownership and Control on Profit Rates", *American Economic Review,* LVIII (1968), 432.

Larner, Robert J., *Management Control and the Large Corporation,* op. cit.

Lewellen, Wilbur G., *Executive Compensation in Large Industrial Corporations.* New York: Columbia University Press, 1968.

Marris, Robin, *The Economic Theory of "Managerial Capitalism."* New York: Free Press, 1964.

Monsen, R. Joseph, John S. Chiu, and David E. Cooley, "The Effect of Separation of Ownership and Control on the Performance of the Large Firm", *Quarterly Journal of Economics,* LXXXII, No. 3 (1968), 435.

Peterson, Shorey, "Corporate Control and Capitalism", *Quarterly Journal of Economics,* LXXIX, No. 1 (1965), 1.

CHAPTER EIGHT

Control: Interlocking Directors

The device of interlocking directors constitutes another avenue of influence or control in corporate decision-making. This achieved national prominence more than sixty years ago and became a major issue in the first Wilson administration. Although, as we will see, there were a number of evils attributed to interlocking directors, a major source of concern was the extent to which it served as the mechanism through which the "Money Trust" in general and J.P. Morgan in particular were seeking to establish control over American industry. Concern with interlocking directors as a device for the domination of major business by financial interests continues to this day.

A. TYPES OF INTERLOCKING DIRECTORSHIPS

Interlocks may be divided into three classes: a) *horizontal,* where common directors link companies that are or may be competitors in the same industry; b) *vertical,* where common directors link companies that deal with each other at different levels in the same industry, or where one provides services to the other although in different industries; c) *general,* where common directors link companies that are not actual or potential competitors and do not deal with one another.

Interlocks may also be classified as: a) *direct,* where common directors are on the boards of the companies in question, b) *indirect,* where there are no common directors, but each company has different representatives on the boards of two competing companies, or a company has a director on the board of another which in turn has a director on the board of a competitor of the first. Financial institutions play a central role in the web of interlocking directorships.

B. THE ATTACK ON INTERLOCKING DIRECTORSHIPS

The Pujo Committee of the House of Representatives investigating the concentration of control of money and credit during 1912-13, and the Stanley Committee of the House investigating violations of the Sherman Act both concluded that interlocking directorates presented serious social and economic evils. The Pujo investigation found that 180 financial leaders held 385 directorships in forty-one banks and trust companies dominating the banking industry and a total of 746 directorships in 134 corporations with total resources or capitalization of $25 billion. The Pujo Committee was disturbed by the elimination in competition among the banks and the control by an "inner group" of financiers over the economy. The Stanley Committee concluded that interlocking directorships had produced "pernicious" conflicts of interest resulting in preferential treatment and excessive costs.

In 1913-14, Brandeis published his well known series of articles in *Harper's* on the "Money Trust," denouncing the interlocking directorship as evil. In an often-quoted passage, Brandeis said,

> The practice of interlocking directorates is the root of many evils. It offends laws human and divine. Applied to rival corporations, it tends to the suppression of competition and to violation of the Sherman law. Applied to corporations which deal with each other, it tends to disloyalty and to violation of the fundamental law that no man can serve two masters. In either event it tends to inefficiency; for it removes incentive and destroys soundness of judgment. It is undemocratic, for it rejects the platform: "A fair field and no favors."—substituting the pull of privilege for the push of manhood. It is the most potent instrument of the Money Trust. Break the control so exercised by the investment bankers over railroads, public-service and industrial corporations, over banks, life insurance and trust companies, and a long step will have been taken toward attainment of the New Freedom.

President Wilson subsequently called on the Congress to deal with the problem presented by interlocking directorships. Following the lines of Brandeis' attack, Wilson stressed a number of factors. He was concerned about the elimination of competition and conflicts of interest impairing business decision. He deplored the denial of opportunity for persons to become directors because interlocks made so many places on the board unavailable, and he was gravely concerned that the "Money Trust" would accumulate such concentrated power through interlocks that it would threaten free government. Of all the evils, concern with power was paramount. In *The New Freedom,* Wilson stated:

> . . . we have . . . to disentangle this colossal "community of interest" . . . no single, avowed combination is big enough for the United States to be afraid of;

> but when all the combinations are combined . . . then there is something that even the government of the nation itself might come to fear . . . [pp. 110-11, 113].

In response to President Wilson's message, the Congress enacted the Clayton Act in 1914. Section 8 of the new law prohibited interlocking directorships involving one or more companies with capital, surplus, and undivided profits of $1,000,000 or more which are or have been competitors so that elimination of competition by agreement between them would constitute a violation of the antitrust laws. Section 8 was weak and ineffective. According to a 1965 Staff Report to the Antitrust Subcommittee of the House Committee on the Judiciary ("1965 Staff Report"), Section 8 was:

> Too incomplete and restricted in scope to reach many significant corporate interrelations and the easy avoidance of section 8's express prohibitions has resulted in a failure of enforcement even as to those interlocks where there is a practical certainty that competition will be adversely affected.

The weakness of Section 8 arose from several factors. Much of the concern over the power of the investment banking community had been removed when Morgan and other leading bankers resigned many of their directorships. Wilson himself had hailed this conciliatory move. The forces for a stringent statute were further weakened when Morgan's death removed the leader and symbol of the "Money Trust."

Professor Travers summarizes four loopholes which have impeded enforcement of Section 8: a) The interlocking person must be a director of both corporations; a director in one and a nondirector officer in another is not proscribed. b) Vertical interlocks are not covered. c) Indirect interlocks are not covered. A partnership—a common form of organization in the investment banking industry—may have different partners on the boards of competing companies.[1] d) Interlocks must relate to companies which are or have been competitors; the existence of potential competition is insufficient.

Section 8 was not only restricted in scope but for decades was not enforced. According to Victor Kramer, the Department of Justice knew of the existence of 1,500 interlocks before 1950. Almost forty years after its enactment, Mr. Justice Douglas observed, "It is only recently that the government has attempted systematic enforcement of Section 8" (*United States v. W. T. Grant,* 345 U.S. 629, 634 (1953). Even then enforcement languished. In 1968 the Department of Justice was successful in achieving voluntary elimination of eleven interlocks involving sixteen companies. In 1973 and 1974 the Federal Trade Commission became increasingly active with respect to interlocking directorates. John A. Mayer, Chairman of the Mellon National Bank

[1]Under the Civil Aeronautics Act, the Civil Aeronautics Board successfully prevented such interlocking where different partners of Lehman Brothers were on the boards of two airlines.

and Trust Company, was a common director of Aluminum Company of America and United States Steel. Because the different metals were substitutable and competed in some markets, the Commission questioned the relationship and forced Mr. Mayer to resign from one of the boards. Similarly, Russell DeYoung, Chairman of Goodyear Tire & Rubber Co. and a director of Aluminum Company of America and Kennecott Copper Company, was forced to choose between the Alcoa and Kennecott Boards. Another executive, Edmund W. Littlefield, chairman of Utah International, Inc., a common director of General Electric and Chrysler, was compelled to resign one of his directorships, because both companies made air conditioners although that was not the major business of either.

The Congress has sought to regulate interlocking directorships in a manner that can only be described as chaotic. In addition to prohibition of horizontal interlocks between competing companies contained in Section 8, the Clayton Act has two other features. It requires express authorization of the Board of Governors for horizontal banking interlocks in the Federal Reserve System. Further, it requires Interstate Commerce Commission approval of vertical interlocks between railroads and suppliers of construction, finance, supply, and maintenance services. In regulated industries, generally, a series of statutes, require approval of interlocks by the appropriate federal regulatory agency, including the Interstate Commerce Commission over common carriers; the Federal Communications Commission over telephone and telegraph common carriers; the Federal Reserve Board over vertical and horizontal interlocks between national banks and securities underwriters; the Federal Power Commission over electrical utilities and vertical interlocks with securities underwriters and equipment suppliers; the Securities and Exchange Commission over vertical interlocks between public utility holding companies and banks, trust companies, and investment bankers; the Securities and Exchange Commission over horizontal interlocks between investment companies and certain vertical interlocks with investment advisers, banks, and securities underwriters; and the Secretary of the Treasury over vertical and horizontal interlocks involving common carriers or aircraft manufacturers.

C. THE NATURE OF THE PROBLEM

As pointed out by Brandeis and Wilson, interlocking directorships present a series of markedly different problems.

1. Market Impairment.

Interlocks can result in the impairment of the market. They can eliminate existing competition or deter potential competition. They can give rise to preferential treatment in the supply of materials and availability of credit. They may even deprive competitors of access to credit. Finally, they can lead to reciprocity and forbearance.

Concerning credit, a 1951 study of the Federal Trade Commission reported:

> . . . A director who is on the board of an industrial company and a financial institution cannot in good conscience encourage the latter to finance expansion by competitors of the former which may jeopardize the former's prosperity; nor can he in good conscience encourage the industrial company to obtain its credit through other channels . . .
>
> . . . Interlocking relations between manufacturing corporations and financial institutions, especially banks and insurance companies, may establish a type of vertical relation that assures adequate credit to favored companies and a withholding of credit and capital from their competitors.

Joint ventures and interlocks can create a "community of interest" that can lead to interdependence and impaired competition or anticompetitive business practices. These are important matters of antitrust policy, but they do not involve the paramount question of the allocation of power in the society. In addition, interlocks may lead to mergers that might otherwise not occur and thereby tend in a minor way to increase aggregate concentration and in some cases market concentration. This essentially involves questions of public policy toward mergers, rather than the more fundamental issue of financial domination of industry.

2. Conflicts of Interest.

Transactions between companies with interlocking directors require careful scrutiny. Loyalties of the common director are divided, and his role is obviously suspect. Where vertical interlocks are involved, representatives of shippers, suppliers, banks, and law firms all have their own objectives to pursue. Even if the common director seeks to reconcile the conflicting objectives of his two principals, it may well be in the best interests of one, or both, or of the society for the corporations to pursue vigorously the policies which produce the conflict. Reconciliation or harmonization (which might well be characterized as collusion) may not be consistent with the free market, or perhaps a free society. The fact that the interlocking director or directors will likely abstain and permit the decision to be made by independent directors does not dispose of the problem. Their "independence" is impaired by social, and perhaps economic, considerations. The directors are in a sense members of a private club who may find it difficult to oppose measures helpful to fellow members. If the interested director or directors represent a powerful institution, the other directors may be hesitant to offend it.

Legal restraints provide limited protection. On shareholder challenge, interested transactions will be set aside by the courts where they are found to be unfair or not to represent the honest judgment of the Board. Litigation, however, is at best an expensive and uncertain remedy. Further, in some states including Delaware and New York, statutes provide methods for authorization of interested transactions which render attack by shareholders more difficult.

Under its proxy rules, the Securities and Exchange Commission requires disclosure of material transactions involving conflicts of interest in listed companies and other companies subject to the 1934 Act. The requirement of disclosure provides a powerful deterrent. Finally, the New York Stock Exchange has also taken measures to deal with problems presented by conflicts of interest.

Conflicts of interest present important questions of fairness to shareholders and the internal conduct of corporate affairs, but they are not matters of fundamental national concern.

3. Reduction of Directorship Opportunities.

The reformers in the Wilson period were much concerned that interlocking directorships pre-empted a significant portion of the pool of available places on the board and thereby restricted or denied opportunity to persons who might otherwise become directors. This seems a relatively trivial matter. Further, it assumes that the number of directorships is fixed, and that boards may not be enlarged to accomodate the additional persons who otherwise might have been elected to the places occupied by the interlocking directors.

4. Burdens of Multiple Directorships.

There is a more important concern with respect to the burdens on the time and energy of the interlocking director. The duties of directors are becoming increasingly onerous, particularly with the growth of the expanded obligations of directors under the securities laws and the increasing importance of issues of public policy concern. To the extent that the executive with pressing primary responsibilities accepts a number of directorships, the question arises whether he is in a position to fulfill all his responsibilities. It is not likely in today's world that anyone will seek to emulate Sidney J. Weinberg's experience of holding directorships in a large number of companies at one time.

These concerns with the appropriate role and functioning of directors are also important, but they too are not fundamental to our inquiry into the concentration of corporate power.

5. Concentration of Social and Economic Power.

The most serious problem presented by the interlocking directorship and the one with which we are primarily concerned is the extent to which interlocks represent a dangerous concentration of economic, political, and social power in the society. As Mr. Justice Douglas stated in *United States v. W. T. Grant,* 345 U.S. 629, 636 (1953), "those intertwined relations [of interlocking directors] are the stuff out of which concentration of financial power over American industry was built and is maintained."

If our concern is corporate power and responsibility, the interlocking director may occupy a central portion on the stage. The existence of interlocking directors aggravates the problems presented by aggregate concentration and institutional concentration of shareownership. The centers of decision-making are largely confined to a relatively small circle of powerful persons managing a progressively smaller number of major enterprises responsible for an increasing share of the sales, assets, and net income of American corporate enterprise.

The 1965 Staff Report made it plain, as Wilson had fifty years earlier, that this concentration of control was the major problem. It found:

> Perhaps the most significant aspect of the common director problem is the concern that, by means of this device, inordinate control over the major part of U.S. commerce would be concentrated in the hands of so few individuals that the normal social and political forces relied upon to maintain a free economy would be ineffective to correct abuses. Ingrown relations, closely knit corporate identities, and the ability to wield power on a wide front, were feared because they would carry the seeds of a business aristocracy that would not be compatible with basic tenets of the political and economic democracy embodied in the anti-trust laws.

Professor Travers observes that interlocks are "visible ties linking a small group of men who wield vast political and economic power," and that "the idea that all interlocking directorates must be smashed has remained one of the intellectual undercurrents coursing beneath the surface of anti-trust activity."

As we have seen, Brandeis was concerned that interlocking directorates enabled the "Money Trust" to control American industry. In today's world the money power no longer seems as formidable a specter as in the past. The reduced reliance on external financing resulting from increased internal generation of funds has helped reduce the power of the great investment banking firms. Concern with interlocks embraces the business establishment generally. Is it wise to concentrate the decision-making responsibility of American major corporations in the hands of a relatively small number of persons, many of whom sit on more than one board, resulting in the development and mutual reinforcement of a common view on the underlying economic, political, and social problems of business and the nation? Are national interests affected by the existence of a relatively small group of persons constituting a "power elite," a "business establishment," or an interrelated "corporate community" controlling the major part of the economy?

This overriding concern arises not from the issues of impairment of competition or conflicts of interest or the malfunctioning of the board. It relates to the fundamental question of the control of the economy by an unrepresentative, self-selected group of persons of like background, experience, and values who will be inclined to think alike. This is a sociological, as well as a political and economic, phenomenon.

D. INTERLOCKING DIRECTORSHIPS AMONG THE LARGEST CORPORATIONS

There is a correlation between corporate size and the frequency of interlocking relationships with other major companies.

The Federal Trade Commission, *Economic Report on Corporate Mergers* (1969) found a total of 1,450 interlocks involving the 200 Largest industrials in 1962. Among the 200 Largest corporations, there were 476 interlocks including 131 interlocks among companies in the same five-digit product class. There were 974 interlocks between the 200 Largest and the 1,000 Largest industrials, including 184 interlocks among companies in the same five-digit product class [see Table 8-1]. These interlocks involved competitors, suppliers, customers, companies producing closely related products, potential competitors, and financial institutions supplying competitors with funds.

The 1965 Staff Report studied management interlocks of twenty-nine major concerns as of 1962. These included the twenty Largest industrials, eight other megacorporations, and American Telephone and Telegraph, the largest utility. The study of these twenty-nine major companies disclosed the existence of 1,262 interlocking relationships, involving 330 with banks, 136 with insurance companies, 745 with industrial and commercial corporations, and fifty-one with other corporations [see Table 8-2]. The Cabinet Committee Study reported that in the same year, 1962, the largest industrial, General Motors, alone was interlocked with sixty-three corporations with total assets of $65 billion.

Although the 1965 Staff Report had some information on interlocks involving banks and industrial corporations, it had more data on insurance companies. It reported that in 1962, the ten largest life insurance companies with 61.4% of the total assets of the industry held 803 interlocking positions in other companies: 195 direct interlocks with commercial banks, fifty-five with other insurance companies, and 550 with industrial or commercial concerns. The largest company, Metropolitan Life Insurance Company, was

TABLE 8-1

Federal Trade Commission, Economic Report on Corporate Mergers (1969), Table 3-11, p. 3-40

Interlocking Directors or Officers Involving the 200 Largest Industrial Corporations, 1962

Company rank	*Total interlocks involving the 200 largest industrial corporations*		*Interlocks among the 200 largest industrial corporations*		*Interlocks with the 201 - 1,000 largest industrial corporations*	
	Total interlocks	*Interlocks among companies in same 5-digit product class*	*Total interlocks*	*Interlocks among companies in same 5-digit product class*	*Total interlocks*	*Interlocks among companies in same 5-digit product class*
1 — 50	520	134	264	80	256	54
51 — 100	379	93	135	38	244	55
101 — 150	308	43	62	12	246	31
151 — 200	243	45	15	1	228	44
Total	1,450	315	476	131	974	184

Source: Bureau of Economics, Federal Trade Commission, derived from *Fortune Plant and Product Directory* and *Poor's Register of Directors and Executives.*

TABLE 8-2

Antitrust Subcommittee of House Committee on the Judiciary Staff Report, Interlocks in Corporate Management, (1965) Table no. 10, p. 117

Summary of Management Interlocks: 29 Industrial and Commercial Corporations, Dec. 31, 1962

					Interlocked corporations							
					Banks and financial institutions				Insurance companies			
Rank	Name of Company	Number of directors	Number of officers	Officers with interlocks	By directors	By officers	Number of directors	Number of officers	By directors	By officers	Number of directors	Number of officers
1	General Motors Corp.	26	25	2	22	1	9	1	4	....	4	....
2	Standard Oil Co. (N.J.)	15	3	....	3	....	3	....	1	....	1	....
3	Ford Motor Co	19	22	1	12	....	9	....	3	....	1	....
4	General Electric Co	20	37	6	17	3	10	2	12	2	7	3
5	Socony Mobil Oil Co	13	10	....	11	....	5	....	2	....	1	....
6	U.S. Steel Corp	18	57	2	20	....	9	....	10	....	7	....
7	Texaco Inc	15	26	....	16	....	10	....	7	....	6	....
8	Gulf Oil Corp	9	16	....	5	....	6	....	1	....	1	....
9	Western Electric Co	13	12	....	7	....	5	....	11	....	5	....
10	Swift & Co	13	16	....	18	....	7	....	5	....	3	....
11	E.I. du Pont de Nemours & Co.	29	9	....	5	....	11	....	1	....	1	....
12	Chrysler Corp	19	18	....	12	....	12	....	9	....	5	....
13	Standard Oil Co. of California	12	11	....	8	....	5	....	1	....	1	....
14	Standard Oil Co. (Indiana)	10	5	....	6	....	4	....	3	....	2	....
15	Bethlehem Steel Corp	16	1	....	....	....	....	....	....	....	....	....
16	Shell Oil Co	15	20	....	2	....	1	....	5	....	3	....
17	Westinghouse Electric Corp	22	45	2	17	2	15	2	7	....	6	....
18	International Business Machines Corp.	17	16	2	18	2	10	2	4	1	3	1
19	General Dynamics Corp	14	25	4	14	2	8	2	1	1	1	1
20	Armour & Co	17	27	....	12	....	11	....	5	....	4	....
24	Lockheed Aircraft Corp	17	29	....	11	....	11	....	2	....	2	....
26	North American Aviation, Inc	11	19	....	7	1	5	1	4	....	3	....
32	Philips Petroleum Co	15	20	....	3	....	6	....	....	....	....	....
35	Sinclair Oil Corp	12	15	....	9	....	5	....	....	....	....	....
39	United Aircraft Corp	13	11	....	11	....	10	....	14	....	10	....
44	American Motors Corp	12	11	1	9	1	5	1	2	....	2	....
55	Continental Oil Co	18	31	2	14	....	7	....	1	....	1	....
64	Douglas Aircraft Corp	15	11	....	7	....	6	....	1	....	2	....
1	American Telephone & Telegraph Co.	18	20	8	18	4	15	4	16	....	9	....
	Total	463	568	31	314	16	220	15	132	4	91	5

Rank	Name of Company	Interlocked Corporations							
		Industrial-commercial				Other			
		By directors	By officers	Number of directors	Number of officers	By directors	By officers	Number of directors	Number of officers
1	General Motors Corp.	32	1	10	1	3	....	2	....
2	Standard Oil Co. (N.J.)	2	....	2	....	1	....	1	....
3	Ford Motor Co.	38	1	11	1	3	....	3	....
4	General Electric Co.	45	2	13	2	3	....	3	....
5	Socony Mobil Oil Co.	7	....	4	....	1	....	1	....
6	U.S. Steel Corp.	54	4	12	2	1	....	1	....
7	Texaco Inc.	25	....	9	....	3	....	2	....
8	Gulf Oil Corp.	24	....	8	....	1	....	1	....
9	Western Electric Co.	18	....	5	....	1	....	1	....
10	Swift & Co.	16	....	7	....	....	....	....	....
11	E.I. DuPont de Nemours & Co.	12	....	8	....	....	....	....	....
12	Chrysler Corp	32	....	13	....	2	....	1	....
13	Standard Oil Co. of California	13	....	5	....	....	....	....	....
14	Standard Oil Co. (Indiana)	3	....	1	....	1	....	1	....
15	Bethlehem Steel Corp.	....	....	....	....	....	....	....	....
16	Shell Oil Co.	15	....	4	....	....	....	....	....
17	Westinghouse Electric Corp.	60	2	16	1	3	....	3	....
18	International Business Machines Corp.	29	2	10	2	2	....	2	....
19	General Dynamics Corp.	35	4	13	3	2	2	2	1
20	Armour & Co.	22	....	12	....	3	....	3	....
24	Lockheed Aircraft Corp.	19	....	11	....	10	....	3	....
26	North American Aviation, Inc.	23	....	7	....	....	....	....	....
32	Philips Petroleum Co.	7	....	3	....	....	....	....	....
35	Sinclair Oil Corp.	26	....	7	....	3	....	3	....
39	United Aircraft Corp.	14	....	9	....	....	....	....	....
44	American Motors Corp.	21	....	5	....	....	....	....	....
55	Continental Oil Co.	39	7	10	2	2	....	2	....
64	Douglas Aircraft Corp.	28	....	7	....	1	....	1	....
1	American Telephone & Telegraph Co.	58	5	17	4	3	....	3	....
	Total	717	28	239	18	49	2	39	1

interlocked with six other insurance companies, fourteen banks, four investment companies, and more than fifty industrial or commercial companies.

A 1974 study of the eighteen major oil companies by Angus McDonald revealed 460 interlocking directorates and advisory committee connections, including 132 banks and other financial institutions, thirty-one interlocks with insurance companies, twelve interlocks with eleven utilities, fifteen interlocks with transportation companies, forty-six affiliations with educational institutions, and 224 interlocks with manufacturing and distributing corporations.

It is plain that the major American corporations are interwoven with interlocking relationships.

Professor Peter C. Dooley[2] has contributed a valuable analysis of interlocking directorates. He studied interlocks in 1965 among the 200 Largest nonfinancial corporations and the 50 Largest financial corporations. The directors of the 250 companies consisted of 3,165 persons who held 4,007 directorships, with 562 persons sitting on two or more boards. Twenty-two companies had as many as twenty or more interlocks with other corporations in the 250 Largest. Three companies had forty or more. Dooley related the existence of interlocking directorates to five factors:

Size: The largest corporations have the most interlocks. Corporations with assets in excess of $5 billion in 1965 had 23.7 average interlocks while those with assets under $2 billion had an average of less than ten. Increased prominence in the business community, more useful business relationships, and greater ostensible ability all contributed to the increased attractiveness of the directors from the largest corporations.

Management Control: As the proportion of management directors on the board increased, the number of interlocks decreased.

Financial Connections: Interlocks involving financial institutions were the most frequent. They are apparently useful both to the financial institution in strengthening its business relationships with customers and to the corporation in furthering its access to credit. Dooley concludes that interlocks may also arise from the effort to provide board representation in recognition of the significant stock ownership of bank trust departments.

Competition: Notwithstanding the prohibition against interlocking directorates among competing corporations in Section 8 of the Clayton Act, Dooley found that nearly one in eight interlocks involved competitors; this is consistent with Kramer's findings fifteen years earlier. Dooley found that interlocks were highest among financial institutions and manufacturers. Because Dooley treated all financial institutions—including banks and insurance companies—as competitors, this result is not surprising. Dooley also

[2]Peter C. Dooley, "The Interlocking Directorate," *American Economic Review,* LIX, No. 3 (1969) 314.

found 133 interlocks among competing industrial firms and twenty-five among competing transportation companies.

Local interest groups: Dooley found a number of relatively tight-knit groups in various metropolitan centers involving links between companies with their head offices in the area. Banks, insurance companies, and to a lesser extent, utilities, formed the center of such groups. Dooley suggests that the presence of outside local business leaders on the board forces management to give greater consideration to community needs. Thus, he asserts that interlocks paradoxically create a constraining influence on the corporation by introducing points of view that prevent management isolation.

It is plain from Dooley's analysis that financial institutions—banks and insurance companies—are the most prominent source of interlocks. This, of course, has been responsible for the deep-seated concern with interlocks as a method by which the "money power" exercises hegemony over the economy. The fifty major financial institutions studied—thirty-two banks and eighteen insurance companies—had a total of 616 interlocks with non-financial companies. Eight giant banks and four giant insurance companies each had twenty or more interlocks.

Financial institutions are of particular interest in view of our concern with institutional control. It is obvious that the interlocks between the thirty-two major banks and 432 nonfinancial corporations reported by Dooley significantly strengthen the implications of potential control that arise from the formidable percentages of stock held by bank trust accounts. Thus, as previously reported, Herman and Safanda have noted that, on occasion, the existence of a common director has caused a bank to vote its shares in favor of management proposals that would otherwise be opposed under the established policy of the bank's trust department.

Contrary to the expectation of a number of observers several decades ago, including A.A. Berle, that major corporations would become free of dependence on the capital markets, reliance on the capital markets has increased, rather than declined. Financial institutions continue to play a dominant role particularly in connection with the issuance of new security issues and the availability of credit generally. In 1974 outstanding bank loans to nonfinancial corporate business amounted to about $117 billion. The vital need for bank support, according to Dooley, helps explain the "presence of knowledgeable men of finance on the board of directors" and the existence of interlocks with financial institutions.

E. SOCIOLOGICAL CONSIDERATIONS

As noted above, it is important not to view interlocking directorships solely as legal devices for achieving economic objectives for the companies concerned. They also involve profound psychological and sociological factors as well.

In a country of more than 200,000,000 people, Dooley found that 3,165 persons held directorships in the 250 Largest companies in his study. These 3,165 individuals comprise the most prominent business persons in the nation. For other companies seeking a new "outside" director, they are the natural candidates in terms of their status, power, record of achievement, experience, and social acceptability. They are already members of the "club." They are the "eligibles" from whom selection is almost irresistible. The group is tiny, and the fact that 562 of them have been selected by one or more other companies to serve on their boards as well should be no surprise. This is a social process that is almost inevitable. These social pressures combine with the economic factors in the process and contribute to the existence of interlocks.

W. Lloyd Warner and D.B. Unwalla[3] studied a selected sample of 500 representative American corporations, including ninety-eight corporations with assets of more than $1 billion and sixty-four with less than $100 million. They found that the 5,776 persons who were directors of the 500 corporations in the sample held a total of more than 20,522 directorships. Of these, 3,696 representatives of large firms held a total of 6,280 directorships in 4,125 large firms and comprised what Warner and Unwalla described as the "elite classes" of the managers of the large corporations; this group also held 3,729 directorships in smaller firms. 1,675 individuals held five or more directorships, and 398 held ten or more; most of these persons holding a substantial number of directorships were managers of large-scale and very large-scale corporations. As noted their prominence in their own highly visible corporations made them especially attractive to other corporations.

Warner and Unwalla concluded that the corporate world formed a social system that has continued through the generations, with the interchange of directors an essential element for the system to function in its present form.

Directorships in the very large companies are psychologically meaningful for the individuals involved. They constitute a valued form of personal recognition. Like an honorary degree, they are a status symbol for "the man who has everything." They provide a form of personal fulfillment that contributes an important degree of psychic incentive leading very busy men to accept additional responsibilities for which there may be increasing risk of personal liability under the securities laws and for which compensation will be modest.

In addition, they are valuable economic associations for the individuals involved. They represent possible access to advantageous business relationships. Lawyer-directors, for example, represent an interesting form of this type of interlock. The major law firms over the nation have numerous representatives on the boards of major corporations as well as serving them as

[3] W. Lloyd Warner and D.B. Unwalla, "The System of Interlocking Directorates" in *The Emergent American Society—Large Scale Organizations,* W.L. Warner, D.B. Unwalla, and J.H. Trimm, eds., (New Haven, Conn.: Yale University Press, 1967).

counsel. In a study by William A. Hudson, Jr., 1,182 law firms were found to have directors on the boards of 1,919 corporations in 1971; these corporations paid $157.5 million in fees to law firms whose partners were on their boards [see Table 8-3]. In 1971 partners of Simpson, Thatcher and Bartlett of New York, for example, sat on the boards of twenty major companies from which their firm received fees of $3.86 million. Shearman and Sterling of New York had partners on the boards of fourteen companies which paid aggregate fees of $3.80 million.

The sociological forces making for interlock have been prominently revealed in a new area. The growing movement for black and women directors has forced major companies to select candidates from very small pools of candidates deemed qualified. The result has been the repeated election of a relatively limited group of prominent blacks and women, contributing further to interlock, at least as a statistical matter. Several examples will illustrate. Patricia Roberts Harris is a director of The Chase Manhattan Bank, International Business Machines, Scott Paper, and the National Bank of Washington. Catharine B. Cleary is a director of General Motors, American Telephone and Telegraph, Kraftco, and First Wisconsin Trust Company. Jerome H. Holland is a director of American Telephone and Telegraph, Chrysler, General Foods, and Union Carbide. Vernon E. Jordan, Jr., is a director of Bankers Trust Company, Celanese, and J.C. Penney. Franklin A. Thomas is a director of First National City Bank of New York, New York Life Insurance Company, CBS, Allied Stores, and Cummins Engine.

Does the coincidence of Mrs. Harris' election to the board of The Chase Manhattan Bank and the National Bank of Washington, on the one hand, and International Business Machines and Scott Paper, on the other, really mean that these banks are extending tentacles of control over these industrial companies? Should we draw a distinction between interlocks involving directors who represent a business interest and those pertaining to directors whose designation reflects social or political factors? It would appear that we cannot stop with a determination of the existence of interlocks but must also ascertain the nature of the underlying forces responsible for their creation.

F. THE MATTER OF PRIMARY LOYALTIES

The discussions in the literature of the implications of interlocking directorates have generally neglected one important element of the problem. The studies have been essentially quantitative, e.g. the determination of the number of interlocking directors between a major financial institution and major industrial companies. The underlying assumption—which is rarely, if ever, articulated—is that the interlocking director is a person whose primary loyalty runs to the financial institution and whose representation on the com-

TABLE 8-3
The Interlocks Between Directorships and Law Fees

Law firm	*Number of companies that report law firm partners as directors*	*Total fees companies paid to interlocking law firms*
Simpson, Thatcher & Bartlett, New York	20	$3,860,704
Shearman & Sterling, New York	14	3,802,174
Baker & Botts, Houston	14	3,525,487
Willkie, Farr & Gallagher, New York	11	2,909,311
Sullivan & Cromwell, New York	17	2,747,748
Jones, Day, Cockley & Reavis, Cleveland	25	2,079,740
White & Case, New York	13	1,849,737
Paul, Weiss, Rifkind, Wharton & Garrison, New York	12	1,835,036
Stroock & Stroock & Levan, New York	18	1,813,800
Cravath, Swaine & Moore, New York	7	1,703,875
Squire, Sanders & Dempsey, Cleveland	11	1,644,091
Mudge, Rose, Guthrie & Alexander, New York	10	1,638,750
Kelley, Drye, Warren, Clark, Carr & Ellis, New York	6	1,494,713
Keating, Muething & Klekamp, Cincinnati	3	1,312,040
Cahill, Gordon, Sonnett, Reindel & Ohl, New York	8	1,243,054
Oppenheimer, Brown, Wolff, Leach & Foster, Minneapolis	3	1,188,627
Price, Cushman, Keck & Mahin, Chicago	5	1,104,772
Donovan, Leisure, Newton & Irvine, New York	1	1,097,724
Mayer, Brown & Platt, Chicago	8	1,089,390
Ropes & Gray, Boston	19	1,074,425
Hogan & Hartson, Washington, D.C.	3	1,065,822
Andrews, Kurth, Campbell & Jones, Houston	5	1,046,836
Foley & Lardner, Milwaukee	9	1,036,510
Pillsbury, Madison & Sutro, San Francisco	6	1,025,211
Parker, Chapin & Flattau, New York	9	1,004,105
Morgan, Lewis & Bockius, Philadelphia	11	1,001,998

Data: Securities & Exchange Commission; William J. Hudson, Jr.

Reprinted from the July 22, 1972 issue of *Business Week* by special permission. Copyright 1972 by McGraw-Hill, Inc.

pany's board is to serve the interests of the financial institution. It is this assumed power on the part of the financial institution that was the basis of the outcry against the "Money Trust." The industrial company is looked upon as the victim of financial colonialism.

In many cases, the interlocking director, is indeed the financial institution's man, and the inarticulate major premise is correct. In many others, however, the interlocking director comes from industry, not from finance, and his presence on the board reflects such facts as the accommodation of mutual business interests, recognition of his ostensible ability and judgment, and perhaps expertise in a specialized area, his position in the business or metropolitan community, his friendship with the chief executive officer or other directors of the institution, or a combination of the foregoing.

Where the primary loyalties of an interlocking director are to the industrial company and not to the institution, or where the primary loyalties may be to a minority group, as in the case of some black or women directors, the interlock has an entirely different significance. It is only when the interlocking director is the financial institution's man that his presence on the industrial company's board serves to strengthen the financial institution's potential of control.

The available data on the interlocking directors of banks and corporations whose stock is held in bank trust accounts does not support the concept of banking colonialism. Persons with their primary loyalty clearly identifiable as owing to the bank represent a relatively small percentage of the interlocks. Most bank interlocks involve directors of prominent nonfinancial concerns who were also on a bank board and in a number of cases on the boards of other companies as well.

In *Monopoly Capitalism,* Paul A. Baran and Paul M. Sweezy essentially agree with this view. They consider interlocking directorates as a method by which a family of great wealth or investment banking firm maintained control over a group of companies. They point to the elder J.P. Morgan, the Mellons, and the Rockefellers as illustrations of this pattern and conclude that this system of common interest groups has disappeared, stating, "The large corporation has won its independence from bankers and shareholders alike."

Indeed, if all interlocking directors between financial and nonfinancial companies are to be proscribed, the result would be to limit severely the extent of "outside" directors on the boards of banks and insurance companies. If the most outstanding men and women in nonfinancial companies are barred, who would be available to bring an outside business input or specialized background to the bank or insurance board?

G. BANK INTERLOCKS AND STOCK OWNERSHIP

In appraising the significance of interlocking directorates as sources of control of the major corporate power centers it is important to determine the extent to which interlocking directorates are reinforced by interlocking stock ownership and therefore represent an even greater base of power than is apparent simply from the fact of board membership. This is particularly true in the case of the banks, in view of the emergence of the trust departments of the commercial banks as the center of the most significant institutional concentration of stock ownership in the nation.

The Staff Report of the Subcommittee on Domestic Finance of the House Committee on Banking and Currency on *Commercial Banks and Their Trust Activities: Emerging Influence on the American Economy* (1969), "Bank Trust Activities Report," contained a study of the interlocking directorships and stock ownership of forty-nine major banks. It found that these forty-nine banks held a total of 768 interlocking directorships, involving 286 of the 500 Largest industrials; they also had 146 interlocking directorships with twenty-nine of the fifty Largest insurance companies, seventy-three interlocking directorships with twenty-seven of the fifty Largest transportation companies, and eighty-six interlocking directorships with twenty-two of the fifty Largest utilities. The interlocks were frequently reinforced by bank stock ownership of 5% of more of the outstanding stock of the interlocked company. One or more of the forty-nine major banks held 5% or more of the common stock of 147 of the 500 Largest with which they were interlocked. The forty-nine banks also held 5% or more of the common stock of seventeen of the 50 Largest merchandising and seventeen of the 50 Largest transportation companies with which interlocks existed.

In the economy as a whole, the forty-nine banks had interlocking director relationships with a total of 6,591 companies. At the same time, they owned 5% or more of the stock in 5,270 companies. Unfortunately, the report does not indicate the extent of the overlap of the two categories.

New York was a center of activity. The Bank Trust Activities Report found that the six major New York banks had a total of 1,489 interlocks involving 1,295 companies and that these banks held 5% or more of the stock of 965 companies. It did not, however, indicate the extent to which the interlocks and the major stock interests involved the same corporation.

Director and Stockholder Interlocks of Major New York Commercial Banks

	Director Interlocks		*Portfolio Companies*
Bank	*Companies per bank*	*Interlocks per bank*	*with 5% or more Stockholding*
Morgan Guaranty Trust	233	251	270
Chase Manhattan	193	208	158
Bankers Trust	224	259	109
First National City Bank	167	188	229
Manufacturers Hanover Trust	200	257	132
Chemical Bank	278	326	67
Total	1,295	1,489	965

Source: Bank Trust Activities Report, vol. 1, p. 694, Table 72.

The following table shows the overlap of interlocking directors and significant voting stock ownership involving the ten major bank trust departments and the 500 Largest industrials, the fifty Largest utilities, insurance, trade, and transportation companies:

Bank	Interlocking Companies	Percentage of Voting Stock Held in Interlocking Companies: Less than 1%	1% to 5%	5% to 10%	Over 10%
Morgan Guaranty	73	50	8	8	7
Chase Manhattan	59	46	10	3	0
Bankers Trust	51	43	2	6	0
First National City	72	56	14	2	0
U.S. Trust Company	56	55	1	0	0
Manufacturers Hanover	53	47	6	0	0
Mellon National	48	42	3	0	3
First National of Chicago	58	52	2	4	0
Continental Illinois	54	51	3	0	0
Bank of America	50	47	3	0	0

Source: Bank Trust Activities Report, vol. 1, pp. 93-215; Report on Disclosure of Corporate Ownership prepared for Senate Committee on Government Operations (1973), pp. 21-114.

Another method to ascertain the extent to which the overlapping of significant bank trust department ownership of voting stock and interlocking directorates reinforces the pattern of concentration of control of the major corporations is to determine the extent to which interlocking occurs between banks and the companies included in their largest twenty-five portfolio holdings:

Bank	Number of Largest 25 Portfolio Companies in which Interlocking Present, 1973	Number of Interlocks Represented by Bank Officers
Morgan Guaranty	8	2
Chase Manhattan	7	0
Bankers Trust	3	2
First National City	8	4
U.S. Trust Company	3	1
Manufacturers Hanover	4	1
Mellon National	4	2
First National of Chicago	5	1
Continental Illinois	3	0
Bank of America	2	1
Total	47	14

It is apparent that significant stock ownership and interlocking directorates are related to some degree and that in some of the major holdings of the banks, interlocks provide reinforcement for the influence arising from stock ownership. Some potential for increased control, or at least for an increased community of interest, is therefore present. On the other hand, in most cases the interlock arises from the presence of one of the portfolio company's senior officers or directors on the bank's board, and only in a minority of cases from the presence of a bank officer on the portfolio company board. The interlocks, therefore, lack much of their apparent significance.

We should not give undue emphasis to the associations between the banks and portfolio companies that may reflect the interlocking relationship but which do not increase the bank's power base or strengthen the concentration of control. These include the following:

(1) Designation as a stock transfer agent or as registrar represents only minor items of banking business that the interlocking relationship may help produce.
(2) Ownership of nonvoting or nonconvertible preferred stock is of no significance.
(3) Portfolio company personnel on the bank board may strengthen the bank's claim to business opportunities, but it does not strengthen bank control.
(4) Fiduciary ownership of common stock, where the bank possesses no voting power, has limited significance.

In summary, interlocking directorates reflect a number of factors. They arise in part from a social pattern which leads megacorporations to select their directors from a relatively small pool of prominent men, and even smaller pools of prominent blacks and women. They reflect an advantageous basis for recruitment for the board that provides corporations with new directors of prominence, experience, demonstrated business success, and in some cases, specialized competence. They may lead to profitable business for the corporations or sources of supply that could be especially valuable in times of shortage.

In many cases, the basis for the selection is personal. In others, the link is institutional; the director is on the board not as an individual but as a representative of his firm. The interlocked firm looks forward to the encouragement of advantageous business relations. It may be a bank, insurance company, investment bank, or law firm enjoying a traditional institutional relationship with the corporation, and the interlocking director may have as one of his major objectives the preservation of the business relationship for his firm to which he owes primary loyalty. While lawyers do not raise the specter of economic colonialism, the presence of representatives of financial institutions on the boards of major firms reflecting such considerations has traditionally been the factor that has provoked much of the concern with interlocking directors, going back to the days of the fear of the "Money Trust".

Interlocking directors may operate as anticompetitive influences and present problems under the antitrust laws. What other significance do interlocking directorates have? They do not appear to be the sinister influences visualized in the past. Where they involve the representatives of financial institutions on boards of corporations in which the institution holds substantial stock, they form an integral part of the problem of the extent of influence or control of the institutions over portfolio companies. However, when the interlocking director is a person—such as the chief executive of a major business—who is on the board of the portfolio company as well as on the board of the financial institution, the relationship takes on a different dimension. The interlocking director may be sensitive to the institution's interests in the discharge of his duties on the portfolio company's board, but he is not the institution's man, he does not represent the institution, and he is not automatically ready to do the institution's bidding. In terms of power relationships, the significance of the interlocking position is significantly diluted. Thus, aside from possible anticompetitive influences, interlocks are primarily significant as illustrative of the relatively small group of highly influential businessmen and women who dominate the centers of power and constitute an elite who possess great power. This is a sociological phenomenon of importance. Except to the extent that interlocks involve the impairment of competition calling for antitrust action, they would not seem to possess the great significance traditionally accorded to them.

BIBLIOGRAPHY

Baran, Paul A. and Paul M. Sweezy, *Monopoly Capitalism,* op. cit.

Brandeis, Louis D. "Breaking the Money Trusts", *Harper's Weekly,* Nov. 22, 1913 to Jan. 17, 1914.

Cabinet Committee on Price Stability, Staff of, *Industrial Structure and Competition Policy,* op. cit.

Dooley, Peter C., "The Interlocking Directorate", *American Economic Review,* LIX, No. 3 (1969), 314.

Federal Trade Commission, *Economic Report on Corporate Mergers,* Washington, D.C.: Government Printing Office, 1969.

Federal Trade Commission, *Report on Interlocking Directorates.* Washington, D.C.: Government Printing Office, 1951.

House Committee on Banking and Currency, *Investigation of Concentration of Control of Money and Credit,* H. Rep. No. 1593, 62d Cong., 3d sess. Feb. 28, 1913. Washington, D.C.: Government Printing Office, 1913.

House Subcommittee on Domestic Finance, House Committee on Banking and Currency, 90th Cong., 1st sess., *Control of Commercial Banks and Interlocks among Financial Institutions.* Washington, D.C.: Government Printing Office, 1967.

House Subcommittee on Domestic Finance, House Committee on Banking and Currency, 90th Cong., 2d sess., *Commercial Banks and Their Trust Activities: Emerging Influence on the American Economy.* Washington, D.C.: Government Printing Office, 1968.

House Committee on Interstate and Foreign Commerce, *Investigation of United States Steel Corp.,* H. Rep. No. 1127, 62d Cong., 2d sess. Aug. 2, 1912.

House Subcommittee on Antitrust, House Committee on the Judiciary, 89th Cong., 1st sess., *Interlocks in Corporate Management.* Washington, D.C.: Goverment Printing Office, 1965.

House Select Committee on Small Business, 85th Cong., 1st sess., *Interlocking Directors and Officials of 135 Large Financial Companies of the United States.* November 30, 1957.

Jacobs, Ephraim, "Interlocks", 29 *American Bar Association Antitrust Section Proceedings* 204 (1965).

Kramer, Victor, "Interlocking Directorships and the Clayton Act After 35 Years", 59 *Yale Law Journal* 1266 (1950).

Note, "Clayton Act Prohibition of Interlocking Directorates in Industrial or Commercial Corporations", 54 *Columbia Law Review* 130 (1954).

Note, "Interlocking Directorates: A Study in Desultory Regulation", 29 *Indiana Law Journal* 429 (1954).

Senate Committee on Government Operations, Subcommittees on Intergovernmental Relations and Budgeting, Management and Expenditures, 93d Cong., 1st sess., *Disclosure of Corporate Ownership.* Washington, D.C.: Government Printing Office, 1973.

Travers, Arthur H., "Interlocks in Corporate Management and the Antitrust Laws", 46 *Texas Law Review* 819 (1968).

Warner, W. Lloyd, and D.B. Unwalla, "The System of Interlocking Directorates" in W. Lloyd Warner, D.B. Unwalla, and J.H. Trimm, eds., *The Emergent American Society—Large Scale Organizations.* New Haven, Conn.: Yale University Press, 1967.

CHAPTER NINE

Conclusion

This empirical review of the dimensions of corporate power has disclosed the serious concentration of economic power in the national economy. Aggregate concentration is high and increasing. Market concentration continues at a high level in about one-third of manufacturing industries and shows no signs of diminishing. Concern with economic concentration has been widened by the growing concentration of share ownership in the hands of financial institutions, which have emerged as a source of potential control over industry. A few hundred industrial megacorporations under the potential control of an even smaller group of financial institutions today represent the central core of economic power. Further, these dominant industrial and financial institutions are tied together with overlapping boards of directors drawn from a limited pool of several thousand unrepresentative men and a few women with the same backgrounds, values, and affiliations.

A. THE DIMENSIONS OF CORPORATE POWER

Aggregate Concentration.

The giant corporations represent an increasing share of the nation's business. In 1973 the 1000 Largest industrials (ranked according to sales) accounted for about 72% of the sales, 86% of the employees, and 85% of the profits of all American industrial corporations. Within this group, the 200 Largest, or the megacorporations, represent the core of concentrated industrial power with about three-quarters of the total sales, assets, employees, and profits of the entire group. The concentration within the 200 Largest has been steadily increasing. By 1968 this relatively small group had approximately the same share of all manufacturing assets as held by the 1000 Largest in 1941. Concentration in value-added by manufacture represented by the 200 Largest has also continued to increase. After a dramatic jump from 30% to 37% in the seven years from 1947 to 1954, the share of the 200 Largest in value-added shows a slower, but nevertheless significant, continuing increase to 43% in 1970.

The remarkable size of the megacorporations elevates their operations to the scale of nation states. In 1972 the total sales of just the ten Largest New York Stock Exchange listed corporations (ranked according to sales) amounted to $136 billion or substantially in excess of the $97.35 billion national product of Austria, Denmark, Finland, Greece, Ireland, Norway, Portugal, and Turkey, with an aggregate population of approximately 80 million persons.

Market Concentration.

Since World War II, the overall level of market concentration has remained remarkably stable in spite of variations in different industries, increases in aggregate concentration, antitrust enforcement, and market forces. One-third of all manufacturing industries appear to be highly concentrated and another one-third moderately concentrated. Although there are highly concentrated industries in which the 200 Largest are particularly active and in which market concentration has been increasing, there does not appear to be any clear link between the megacorporations and undue concentration in the economy as a whole.

In 1970 more than one-half of the shipments of the most highly concentrated four-digit industries (with shipments in excess of $500 million and four-firm concentration ratios over 60%) was represented by only five industries (autos, steel, computers, aircraft, and tires and tubes) out of the total of thirty-nine, reducing the implications of concentration in the economy as a whole.

Concentration ratios in different industries have not moved uniformly. Concentration in producer goods with generally undifferentiated products has been declining while concentration in consumer goods has been increasing, particularly in consumer goods industries involving product differentiation and experiencing increased advertising expenditures. Although the Federal Trade Commission *Economic Report on Corporate Mergers* found a close relation between the 200 Largest and the industries showing increases in market concentration, the conclusion that this rests on control over the market rather than superior efficiency has been challenged.

Interlocking Directorates.

Since the Wilson Administration, the control of major industrial enterprises by financial interests through interlocking directorates has been regarded not merely as a source of anticompetitive practices but as a concentration of financial power that could conceivably constitute a threat to a free society. Concern with interlocking directorates as a technique for extension of the power of financial institutions has persisted to this day.

Notwithstanding such concern, governmental regulation has been spotty and ineffective, and interlocking directorates have continued as a prominent feature of the corporate world. The continued existence of interlocking directors aggravates the problems presented by increasing aggregate concentration and institutional concentration of share ownership. This is a question of the concentration of power. The centers of decision-making are largely confined to a relatively small circle of powerful persons managing a progressively smaller number of major enterprises responsible for an increasing share of the sales, assets, and net income of American corporations. With the decline in the power of the great investment banking firms as a result of the reduced dependence of the large corporations on external financing, concern with interlocks relates to the business establishment generally and is not confined to the financial institutions. It involves not merely possible anticompetitive practices or conflicts of interest. It presents the fundamental question of the control of the economy by a relatively small unrepresentative, self-selected group, with like background, experience and values, inclined to have a common view on the underlying problems of business and the nation, who comprise an elite which dominates the centers of power.

B. POTENTIAL INSTITUTIONAL CONTROL

The enormous increase in the size of financial institutions and changes in investment philosophy resulting in a sharp increase in the proportion of portfolios invested in common stocks have produced a fundamental change in the allocation of corporate power. The financial institutions, and particularly the trust departments of the commercial banks, have accumulated tremendous holdings of the common stocks of the major American corporations, resulting in a high concentration of securities in institutional hands and increasing institutional domination of the securities markets. By 1972 the New York Stock Exchange estimated that total institutional holdings exceeded 45% of all NYSE-listed shares.

As we have seen, the portfolios of the major financial institutions represent surprisingly high percentages of the stock of the largest American corporations and, as the Institutional Investor Study Report of the Securities and Exchange Commission concluded, the institutions now possess the potential power to control or influence corporate affairs. Such power requires an unlikely degree of concerted action among the institutions involved and indicates that community of values and outlook rather than deliberate, concerted action will be the likely avenue of institutional influence.

C. THE REACH OF CORPORATE POWER

The concentration of economic power in the megacorporations and of potential control in the leading financial institutions inter-connected as a result of multiple or interlocking directorships presents serious questions for the nation. These questions are all the more important because of the far-ranging reach of corporate power. The scope of corporate decision-making has widened markedly and increasingly involves major questions of public policy concern. Corporate decisions affect many groups, communities, and even the nation in major respects. Corporate influence, moreover, transcends economic matters and has important political and social dimensions as well.

The concentration of power goes beyond the more limited question of the antitrust laws, with which we are only incidentally concerned. It goes to the nature of the society itself. The fundamental question is the relation between size and liberty. To what extent does the compounded concentration of economic power and control threaten the primacy of political decision-making by democratic institutions and the maintenance of social and political controls over the major centers of power, which are essential components of a free democratic society?

D. DISAPPEARING CONFIDENCE IN THE CORPORATE INSTITUTION

The great power of the megacorporations and the possible role of the financial institutions with the potential power to control or significantly influence their portfolio companies is of especial concern because of the existing confusion on the part of business as to the proper goals of the large corporation. The corporate institution is undergoing attack from without and suffering lack of confidence within. The ideological foundations of the business society are being severely shaken. Business is no longer able to articulate its objectives in a way that will command support. Many businessmen are no longer willing to assert profit maximization as the overriding goal of the corporation. Business is in search of an ideology that will embrace not only the drive for profit but the social responsibilities business has increasingly assumed. With the erosion of confidence in the ideological foundations of the business society the legitimacy of the corporation as an institution has been challenged. Its acceptance is increasingly suspect. A 1974 poll of the Opinion Research Corporation showed that only 11% of the American public believed that the performance of business was good.

Further, the fragmentation of share ownership among millions of individual investors, the reluctance of the financial institutions to exercise the potential influence or control represented by their substantial holdings in the megacorporations, and management control of the corporate electoral process have made management a self-elected, self-perpetuating group. Shareholders lack power, the annual meetings are ceremonial, and accountability on the part of the directors has disappeared. As a result of all the foregoing factors, the future role of business in the society is in doubt.

E. THE TAMING OF CORPORATE POWER

For the time being, management fortified by its control over the corporate electorate machinery continues to be supreme. Restraints of the capital market, of the securities market (including possible take-over attempts) and of the climate of public opinion, provide nongovernmental limitations on corporate power. Actual governmental intervention asserts direct restraints, and the fear of potential governmental intervention serves as a highly salutary prophylactic pressure. These restraints and others which serve to limit corporate power are of vital significance in the preservation of a free society. In a companion volume on the taming of corporate power, these restraints will be examined in detail, along with structural and other reforms that would help assure legitimacy and accountability for the large corporation, preserve the primacy of decision-making by democratic institutions, and thereby contribute to the continued survival of a reformed corporate order.

In summary, I have endeavored to set forth the dimensions of corporate power in the United States, the concentration of economic power in the hands of the megacorporations, and the emergence of potential corporate control in the financial institutions. The concerns that these developments present for a free society are fundamental. The extent of corporate power is plain. The basic issue is how to limit it in a way that will be compatible with the preservation of free institutions.

Index

Q

R

S